CASTING OUT
The Eviction of Muslims from Western Law and Politics

Three stereotypical figures have con̶   ̶'
– the 'dangerous' Muslim man, the   ̶
the 'civilized' European. *Casting Out*   ̶
terizations in the creation of the my̶   ̶ ̶ ̶ ̶ democratic
Western nations obliged to use politi̶ ̶ ̶ ̶, ̶military, and legal force to
defend itself against a menacing third world population. It argues that
this myth is promoted to justify the expulsion of Muslims from the
political community, a process that takes the form of stigmatization,
surveillance, incarceration, torture, and bombing.

In this timely and controversial work, Sherene H. Razack looks at
contemporary legal and social responses to Muslims in the West and
places them in historical context. She explains how 'race thinking,' a
structure of thought that divides the world between the deserving
and undeserving according to racial descent, accustoms us to the idea
that the suspension of rights for racialized groups is warranted in the
interests of national security. She discusses many examples of the institution and implementation of exclusionary and coercive practices, including the mistreatment of security detainees, the regulation of
Muslim populations in the name of protecting Muslim women, and
prisoner abuse at Abu Ghraib. She explores how the denial of a
common bond of humanity between European people and those of
different origins has given rise to the proliferation of literal and figurative 'camps,' places or bodies where liberties are suspended and the
rule of law does not apply.

Combining rich theoretical perspectives and extensive research,
Casting Out makes a major contribution to contemporary debates on
race and the 'war on terror' and their implications in areas such as law,
politics, cultural studies, feminist and gender studies, and race relations.

SHERENE RAZACK is a professor in the Department of Sociology and
Equity Studies in Education at the Ontario Institute for Studies in Education, University of Toronto.

SHERENE H. RAZACK

Casting Out

The Eviction of Muslims from Western Law and Politics

UNIVERSITY OF TORONTO PRESS
Toronto Buffalo London

© University of Toronto Press Incorporated 2008
Toronto Buffalo London
Printed in Canada

ISBN 978-0-8020-9311-0 (cloth)
ISBN 978-0-8020-9497-1 (paper)

Printed on acid-free paper

Library and Archives Canada Cataloguing in Publication

Razack, Sherene
  Casting out : the eviction of Muslims from western law and
  politics / Sherene H. Razack.

  Includes bibliographical references and index.
  ISBN 978-0-8020-9311-0 (bound)
  ISBN 978-0-8020-9497-1 (pbk.)

  1. Muslims – Western countries.   2. Race discrimination –
  Western countries.   I. Title.

  BP173.5.R39 2007   305.6'97091713   C2007-903885-9

University of Toronto Press acknowledges the financial assistance to its
publishing program of the Canada Council for the Arts and the Ontario
Arts Council.

University of Toronto Press acknowledges the financial support for its
publishing activities of the Government of Canada through the
Book Publishing Industry Development Program (BPIDP).

To my mother, Acclema

Contents

Acknowledgments

It is hard to know who *not* to thank for assistance with this book. I have benefited from the advice, love, and support of virtually everyone I would call a friend and family member, and from the ideas of countless colleagues, and from audiences where I presented this work. Of course, the wonderful students of the Ontario Institute for Studies in Education of the University of Toronto influenced the final version. Perhaps it is a good idea to start with research assistance and to confess that I have had extraordinary research assistants without whom I could not get along. Time and time again, Carmela Murdocca, Gada Mahrouse, and Leslie Thielen Wilson have offered me the best of themselves, and I am deeply grateful. To Leslie, I extend a special thanks for saving me from myself when I thought the sky was falling and for never failing in her enthusiasm for the project. Honor Ford Smith, Amina Jamal, and Homa Hoodfar were always willing to listen and to theorize about what has been happening to Muslims since 9/11. Barbara Buckman, Donna Jeffery, Sheryl Nestel, Helene Moussa, and Ruth Roach Pierson encouraged me in times of crisis. My family are always the ground on which I stand to write. I thank them for material and emotional support and for inspiring me with their own capacity to work hard and to care. Lots of love goes to Larry, Ben, and Ilya and to my siblings, nieces, and nephews. This book was always a collective family project discussed over many meals. I dedicate it to my dearest mother, who showed me early on all the things a Muslim woman can be. Her unshakeable belief that her children are special is the best gift she gives, and I want to thank her for it and for the privilege of growing up with a hard-working, loving, and above all joyous mother who loves cricket and hockey games and going to the beach as much as she loves going to the mosque.

I owe Sharry Aitkin, Barbara Jackman, Andrew Brouwer, John Norris, Kike Roach, and the African Canadian Legal Clinic a special debt for sharing their insight and materials and for supporting the research on security certificates, my colleague Megan Boler for reading a draft of the working paper, and Laura Gomez for helping me to get the work out. Kari Dehli, Anja Bredal, Nita Kapoor, and Rachel Paul were of considerable help for research on the Norwegian context, and Ulla Johanson translated Norwegian texts. The Social Sciences and Humanities Research Council supported the book with a grant for which I am grateful. Versions of these chapters appeared in the following journals and I am grateful for permission to reproduce them: *Canadian Journal of Women and the Law*, *Feminist Legal Studies*, *Social Justice Review*, and *Studies in Law, Politics and Society*.

CASTING OUT
The Eviction of Muslims from Western Law and Politics

Introduction: Race Thinking and the Camp

That colonies might be ruled over in absolute lawlessness stems from the racial denial of any common bond between the conqueror and the native.

Achille Mbembe[1]

The state of exception is an anomic space in which what is at stake is a force of law without law (which therefore should be written: force of ~~law~~).

Giorgio Agamben[2]

A Typical Month in the 'War on Terror' in Canada

In the month of June 2006, there were 'terror sweeps' of seventeen young Muslim men in Toronto who were allegedly planning to blow up the CN Tower and the headquarters of Canada's security services. The young men, five of whom are teenagers, were brought to the courtroom in leg irons, surrounded by the heavy presence of police snipers, a spectacle of 'dangerous' Muslim men whose meaning few could fail to grasp. Uncharacteristically naming race, Canadian newspapers covering the June terror arrests openly referred to Muslims as 'brown-skinned' and were at pains to make the distinction between those who were merely 'Canadian-born,' as the seventeen accused are, and those who are truly Canadian by virtue of possessing Canadian values, if not Canadian skin. Few reporters bothered to consider the presumption of innocence. At the same time as four hundred Royal Canadian Mounted Police officers in battle fatigues were engaged in arresting the seventeen young men, the Supreme Court was getting ready to hear challenges to the constitutionality of security certificates, a legal mechanism contained in the *Immigration and Refugee Protection Act* that permits the detention without due process of non-citizens suspected of involvement in terrorism and, more significantly, those considered to have the *potential* to commit terrorist acts. The Canadian government contemplated extending similar provisions in the *Anti-Terrorism Act,* which applies to citizens and non-citizens alike. In the same month, the government was also seeking support for sending more troops to Afghanistan and those already present there were beginning a major offensive against the Taliban. Terror arrests at home undoubtedly invested these latter activities with greater legitimacy, particularly when the bodies of Canadian soldiers killed in Afghanistan began coming home. Canadians are reminded daily that we are a nation at war, and even hockey games can now begin with soldiers parachuting on to the ice.

In this climate, where the suspension of rights is legally authorized as necessary in what is called the 'war on terror,' there are also calls to end multiculturalism, to increase the surveillance of immigrants and refugees, and to further limit their fundamental rights. Confronted with the possibility of an imminent terror threat, few protest such erosions of citizenship. Barely a murmur arose, for example, when it emerged that Canadians born in Syria and Iran who were working on U.S. defence contracts awarded to Bell Canada were fired from their jobs or reassigned owing to a U.S. stipulation that such workers cannot be employed on projects that involve the construction of American strategic military weapons.[3] In the same vein, when Canada's largest bank initially agreed to prohibit Canadians with dual citizenship in countries under American sanction (Iran, Iraq, Cuba, Sudan, North Korea, and Myanmar) from opening U.S. dollar accounts, few saw in such penalties an ominous sign of the racial structure of citizenship.[4]

Globally, while Muslim men have been the target of an intense policing, Muslim women have been singled out as needing protection from their violent and hyper-patriarchal men. The wearing of the hijab in public schools has now been prohibited in France and there are calls to extend the ban to all public spaces. In the province of Ontario, Canada, the government has banned faith-based arbitration, long permitted in the province, for fear that fundamentalist Muslims will now use the opportunity to introduce Sharia law against vulnerable Muslim women. Several European countries ban what they describe as forced marriages between European Muslim girls and men from Muslim countries. The headlines warn that unless we are vigilant against conservative Muslims, soon the stoning of women will be allowed in the Western world. Perhaps nothing expresses the rising hysteria better than the action taken by a small rural town in Quebec to declare formally that the town forbids the stoning of women and the burning of them with acid.[5] Explaining why a town of three hundred white citizens in which there are no Muslims felt compelled to proclaim its 'standards' publicly, the town's mayor simply declared: 'I like the way we live and I don't want it to change.'[6] Throughout these various media spectacles and legal campaigns, the pundits, politicians, lawyers, and journalists warn of a deadly clash of civilizations between a medievalist Islam and a modern, enlightened West, and declare the urgent need for the West to defend itself against the Islamic threat.

Three allegorical figures have come to dominate the social landscape of the 'war on terror' and its ideological underpinning of a clash of civilizations: the dangerous Muslim man, the imperilled Muslim woman, and the civilized European, the latter a figure who is seldom explicitly named but who nevertheless anchors the first two figures. This book explores some of the places in law and society in the West where these figures animate a story about a family of white nations, a civilization, obliged to use force and terror to defend itself against a menacing cultural Other. The story is not just a story, of course, but is the narrative scaffold for the making of an empire dominated by the United States and the white nations who are its allies. Supplying the governing logic of several laws and legal processes, both in North America and in Europe, the story underwrites the expulsion of Muslims from political community, a casting out that takes the form of stigmatization, surveillance, incarceration, abandonment, torture, and bombs.

While conferences are held on the 'deadly threat of Islam,'[7] and a rise in anti-Muslim racism is in evidence, it is also true that the 'war on terror' began with the destruction of the World Trade Center and the attack on the Pentagon in 2001 and the loss of nearly three thousand lives; since then there have been bombings of trains in Madrid and London. In view of European and North American loss of life, until now a rare outcome of political conflict, it may seem not entirely surprising that there has been such a strong resurgence of an old Orientalism and an immediate intensification of surveillance, detention, and the suspension of rights for those who are 'Muslim-looking.' As Western governments have argued, these are times of emergency and a deadly threat confronts the nation, a threat that warrants the suspension of rights. The threat explains, if not excuses, the rise in anti-Muslim racism. Such responses naturalize the suspension of rights and the rise of anti-Muslim racism in the post-9/11 period, uncoupling them from the past and, significantly, from the *ongoing* management of racial populations of which they are a part.

It is my intention in this book to situate contemporary legal and social responses to Muslims in the West within a history, a history of the encounter between the West and its racial Others. To historicize the legal projects that are discussed here requires that we ask not only about the old structures from which they emerge, and upon which they rely, but, most of all, that we explore what they *accomplish* in the present. When Muslim-looking terror suspects are rounded up and denied fundamental rights, when the rule of law is no longer considered relevant, and when ordinary Canadians wake up one morning and decide that something must be done to safeguard their values from fundamentalist Muslims, we must consider the productive function of these practices. A particular kind of nation state comes into being, as does a particular kind of national subject. In the case of the nation state, we can say immediately that what is born, or perhaps born again, is a national community organized increasingly as a fortress, with rigid boundaries and borders that mark who belongs and who does not. The national subject of this securitized state understands himself or herself as being under siege. When both developments draw upon, even as they sustain, old notions of the nation as a racial kin group, we are witnessing the consolidation of a racially ordered world.

In this book I offer two interlinked arguments about the contemporary context of the 'war on terror.' First, race thinking, the denial of a common bond of humanity between people of European descent and those who are not, remains a defining feature of the world order. Second, this 'colour-lined' world is one increasingly governed by the logic of the exception and the camps of abandoned or 'rightless' people it creates. The camp, created as a state of exception, is a place where, paradoxically, the law has determined that the rule of law does not apply. Since there is no common bond of humanity between the camp's inmates and those outside, there is no common law. For those marked as outside humanity, law reserves the space of the exception. I argue in this book that the abandonment of populations, an abandonment configured as emergency, is accomplished as a racial project.

It is now widely argued that today's empire is most distinguished by the proliferation of camps and by the culture of exception that underpins the eviction of increasing numbers of people from political community. Camps range from those whose inmates are 'terror' suspects wearing black hoods (as the cover of this book shows) to those of asylum seekers and their children, facilities hidden away in the deserts of Australia or the suburbs of Texas and Toronto, camps for migrant workers on the Niagara peninsula where workers live in barrack-like surroundings and do not have freedom of movement, and conventional prisons whose inmates nevertheless do not enjoy prisoners' rights and spend long periods in solitary confinement. Camps may even extend to an entire state, as several have argued of the Israeli occupation of Palestine.[8] All such spaces are distinguished by a legally authorized suspension of law and the creation of communities of people without 'the right to have rights,' as Hannah Arendt put it long ago when describing the impact of the First World War and the creation of large groups of people who were homeless, stateless, and 'rightless.' Camps are places where the rules of the world cease to apply.[9]

Communities without the right to have rights are significantly different from communities who are merely discriminated against. They are constituted as a different order of humanity altogether by virtue of having no political community willing to guarantee their rights, and whatever is meted out to the 'rightless' becomes of no concern to others. Indeed, their very expulsion from political community fortifies the nation state. As Hanson and Stepputat observe:

> The expulsion of someone who used to have rights as a citizen, or simply to categorize some individuals in a society as a form of life that is beyond the reach of dignity and full humanity and thus not even a subject of a benevolent power, is the most elementary operation of sovereign power – be it as a government in a nation-state, a local authority, a community, a warlord, or a local militia.[10]

For many who observe the increasing numbers of 'rightless' people and the creation of camps, it is clear that those most often evicted from political community are racialized. I am particularly interested in how such evictions of racialized peoples make possible the production of white identities – as kin groups, families, nations. Materially and symbolically, camps help to create and sustain a racial and neoliberal order in which white people come to know themselves as a superior people, a community that must fortify itself against pre-modern racial Others who do not share its values, beliefs, practices, and level of civility. Such a racially homogeneous community is nevertheless one made up of subjects who imagine themselves as raceless individuals, consumers, and agents without defining links to community – in other words, as citizens who have the freedom to make their own choices.

Race Thinking

To understand the place of race in the concept of a modern world menaced by a pre-modern one, a world of camps, it is useful to consider what Hannah Arendt, in *The Origins of Totalitarianism*, called race thinking. Race thinking is a structure of thought that divides up the world between the deserving and the undeserving according to descent. As Irene Silverblatt has suggested, race thinking encapsulates a much broader phenomenon than racism, since it refers to 'any mode of construing and engaging social hierarchies through the lens of descent.'[11] Race thinking enables us to understand 'how a relatively innocent category (like color) could become virulent, how politically defined characteristics (like nationality) could so easily become inheritable traits.'[12] In our context, race thinking reveals itself in the phrase 'Canadian values' or 'American values,' uttered so sanctimoniously by prime ministers and presidents when they articulate what is being defended in the 'war on terror.' Drawing on the modern idea of race traced by David Goldberg as 'shared social characteristics, ones perhaps deemed as natural properties of the group,' and bolstered by what Goldberg identifies as the four features of race thinking (the rhetoric of descent, claims of common origins, a sense of kinship and belonging, and the naturalization of social relations), values talk conceals the hierarchy it expresses.[13] Echoing a long-standing imperial belief that Northern peoples possessed an innate ability to govern themselves and were by nature more rational (for Rudyard Kipling, it was 'the climate that puts iron and grit into men's bones'),[14] these statements simply reinstall bloodlines through the idea that some groups have a greater innate capacity for rationality than others.

For Arendt, who drew on Erich Voegelin,[15] race thinking matures into racism through its use as a political weapon. Racism's graduation from an obscure free opinion to a full-fledged ideology occurred with imperialism and the 'fateful days of the scramble for Africa.'[16] In imperialism, race thinking combined with bureaucracy, 'the organization of the great game of expansion in which every area was considered a stepping stone to further involvements and every people an instrument for further conquest.'[17] As a 'scavenger ideology' (to use George Mosse's words),[18] race thinking picks up political projects here and there and annexes itself to ideas such as evolutionist doctrines or romanticism with its notions of inherited genius, eventually growing into the full-blown power of racism. We may not find that President George W. Bush pursues a race project as single-mindedly as did Adolf Hitler, but we can see how race thinking (the clash of a modern and pre-modern civilization) is annexed to a political project (control of oil, capitalist accumulation, power) and erupts into a full-blown racism when united with ideas about universal values, individualism, and the market.

When race thinking unites with bureaucracy, when, in other words, it is systematized and attached to a project of accumulation, it loses its standing as a prejudice and becomes instead an organizing principle. In our time, one result is a securitized state in which it is possible to know that 'the passenger who has ordered a special meal is a non-smoking Muslim in seat 3K'[19] and to arrange for that passenger's eviction from the aircraft. Racial distinctions become so routinized that a racial hierarchy is maintained without requiring the component of individual actors who are personally hostile towards Muslims. Increasing numbers of people find themselves exiled from political community through bureaucratic processes in which each state official can claim, as did Adolf Eichmann about arranging the transport of Jews to Nazi Germany, that he was only doing his duty. In the 'war on terror,' race thinking accustoms us to the idea that the suspension of rights is warranted in the interests of national security. Captured in the phrase 'they are not like us,' and also necessarily in the idea that 'they' must be killed so that 'we' can live, race thinking becomes embedded in law and bureaucracy so that the suspension of rights appears not as a violence but as the law itself. Violence against the racialized Other comes to be understood as necessary in order for civilization to flourish, something the state must do to preserve itself. Race thinking, Silverblatt reminds us in her study of the Spanish Inquisition, usually comes clothed in an 'aura of rationality and civilization.'[20]

Although race thinking varies, for Muslims and Arabs it is underpinned by the idea that modern enlightened, secular peoples must protect themselves from pre-modern, religious peoples whose loyalty to tribe and community reigns over their commitment to the rule of law. The marking of belonging to the realm of culture and religion, as opposed to the realm of law and reason, has devastating consequences. There is a disturbing spatializing of morality that occurs in the story of pre-modern peoples versus modern ones. We have reason; they do not. We are located in modernity; they are not. Significantly, because *they* have not advanced as we have, it is our moral obligation to correct, discipline, and keep them in line and to defend ourselves against their irrational excesses. In doing all of these things, the West has often denied the benefits of modernity to those it considers to be outside of it. Evicted from the universal, and thus from civilization and progress, the non-West occupies a zone outside the law. Violence may be directed at it with impunity.

To divide up the world between the civilized and the uncivilized according to a line of descent requires a racially delineated community of 'original' citizens, a 'volk' constituted against foreigners.[21] Foucault has argued that the modern state, in constituting itself as sovereign and as having the power over life, requires racism. Racism enables us to live with the murderous function of the state and to understand the killing of Others as a way of purifying and regenerating one's own race: 'The fact that the other dies does not mean simply that I live in the sense that his death guarantees my safety; the death of the other, the death of the bad race, of the inferior race (or the degenerate, or the abnormal) is something that will make life in general healthier: healthier and purer.'[22] George Mosse developed a related argument with respect to European racism, pointing out that racism is 'no mere articulation of prejudice,' but is instead 'a fully blown system of thought.'[23]

> All racists held to a certain concept of beauty – white and classical –to middle-class virtues of work, of moderation and honor, and thought that these were exemplified through outward appearance. Most racists consequently endowed inferior races whether black or Jew with several identical properties such as lack of beauty, and charged them with the lack of those middle-class virtues, and finally with lack of any metaphysical depth.[24]

In the context of Nazi Germany, Mosse has written, racism 'defended utopia against its enemies.'[25] Racism could embrace people who were not themselves racists, Mosse argued, principally through appeal to 'the thought that some had to be killed so that others could live to the full.'[26] When we look for signs of racism's presence, then, it is not simply to be found in the racial hostility some individuals bear towards others not of their race, but also in the ideas that the state must protect itself from those who do not share its values, ideals of beauty, and middle-class virtues. It is by virtue of the foreigner's *inherent* difference (manifested, as Mosse has suggested, through outward appearance, including cultural and religious practices and accent) to an imagined homogeneous citizenry, a difference understood as inferiority, that states make the claim that utopia is threatened and invoke state-of-exception measures.

The Camp

Legal measures that suspend rights in the interests of national security have been variously described as state-of-exception, state-of-emergency, war measures or state-of-siege measures. Whether they are found in immigration provisions, as are Canadian security certificates, whereby detainees are not entitled to see all the evidence against them, or in anti-terrorism acts, they share the paradox that they are laws that suspend the rule of law. It should be noted that the threats against which society must be defended, to use Foucault's memorable phrase, are multiple. As Balibar has observed, they can be threats 'stemming from the economic forces of 'globalization,' 'criminal' immigration networks, religious or cultural 'communitarianism,' and finally cosmopolitan intellectuals and nongovernmental organizations that allow themselves to be seduced by a 'postnational' ideology.'[27] As Aihwa Ong argues, at the heart of neoliberalism is the idea and the practice of the exception, the notion that the government has the right to do anything in the interest of governance. Capital constructs spaces of exception, and a graduated or variegated sovereignty – where, for example, corporations have the right to suspend the law – is the hallmark of neoliberalism. Exceptions operate with varying regimes of incarceration, imprisoning some in migrant worker camps or domestic worker zones and confining others within gated communities but removing all such communities from the reach of the law.[28]

There is now a great deal of scholarly attention given to states of exception and to the camps they authorize, not only because the 'war on terror' has brought us Guantanamo Bay with its inmates who are held without charge and indefinitely detained, but also because of the large numbers of migrants and refugees in detention centres throughout the Western world. It is useful to recall that before it became an interrogation centre for terror suspects in the 1990s, Guantanamo Bay held Haitian refugees who were declared to pose an HIV threat. The Clinton administration attempted to justify the inhumane treatment meted out to these refugees on the grounds that Guantanamo was a law-free zone.[29] The 'war on terror' did not mark the beginning of a resurgence of camps or the spread of camp logic. Indeed, when, in 1995, Zygmunt Bauman posed the question of whether or not the twentieth century would be remembered as 'the age of camps,' he had in mind Auschwitz, the Soviet Gulag, the Rwandan genocide, refugee camps, and prisons in the United States with their ever-growing pop-ulations of colour and their increasing suspensions of prisoners' rights.[30] Similarly, Giorgio Agamben, in *Homo Sacer: Sovereign Power and Bare Life* (1995), analyses the stadium in Baril (where Italian police rounded up illegal Albanian immigrants in 1991 before deporting them) as a camp. Agamben's examples include airport detention centres for refugees and the camps into which the Weimar government rounded up Jews.[31]

What the 'war on terror' has prompted, however, is an answer in the affirmative to Bauman's question. The camp has become the rule, and our culture is now globally one of exception.[32] In their much-discussed book *Empire*, Michael Hardt and Antonio Negri consider today's empire a new phenomenon, one that builds on the imperialism of old but is nonetheless a new juridical formation. Empire, they argue, proj-ects a single supranational figure of political power and is based on a new notion of right. The exception is central to this new form of sov-ereignty: 'The concept of empire is presented as a global concert under the direction of a single conductor, a unitary power that maintains the social peace and produces its ethical truths. And in order to achieve these ends, the social power is given the necessary force to conduct, when necessary, "just wars" at the borders against the barbarians and internally against the rebellious.'[33] The exception grants the 'right to police' an enemy who is so routinely persecuted that it is banal or, con-versely, an archetypical enemy who poses an absolute threat.[34] When scholars emphasize the proliferation of camps in today's 'war on terror,' it is in order to note the sheer numbers of people exiled from political community, their status as non-persons, and the fact that the eviction from political community is a legally authorized one inspired by a sense of permanent emergency and endless war.[35] Camps, then, are not simply contemporary excesses born of the West's current quest for security, but instead represent a more ominous, permanent arrangement of who is and is not a part of the human community. The exception, Ong shows, produces new kinds of citizens, principally those who are subjected to neoliberal considerations and those who are excluded from it. Cautioning us that it would be a mistake to understand citizenship as structured by a simple opposition between those within the state and those outside of it, Ong emphasizes that the exception be considered as a practice of governance. It can create 'new economic possibilities, spaces and techniques for governing a population.'[36] With this caution in mind, we can consider the logic of the exception, its confirmation of sovereign power, its multiple practices of inclusion and exclusion, as sustaining a neoliberal and racial order that is nonetheless one filled with contradictions and fissures.

Law and the Right to Punish Strangers

Because suspensions of the rule of law turn on a logic that normative citizens must be protected from those who threaten the social order, a category to which race gives content, those who consider themselves 'unmarked' or original easily find them defensible. Agamben has proposed that we see the state of exception as the 'preliminary condition' for understanding the relationship of law to the living. Following his own directions, and understanding a state of exception as 'a legal civil war that allows for the physical elimination not only of political adversaries but of entire categories of citizens who for some reason cannot be integrated into the political system,'[37] Agamben takes us on a sobering journey through American, English, Italian, and German law to show how states of exception become lasting practices of government that enable the state to mark who is a member of political community and who is not. Although we might contest the rigidity of Agamben's account, it is the extraordinary power to cast out that he documents that should stop us in our tracks. Offering a contemporary example, Agamben writes of the 13 November 2001 American presidential decree that authorizes indefinite detention and hearing by military tribunal of non-citizens suspected of involvement in terrorist activity. While aliens suspected of terrorist activity could be taken into custody under the *Patriot Act*, the 13 November presidential decree 'radically erases any legal status of the individual, thus producing a legally unnamable and unclassifiable being.'[38]

Neither prisoners nor persons accused, but simply 'detainees' they [the prisoners at Guantanamo Bay] are the object of a pure de facto rule, of a detention that is indefinite not only in the temporal sense but in its very nature as well, since it is entirely removed from the law and from judicial oversight. The only thing to which it could possibly be compared is the legal situation of the Jews in the Nazi *Lager* [camps], who, along with their citizenship, had lost every legal identity, but at least retained their identity as Jews.[39]

Several scholars draw attention to the relationship between race, violence, and the law that are evident in states of exception. In pointing out that the slave plantation was a space of exception, Paul Gilroy reminds us not to overlook 'how colonial societies and conflicts provided the context in which concentration camps emerged as a political administration, population management, warfare, and coerced labor.'[40] It is the idea of a modern civilization encountering a premodern one that produced the colonial world as 'a permanent, tropical exception from common law applicable in Europe,' Hansen and Stepputat note.[41] What the state of exception made possible in the colonies was a brutal inscription of the power of the colonizers on the bodies of the colonized, a violence that was legally authorized. Such violence became socially acceptable, Edward Said brilliantly showed, through ideas that the colonized only understand force and cannot be governed through the rule of law as it applied to Europeans.[42]

Race perpetually tested the limits of universal law and the exception resolved this tension by providing two different regimes of law under one banner.[43] Mbembe shows for the African context how colonial governance was based on a state of exception, with bureaucrats and company officials possessing a different power than other citizens. The violence of such regimes acted as authority and as morality, instructing all in the *power* of the law and its spaces of non-law, and consequently in who belonged to political community and who did not.[44] Nasser Hussain provides an example of the logic of the jurisprudence of emergency as authority and morality in his analysis of the Amritsar massacre in nineteenth-century British India. Relying on the authority of martial law, the British General Dyer ordered his troops to fire into a crowd of Indians until 379 lay dead and thousands injured. Despite the best efforts of the Home Office to depict Dyer's actions as those of a madman driven to excesses, Dyer himself explained his behaviour as duty – the duty to teach the natives a lesson or, in his words, 'to produce a sufficient moral effect from a military point of view.'[45] The killing would have gone on, Dyer asserted, until the lesson was learnt. Only the lack of bullets stopped it. Dyer, Hussain comments, 'unabashedly links the performativity of violence to the project of moral education,' understanding completely that martial law's purpose was none other than the reconstitution of the authority of the state and the inscription of obedience on the bodies of the colonized.[46] Through emergency, colonial law provided for its own failure, a practice born out of the need to set up a political system that both maintained the rule of law and was able to respond to the exigencies of the colonial situation, one that was rife with 'dissent' and 'disobedience.'[47]

Wherever sovereign power is exercised, and whether or not the performances of sovereignty are spectacular and public as they were in the Amritsar massacre or appear as 'scientific/technical rationalities of management and punishment of bodies,'[48] as I shall argue they are in terror arrests and security certificate hearings, such power remains embedded in the idea of the citizen and thus in the boundary between members of political community and those outside of it. Violence is 'fetishized as a weapon of reason and preservation of freedom of the citizens vis-à-vis the threats from outsiders, from internal enemies, and from those not yet fit for citizenship – slaves and colonial subjects.' Sovereignty thus becomes 'embodied in citizens sharing territory and culture, and sharing the right to punish strangers.'[49]

If we look for how sovereign power constructs its authority through its 'capacity for visiting violence on human bodies,' colonial forms of sovereignty were always more excessive than those that prevailed in Europe.[50] However, the colony as a formation of terror revealed the structure of the *European* juridical order. That order rested on the logic of the juridical equality of all states (each possessed the right to wage war – to kill – and no state could make claims to rule outside its borders), but also on the equally fundamental tenet that this logic did not apply to those parts of the globe outside Europe available for colonization. If Europe laid claim to humanity, Gilroy notes, that humanity 'could exist only in the neatly bounded, territorial units where true and authentic culture could take root under the unsentimental eye of a ruthlessly eugenic government.'[51] If the nation existed within the higher logic of a natural hierarchy, that logic also ordered those *within* the nation itself. Extending Foucault's argument that racism was the ordering principle establishing who shall live and who shall die, Gilroy suggests that at the summit of imperial power, race thinking and race science combined with nationalism to invest the nation with

characteristics associated with biocultural kinship in which new forms of
duty and mutual obligation appeared to regulate relationships between
members of the collective, while those who fell beyond the boundaries of
the official community were despised, reviled, and subjected to entirely
different political and juridical procedures, especially if they did not
benefit from the protection of an equivalent political body.[52]

Gilroy's reminder of the nation imagined as a biocultural kin group
that must be fortified against culturally and racially different others is
especially relevant to today's empire of camps.

Gender and the Camp

Etienne Balibar has remarked that in this time of a single supranational
power, it is through the right to exclude that the weakened nation state
'*demonstrates* (at low cost) the force that it claims to hold and at the
same time *reassures* those who suspect its destitution.'[53] In the 'inten-
sive universalism' of contemporary nation states, Balibar argues,
'anthropological differences' become the reason to exclude. If all citizens are entitled to equal rights, then those who are considered
unequal by virtue of pathological, sexual, or cultural difference can be
summarily excluded from citizenship on the grounds that they pose a
threat to the nation.[54] The racism of empire treats differences between
cultures and traditions as insurmountable; racial hierarchy becomes in
this way an effect of culture, an outcome of what are considered
immutable cultural differences.[55] In the 'war on terror,' Muslim cultures and traditions become innate characteristics that permanently
mark Muslims as belonging outside the polity. Gender is crucial to the
confinement of Muslims to the pre-modern, as post-colonial scholarship has long shown.[56] Considered irredeemably fanatical, irrational,
and thus dangerous, Muslim men are also marked as deeply misogynist patriarchs who have not progressed into the age of gender equality, and who indeed cannot. For the West, Muslim women are the
markers of their communities' place in modernity.

How does it come to be that visions of veiled women dance in the
heads of so many that 'codes de vie' must be devised declaring that all
women must show their faces in the small North American town of
Hérouxville, Quebec? In the unconscious structure of Orientalism, the

veiled Oriental woman, Yegenoglu observes, signifies the Orient as seductive and dangerous, but the powerful allure and productive power of the fantasy of Orientalism has meant that the European man must dream a dream of possession of the veiled woman if he is to know himself as modern, all-knowing and rational. The longing to possess, to unveil, is often expressed as rescue, and in this way it is a fantasy shared by both men and women. Saving Brown women from Brown men, as Gayatri Spivak famously put it, has long been a major plank in the colonial ship since it serves to mark the colonizer as modern and civilized and provides at the same time an important reason to keep Brown men in line through practices of violence. In the post-9/11 era, this aspect of colonial governance has been revitalized. Today it is not only the people of a small white village in Canada who believe that Muslim women must be saved. Progressive people, among them many feminists, have come to believe in the urgency of saving Muslim women from their patriarchal communities. As a practice of governance, the idea of the imperilled Muslim woman is unparalleled in its capacity to regulate. Since Muslim women, like all other women, *are* imperilled in patriarchy, and since the rise of conservative Islam increases this risk (as does the rise of conservative Christianity and Hinduism), it is hard to resist calls to 'save the women.'

Empire is a gendered project not only in the sense that what happens to colonized men often differs from what happens to colonized women, but because the work that the ruling race *does* is also stratified along gender lines. Whereas it is principally the men of the West who engage in actual policing (with notable exceptions in camps such as Abu Ghraib where there were also some women guards), it falls to the women of the ruling race to police the colour line in a different way. They mark the West as a place of values, and the non-West as a place of culture, a line in the sand drawn by comparing their own apparently emancipated status with that of their non-Western sisters. The Western subject is 'an unavoidably masculine position,' and Western women, Yegenoglu notes, can access the universal only through asserting themselves in the same fantasy of possessing of the Oriental woman.[57]

In this book, I devote considerable space to how some Western feminists participate in empire through the politics of rescue, unhesitatingly installing the idea that it is through gender that we can tell the difference between those who are modern and those who are not. As I argue in several chapters, Western feminists fail to see their own implication in the neoliberal politics of empire, understanding only that they are more enlightened than their worse-off sisters in the South. Gender operates as a kind of technology of empire enabling the West to make the case for its own modernity and for its civilizational projects around the globe. Where gender is relied upon in this way, Muslim women find themselves stranded between the patriarchs of their own community and the empire's bombs. That is, either we accept the diagnosis that our cultures and our men are barbaric and take the cure (the bombs on our heads and the camps), or we endure patriarchal violence. From laws against forced marriages in Norway to the banning of faith-based arbitration in Canada, I will offer several examples of how Muslim women are socially constructed on the horns of this dilemma. My own concern as a feminist with a Muslim name is the enormous difficulty of practising a feminist politics when feminism can be so easily co-opted. In the post-9/11 environment, how can feminists respond to the very real threats posed by religious conservatives for whom the control of women is paramount? I answer this question through an exploration of the kinds of anti-violence strategies that have gained ground since 9/11, strategies about control and surveillance of communities of colour. These, I argue, do little to confront violence against women and they enable a marking of Muslim communities as insufficiently modern, a branding that has grave consequences.

The Organization of This Book

I divide the book into two parts. Part one, composed of chapters 1 and 2, focuses on the figure of the 'dangerous' Muslim man and examines the camp as a place in which are incarcerated 'terror suspects' and those marked as outside political community. Part two, composed of chapters 3 to 5, focuses on imperilled Muslim women, exploring in detail feminism's connection to race thinking and the legal projects that regulate Muslim communities in the post-9/11 era. Given the two arguments I advance, that race thinking undergirds the making of empire, and that the world is increasingly governed by the logic of the exception, each chapter is an example of a camp – that is, a place where law is suspended (the force of law without law) and Muslims are evicted from the national community. The camps I discuss range from literal prison camps, where terror suspects do not have the right to *habeas corpus*, to Muslim immigrant communities, for whom the rights and privileges of citizenship, such as the right to marry once the age of consent has been reached to the right to practise their faith as do others, do not apply. Ultimately, all Muslims become marked as outside political community when they are assumed to carry *within* them the possibility of threat to the nation.

In chapter 1, on the incarceration of Muslim men in Canada and the restriction of their rights to due process, I show the micro-processes through which the camp is legally authorized. In examining closely how suspensions in rights are justified in security certificate hearings, I show that the 'dangerous' Muslim man who threatens the West is depicted as a 'monster terrorist' who is an Islamic extremist. The danger is made believable largely through appeal to racist narratives about intrinsically savage, pre-modern Muslims. Under this logic, it is possible to defend the idea that Muslim men must be detained indefinitely and denied due process on the grounds that they may carry within them the seeds of terrorism.

In chapter 2, I turn my attention to the sexualized torture enacted on Arab men at Abu Ghraib. Here I argue that sexualized torture, or what has euphemistically come to be called 'prisoner abuse,' is more appropriately named racial terror. Terror is how colonizers come to know their own power as well as how they come to make it known. In showing that what went on at Abu Ghraib convinced the American men and women who engaged in torture that they were themselves members of a racially superior race and nation, I emphasize, drawing on Michael Taussig, that terror is a mythology, a narrative meant to teach us who must be kept in line through force and who are the enforcers. Acts of terror make the nation and the empire, and as such they will continue to happen. The practices of torture at Abu Ghraib were sexualized and recorded in photos and videotapes. These two aspects suggest the psychic underpinnings of empire, whereby the boundary between self and Other must be policed through violence, lest it collapse. At Abu Ghraib, the acts of violence afforded American soldiers an intimacy that would otherwise be forbidden as well as a chance to establish forever who is in control. In attending to the ambivalence at the heart of the fantasy of Orientalism, the multiple ways in which individuals participate in empire through desire and fear, I suggest that if we pay attention to how empire is embodied, to the deep, psychically structured ways in which race, class, gender, and sexuality shape the encounter between the West and its Others, we can begin to understand how casting out takes place and how it must be resisted.

In chapter 3, I turn to gender as a technology of the 'war on terror,' exploring how the violence that is unleashed on Muslim communities is transformed into a civilizing narrative about saving Muslim women. I begin with popular culture, exploring three books – by an American, European, and Canadian author respectively. What marks these popular books as emblematic of the post-9/11 era is their authors' positioning as feminist and their common insistence that the violence Muslim women endure at the hands of Muslim men is not only an indicator of barbarism but, more importantly, a reason to invade, occupy, and civilize Muslim communities. In tracing the role that gender plays in the ideological justifications underpinning the American bid for empire, I show how white nations are invited into the project of empire as members of a superior race, a race distinguished by a commitment to gender equality, democracy, and human rights. Here Muslims are imagined as camp inmates by virtue of being insufficiently modern, a condition that is assumed to be innate.

The policing of Muslim communities in the name of gender equality is now a globally organized phenomenon, an argument I make in chapter 4 through an examination of Norwegian laws on forced marriages. Several European states have sought to regulate the conduct of Muslim populations in Europe in the name of protecting Muslim women from their violent communities. Typically, these initiatives are understood as necessary in order to forcibly 'deculturalize' feudal and hyper-patriarchal migrants to Europe who are Muslim. In exploring the tension between meaningful anti-violence initiatives and those that simply reinstal Europeans as normative citizens and Muslims as outside the nation (literally and figuratively), I show how an unequal structure of citizenship is achieved in Europe through the deployment of the idea of the imperilled Muslim woman. Through such moves as regulating the age of consent and family reunification, European states create a category of citizen whose private life choices are controlled. For Muslims, public space is literally shrinking as they encounter constraints on their social and cultural practices that do not apply to other citizens.

In chapter 5, I explore how gender as a technology of empire operates in Canada, a white settler context that is without colonial history in the Muslim world, and thus without the large Muslim migrant populations such histories usually produce. As in Europe, laws that stigmatize Muslim populations and regulate their conduct usually begin in a media spectacle. In Canada, the idea advanced by a small group of Muslim men that faith-based arbitration could be utilized to implement Sharia law in Canada quickly became the basis for a moral panic that feudal Muslims who are likely to be terrorists had now successfully contaminated Canadian civilization. Attending to the risks posed to women if conservative Muslims were to have their way, I thread my way through feminist opposition to faith-based arbitration and conclude that Muslim women were stranded between the rock of a rising conservatism in their communities and the hard place of an even more vigorous policing by the state. The latter, I conclude, poses the greater threat at this moment. In this chapter I focus on one salient aspect of the clash-of-civilizations thesis, the notion that the West is secular and thus modern, while the non-West is religious and pre-modern. I show how the idea of secularism operates as a governmentality, Foucault's concept referring to the ways in which individual subjects are governed through various institutions and processes that organize modern life. Muslims are produced in this framework as undeserving of full citizenship, including the right to practise their faith as they see fit, a restriction that both marks them as not yet ready for citizenship even as it insists that the public sphere is a universal one where citizens have equal rights.

In bringing together case studies that explore the eviction of Muslims from political community, I hope to stress the various paths through which we are drawn into the project of empire. Feminist activists, no less than soldiers at Abu Ghraib, are invited to defend country and civilization and to join in the creation of a world that requires camps. What these chapters show is that no one stands outside of empire. As in my other books, I have sought to give some content to the notion of complicity, exploring the multiple ways in which we come to know ourselves as modern, democratic, and feminist and the actual practices of violence underwritten by this knowledge.

This book is written with the conviction that we can reorient ourselves in this age of the 'war on terror,' unlearning ourselves as modern and coming instead to understand ourselves as responsible. Suspending the rule of law and engaging in violence with impunity are practices undertaken in the name of civility. Violence as civility suggests a critical pedagogy and radical politics. If we are to stop the violence unleashed by camp thinking, we will need to confront ideas of a clash of civilizations, torture for the sake of keeping the natives in line, occupation as a means of improvement of savage peoples and savage lands, secularism as simply about freedom from tradition and the triumph of free will, and the primacy of the market, contract, and choice.[58] We will also have to confront the unconscious processes that structure how individuals come to participate in empire. This book approaches this task by arguing that race thinking structures the conceptual arsenal of the 'war on terror' and its reliance on the logic of the concentration camp. What I have tried to do is document what at times has been an intensely personal, that is to say, bodily awareness of the world as camp.

PART ONE

'Dangerous' Muslim Men

1 'Your client has a profile': Race in the Security Hearing

Whoever entered the camp moved in a zone of indistinction between outside and inside, exception and rule, licit and illicit, in which the very concepts of subjective right and judicial protections no longer made any sense.

Giorgio Agamben[1]

34 (1) A permanent resident or a foreign national is inadmissible on security grounds for (f) being a member of an organization that there are reasonable grounds to believe engages, has engaged, or *will engage* in acts referred to in paragraphs (a) [espionage or subversion], (b) [subversion by force] or (c) [terrorism]. (Emphasis added)

Immigration and Refugee Protection Act [2]

At a hearing on 27 November 2003 to determine the validity of the security certificate that declared Hassan Almrei inadmissible to Canada on the grounds that he will engage in acts of terrorism, an agent from the Canadian Security Intelligence Service (CSIS) confidently clarified for Almrei's counsel the heart of the Service's case against his client:

What I am saying today is that *your client has a profile* which makes him of use to Al Qaeda and his connections to the organization through various individuals is what leads us to conclude that he is a threat to the security of Canada. I am afraid that I can't get into any more detail than that.

We are not hanging our case on this notion that he was among the cream-of-the-crop recruits in the early 1980s. I never said that.[3] (Emphasis added)

Not the cream of the crop of recruits, and possibly not even recruited by Al Qaeda, Almrei has the profile of someone of *possible* use to Al Qaeda, and that seals his fate. Almrei's profile is that of an Arab man who went to Afghanistan as a teenager to fight the Soviets in the late 1980s and early 1990s. When combined with the fact that he seems to know other Arab men, some of whom have similar histories, the profile is enough for CSIS, and ultimately the court, to believe that he is someone who will engage in terrorism.

In the post-9/11 environment, few are surprised that individuals with life histories such as Almrei's should come to the attention of security services. What is noteworthy, however, is that at his hearing, Hassan Almrei's life history *suffices* to make the case that he is a terrorist or will become one. No longer simply about 'targeting individuals who possess identifiable attributes that is [*sic*] believed to bear positive statistical correlations to particular kinds of misconduct,'[4] in the post-9/11 period the profile now performs an additional function. It targets *and* condemns through launching Hassan Almrei into a state of exception, a place in law where he has limited due-process rights.

Hassan Almrei's situation arises out of a section of the *Immigration Act* that authorizes security certificates, and thus the state of exception into which he is plunged is part of the legal structure in which non-citizens have fewer rights than do citizens. Security certificates did not begin with the 'war on terror,' but they have become the 'front-line tools' used by Canada to fight terrorism, and their usage is now primarily directed at Arabs and Muslims.[5] A security certificate, issued by the minister of citizenship and immigration and the solicitor general, and authorized under the *Immigration and Refugee Protection Act*, permits the detention and expulsion of non-citizens who are considered to be a threat to national security. Detainees have no opportunity to be heard before a certificate is issued, and a designated judge of the federal court reviews most of the government's case against the detainee in a secret hearing at which neither the detainee nor his counsel is present. The detainee receives only a summary of the evidence against him. Detention is mandatory for non-permanent residents held under a security certificate, and there is no possibility of release unless a person leaves Canada, or the certificate is struck down, or if 120 days have elapsed and deportation has still not taken place. At this point, an application for release can be made. In contrast to non-residents, permanent residents are entitled to a review of the detention order after the first forty-eight hours and subsequently at six-month intervals until a final decision is made by a federal court judge concerning the security certificate. For 'foreign nationals' and permanent residents alike, however, there is no appeal with respect to the judge's decision on the security certificate and the test for the finding of the reasonableness of the certificate is a low one, the ministers needing only to satisfy the court that there is a *possibility* that the person is a terrorist or a member of a terrorist organization.[6] The five men currently detained under security certificates are all Muslim men of Arab origin each of whom has been detained for three to seven years.[7] The detainees – Hassan Almrei,[8] Mohammed Mahjoub,[9] Mohammed Jaballah,[10] Mohamed Harkat,[11] and Adil Charkaoui[12] have served varying periods of time in solitary confinement, and each is detained without charge indefinitely. Adil Charkaoui, the only permanent resident of the five, was released on strict bail conditions after twenty-one months in prison. Mohammad Harkat was released on even stricter bail conditions after three and a half years in prison, and Mohammed Mahjoub's bail was finally granted in February 2007, seven years after his initial detention.

On 23 February 2007 the Supreme Court of Canada ruled that it is unconstitutional to detain people based on secret evidence. In a unanimous decision the court ruled that the sections of the *Immigration and Refugee Protection Act* that permit secret evidence to be used in the judicial confirmation of security certificates unfairly denies detainees their fundamental right to a fair trial. Equally, the section of the act that denies a prompt hearing to foreign nationals violates the *Charter of Rights and Freedoms*. The court also recognized that returning detainees to countries where they might be tortured is not a viable option, although it did not declare such an action unconstitutional. Importantly, the court did not strike down security certificates per se and it gave parliament a year to amend the law in a way that protects detainees' due-process rights to a greater extent than they are protected now. The court favours the solution of lawyers specially appointed to review secret evidence, a solution that may not in fact protect detainees if such appointees are more likely to keep the government's position in mind than the detainees', and especially if special advocates are not allowed to share the secret information with the detainees.[13] As law professor Kent Roach has suggested, it would be a mistake to consider the Supreme Court ruling an outright victory. The court did not condemn indefinite detention of terror suspects

under immigration law as discriminatory nor did it regard such detention as cruel and unusual punishment.[14]

The five detainees are more than simply victims of racial profiling.
Their Arab origins, and the life history that mostly Arab Muslim men
have had, operate to mark them as individuals likely to commit terrorist acts, people whose propensity for violence is indicated by their
origins. When race thinking, the belief in the division of humanity into
those prone to violence and those who are not according to descent, is
accompanied by the idea that there must be two different, hierarchical
legal regimes for each, and when we begin to grow accustomed to
places without law and to people to whom the rule of law does not
apply, we enter the terrifying world of the colonies and the concentration camp. This chapter examines how a space where law is suspended
operates in the 'war on terror,' and it attends to the work that ideas
about race do in the environment of the exception.

Whether with respect to non-citizens or citizens, at the heart of the
state of exception, the place Agamben described as 'the force of law
without law,' is the idea that only an unfettered state power can properly confront threats to the nation. Race thinking helps us to believe in
the necessity of an all-powerful sovereign. If the threat can be contained in no other way than through this extraordinary power to
suspend fundamental rights, it is surely because 'they (those who
threaten us)' are not like 'us' and can only be stopped with brute force.
As Angelina Snodgrass Godoy perceptively notes, two assumptions
remain unchallenged in the culture of exception: we can tell them from
us, and the suspensions of the rule of law will not affect those of us
who are deemed to be within political community.[15] In this way, the
exception instals the idea that the nation is a kin group that must be
fortified against outsiders whose disloyalty we will *recognize*, a disloyalty that is visible not in what people do but in who they are. As I show
below, who people are is formulated in terms of an unchanging
essence derived from their histories, associations, and religious practices, a constellation of *invariant* characteristics inherited from a
culture, religion, and region. A race fiction thus grounds the nation and
inheres in the power of the state to decide who is part of the kin group
and who is not.

How does one end up in the place of exception, 'where judicial protections no longer make sense,' a world of secret evidence in which
there is no right to *habeas corpus*? Hassan Almrei and the other security-
certificate detainees discussed in this chapter are detained on the basis

that they are 'Islamic terrorists,' men who come from a culture in which religion, and not rationality, produces individuals with an *inherent* capacity for violence. A 'Jihadist,' as the 'Islamic terrorist' is called, is forever unable to escape the marking of his religion, culture and history. If Jihadists exist in a space where judicial protections no longer make any sense, their eviction from the law is argued on the basis that the West must necessarily be vigilant when such monsters are let loose on the world. The terrorist as monster draws on a number of Orientalist images, as others have shown.[16] Significantly, monster terrorists lie forever beyond the law, and through them we become accustomed to the idea that there should be places where human beings have no rights. In security-certificate hearings there is a casual, unreflected-upon lawlessness, an abandonment of the rule of law that only race thinking can make defensible. What else can explain the unquestioned absence of evidence, the incoherence of the arguments, and the retreat to the simple logic that 'they' are not like 'us' and cannot be given the benefit of the rule of law?

Pre-emptive Punishment

The domestic philosophy of pre-emptive punishment argues that if there is a possibility that a crime might be committed, it ought to be pre-empted by government action.[17]

Shortly after 9/11, men and some children rounded up from the villages and battlefields of Afghanistan were herded into shipping containers by the Northern Alliance (at the behest of the United States). Many died; it is estimated that only thirty to fifty in each container of three to four hundred apparently survived.[18] Those who survived typically were taken to prisons at Bagram and Kandahar, Afghanistan, and were shipped to third countries (the process known as extraordinary rendition) or to the U.S. base at Guantanamo, Cuba, where they were detained on the basis that the president, as the commander-in-chief, possessed the unilateral authority to arrest and detain anyone. Detainees were declared 'enemy combatants,' a designation that left them in a no man's land of rights, neither prisoners of war nor criminals.[19] In the United States, Canada, and Europe, security programs concentrated on immigrants, utilizing those places of exception long existing in immigration law, as well as new powers to arrest, detain, and deport without due process. Mainly Arab/Muslim men were

swept up in these terror arrests and deported or detained indefinitely.[20] The practices that facilitate the rounding up of Muslims and
Arabs and result in their exile to places without law include strengthened surveillance powers and powers to detain, prosecute, and convict
without any procedural protections or oversights by the courts.

In the Canadian context, fewer due-process rights remain in the
Immigration Act than before 9/11, although it is important to note that
here, as in the United States, many changes pre-date 9/11 and simply
received more widespread support in the ensuing events. The federal
government's allocation of individuals for immigration detention has
increased.[21] An important change introduced into the *Immigration and
Refugee Protection Act* mandates security checks before asylum
processes even begin, a front-end screening that has deeply concerned
refugee advocates.[22] Those marked as security risks now become inel-
igible for a refugee hearing and are immediately deported. Small
openings that once existed – for example, the seeking of ministerial
relief after showing a record of stable residency in Canada – have
mostly closed. Bureaucrats now understand the relief provisions as relevant only in exceptional cases, and there is little expectation that
anyone marked as a security risk will be able to clear himself through
demonstrating 'good behaviour.'[23] It is now the minister of public
safety and emergency preparedness who grants ministerial relief, a
decision so enmeshed in post-9/11 security considerations that it is an
option that appears to be rarely granted.[24]

Those who are found inadmissible for reasons of national security
have now lost all appeal rights. The *Immigration and Refugee Act* passed
in 2002 greatly expanded the powers of immigration officers. It is no
longer possible to complain about the practices of CSIS. Those subject
to security certificates need not pose any actual security risk, but
merely have to be shown to have possibly been a member of a terrorist organization, and to have the potential to engage in terrorist acts. It
is the notion of prevention, the detaining and deporting of individuals
before they have committed a crime, that best sums up the post-9/11
changes and the increasing logic that law must be suspended in the
interests of national security.

The justifications offered for the considerable expansion of state
powers and the suspension of fundamental rights rest on the notion
that it is necessary to strike at the enemy before he strikes at us. Mirzoeff notes that the wall built by Israel in the Occupied Territories, the
physical barriers built by the United States at its Mexico border, and

the detention camps established through the Western world that keep asylum seekers incarcerated indefinitely are all pre-9/11 examples of pre-emptive punishment, an abandonment of law, and the creation of categories of people without rights, all justified on the basis that they may pose a threat to the nation. While globalized pre-emptive punishment means invading and occupying countries on the basis that they *will* pose a threat, as happened in Iraq, domestically it entails an aggressive use of immigration law. Importantly, the goal of detention is 'to keep its inmates invisible with the goal of having them forgotten.'[25] 'Their location is meant to emphasize that they are not part of the nation state and that their inmates will not achieve asylum, let alone citizenship.'[26] The logic of detention, Mirzoeff comments, is that 'there is no such thing as society but only people who belong to the nation and those who do not.'[27] For Zygmunt Bauman, the refugee is placed in the category of the unthinkable and the camps to which they are confined are 'artifices made permanent through blocking the exits.' We refuse to imagine the camp's inmates as members of political community.[28] The very physical location and anonymity of the camp – in the case of Canada's security detainees, a special wing of a maximum-security prison – is meant to convey this eviction from humanity.

Race is crucial to pre-emptive punishment. Mirzoeff notes that pre-emptive punishment has depended heavily on the racial notion that 'they' are not like 'us' and owing to their natures/cultures are likely to erupt into violence against us.[29] The logic is once again a colonial one, whereby states of exception are justified because the colonized cannot be governed through the rule of law as can Europeans. Prevention based on the irrationality and unpredictability of their natures and cultures justifies the camp as well as the practices associated with it. For example, as Nancy Baker and others show, the United States government has defended its practices of limiting press and public access to information, refusing to disclose the names and locations of, and charges against, those detained, conducting immigration hearings in secret, and denying bail even to minor violators on the grounds that anything and anyone can potentially be of use to terrorists.[30] Following what the CIA has described as the mosaic theory, the government has argued that small pieces of information might later fit into the larger terrorist picture. The mosaic theory hinges, however, a great deal on ideas about the natures of those who threaten us.

Risk is read on the body. If it is true that the profile is one way to sort out who goes to the camp and who does not, then those marked as bearing an inherent capacity for disloyalty are not simply being profiled, but are in fact exiled from political community. This process, whereby to be profiled is to be denied due-process rights and to be detained indefinitely, shifts radically what racial profiling now means. The very concept of racial profiling seems inadequate to describe what actually happens to those whose race, read as origins, life histories, and religious practices, marks them as potential terrorists. As Reem Badhi has shown for Canada, public debate over racial profiling has shifted from being about whether racial profiling has happened at all to being about its necessity in this time of emergency.[31]

Although some argued that detaining Muslim or Arab men was not race discrimination most commentators have acknowledged that post-9/11 profiling used 'race as a proxy for risk, either in whole or in part'[32] and accepted that brown skin, 'Middle Eastern looks,' beards, and Muslim or Arab names provided good reasons to detain. In the United States, much of this thinking was overt and legally authorized, while in Canada such practices have been for the most part informal. For example, shortly after 9/11, the U.S. Department of Justice sought to interview male non-citizens between the ages of eighteen and thirty-three from Middle Eastern or 'Islamic' countries or countries with some suspected tie to Al Qaeda.[33] In a less direct fashion, the Canadian government has not officially endorsed racial profiling of Arabs and Muslims, but its practices, particularly in much publicized 'terror sweeps,' suggest that profiling takes place regularly on much the same basis.[34] The argument for racial profiling is risk management and gains are considered to outweigh losses (for instance, the humiliation and stigmatization of Arab and Muslim communities). For example, Professor Stephen Legomsky argues:

> Certainly, I agree that only a minuscule percentage of noncitizens who appear to be Arab or Muslim are involved in any way with terrorism. But that is not the point. The more relevant figure, I maintain, is the converse – the percentage of those noncitizens involved in terrorism who are Arab and Muslim. If there is credible evidence that this percentage is higher in this subgroup than in the general population, then, it seems rational for the government to focus particular attention on that group. It is simply a matter of channeling inspection resources to places where they are statistically most likely to detect real terrorists.[35]

Legomsky's view is one that is gaining in popularity as the fear of a terrorist attack increases. After uncovering what it declared to be a terrorist plot to bomb U.S.-bound passenger jets leaving Britain, the former head of London's metropolitan police expressed the view that it made sense to concentrate searches on young Muslim men travelling by themselves, and to leave those who do not fit this profile alone.[36] Certainly everyone could not be searched, an option suggested by Canadian legal scholar Sujit Choudrhry.[37]

When racial profiling becomes so thoroughly recast as bureaucracy, it becomes easy to miss the inclining rather than declining significance of race. U.S. authorities did not go around detaining white men simply because Timothy McVeigh, a white man, had blown up the Oklahoma City buildings, legal scholar Leti Volpp comments, since whites remain individuals while Arabs and Muslims are understood only as a group with the group characteristic of violence.[38] Historically, it is not hard to trace the racial basis to the profiling practised in the 'war on terror.' Before the Gulf War, Canadian and American Arabs and Muslims were the subjects, both in the media and in scholarship, of what Edward Said described as 'a trafficking in expert Middle East lore': 'All roads lead to the bazaar; Arabs only understand force; brutality and violence are part of Arab civilization; Islam is an intolerant, segregationist, 'medieval,' fanatic, cruel, anti-woman religion.'[39]

Scholars such as Edward Said long ago documented a consistent anti-Arab and anti-Muslim bias in the media. In the Canadian context, Karim Karim examined the media for the period 1980 to 2000, and showed how Islam became 'the new red scare.' The Muslim Other replaced the cold war script in the Canadian media, starting primarily with the overthrow of the Shah of Iran in 1979. Muslim political violence was nearly always described as terrorism, Karim shows, and the media prepared the public to think of all Muslims and Arabs as irrational, terrorist fanatics.[40] During the Gulf War, in 1991, many of these Hollywood-inspired stereotypes were marshalled in Canada, as journalist Zuhair Kashmeri showed in *The Gulf Within*.[41] Scholars in the United States have similarly documented a consistent racialization of Arabs, Muslims, and South Asians in the United States and have noted that the basis for racial animus facing these groups is not always the same.[42] Gott suggests that scholars have described the racism directed at Arab, Muslims, and South Asians as originating in specific political contexts, for example, hostility towards the Palestinian cause, nativistic racism that affects all Asian Americans, and white racism spawned by a hyper-ethnocentrism.[43] The attacks on the World Trade Center and the Pentagon escalated the hostility and racism coming from all these directions. Anti-Muslim racism, often described as 'Islamapho-bia,' has resulted in the 'Arabification' of Muslims and the 'Muslimifi-cation' of Arabs, even though approximately 60 per cent of Canadian Arabs are Christian.[44]

What remains significant about the contemporary racial profiling of Arabs and Muslims, however, is not this well-established history but the fact that anti-Muslim racism now operates in a culture of excep-tion, where to be profiled as a terrorist is to have a high chance of being taken to a place of law without law. Those who are profiled soon find themselves on lists, under surveillance and under suspicion, and in detention – states from which they cannot easily emerge. Diken and Lausten suggest that if 'power is to be total, it must defy regularity and rationality.'[45] Power must become terror, arbitrary and unpredictable. If, in the security-certificate hearings discussed below, we do not yet glimpse the full outlines of a regime of terror, we can see the arbitrary character of the law whereby stereotypes hold sway and arguments, in the absence of evidence of wrong-doing, rests primarily on the idea that they are not like us and they will pose a threat to us.

The Case of Hassan Almrei

Courts called upon to determine the presence of the potential to commit a terrorist act, as opposed to determining whether illegal acts have been committed, must operate in ways that are strikingly similar to those of the Spanish Inquisition, a creation of another state of exception. As Irene Silverblatt has shown, the Spanish Inquisition was one of the most modern bureaucracies of its time, 'established to meet a perceived threat to national security from Jews, Muslims, and 'all manner of Heretics.'[46] The Inquisition ran according to proce-dures and rules and was overseen by bureaucrats. Its function was to clarify publicly and powerfully who 'held beliefs or engaged in life practices that were considered threats to the colony's moral and civic well-being.'[47] Spanish citizens learned from the Inquisition what citi-zenship was, and who would be forever beyond it. In a similar manner, security-certificate cases establish whose beliefs and life practices are a threat to the state and who must therefore be cast out of political community.

Inquisitors dominated a special kind of knowledge, for they could determine the most profound of societal truths – membership in a human community. Inquisitors were charged with certifying Spanish 'purity of blood' (i.e. the absence of Jewish or Moorish ancestry); and they oversaw religious orthodoxy – a determination often attached to purity of blood – that in its modern form, was linked to a budding spirit of Spanish nationalism.[48]

In security-certificate cases, CSIS establishes who possesses 'Islamic extremist' ideology. Once marked as bearing the stain of disloyalty and violence associated with this ideology, a detainee can hardly challenge the determination owing not only to secret evidence but also to the very amorphousness of a charge built on latent qualities. The 'crime' in security cases is not a crime but something born in the blood or the psyche, a hidden indicator of a latent capacity to be violent. Because the capacity to be violent is an internal quality, people are condemned for what they might do (based on who they are) and not for what they have done. In the same way, the Inquisition did not concern itself with crime but with those who 'could not erase the stains of a heretical religious past.' Individuals with 'stained blood' might well have been Christian for centuries, but evidence of a connection to Judaism, whether centuries old or not, and however tenuous, predicted an inherent capacity for disloyalty that could someday emerge. Since heresy and treason were latent, however, proof could not be expected to be at the standard expected for crimes.

Discovering 'the stains of a heretical religious past' required that Spaniards accused of practising Jewish or Muslim rituals be interrogated on more than questions of faith. The questions of the Inquisitors 'were used to reconstruct a certain kind of life history, one built on a predefined set of variables' that would reveal the hidden stain. Inquisitors tried to fit the accused's life into a pattern 'from birth to present, including all places of residence, travel, and major life events.'[49] Silverblatt considers that the Spaniards were 'participating in a vision of the world reminiscent of what we today call "racial profiling."'[50] Crucially, here racial profiling has two components. First, it is the practice of attributing disloyalty, treason, or criminality to an identified group on the basis of race, religion, and life history. Second, it is a practice that determines who shall have fundamental rights and who shall not. Seen as such, racism lies both in the practice of profiling (e.g., all Jews are disloyal) and in the processes of law and bureaucracy that support the profile as a reason to evict specific groups from law itself. It is in the profile's connection to the place of law without law that we find race doing the work of making this exile from political community permanent.

Signs of Disloyalty

In certificate hearings, a number of markers indicate who holds the ideology of an Islamic extremist. First, an Islamic extremist is someone who has participated in 'Jihad,' understood principally as participation in anti-Soviet activities in Afghanistan during the late 1980s and early 1990s. He (no women have the label) has had either a direct or indirect association with Osama bin Laden or others who associated with him. These associations need not be close, and sometimes merely agreeing with some of Bin Laden's criticisms of the West will suffice to raise a red flag. Anyone who is involved, however peripherally, in activities that are likely to be of some use to terrorist organizations, for example, passport forgery, is suspect. Finally, any associations with Muslim countries or people are red flags. Terrorists have these histories. Any individual with this history must be a terrorist.

In the first summary[51] of secret evidence held against him, prepared by CSIS, Hassan Almrei's story begins when he applied for a visitor's visa in April 1998 in order to visit Hoshem Al Taha. He applied for asylum. CSIS alleges that Almrei behaved in a clandestine manner and that he visited a number of Arab Afghans, individuals whom CSIS defines in a footnote as 'mujahedin' and 'Islamic fighters in a jihad.'[52] The footnote further explains that 'Jihad' is 'a religious war of Muslims against unbelievers in Islam, inculcated as a duty by the Koran and traditions.' The Service reiterates its belief that there are reasonable grounds to believe that Almrei, a participant in anti-Soviet activities in Afghanistan in the early 1990s, has engaged in or will engage in terrorism and that he is a member of Osama bin Laden's network, an organization 'that there are reasonable grounds to believe will engage in terrorism or was engaged in terrorism.'[53]

The case against Almrei rests on the interpretation of a past history as a predictor of future behaviour and its construction depends on specific characterizations of Bin Laden's network Al Qaeda, notably its ideology of jihad, bonds between members, and its 'sleeper-cell' structure. The sleeper cell theory is not a new one, as Volpp reminds us. It was used to justify the internment of Japanese Americans during the

Second World War; in this instance too it turned on the logic that as inscrutable 'Orientals,' Japanese Americans were 'patiently waiting to strike' at America and therefore must be interned.[54] Indeed, all three characteristics (jihad, bonds between members, and the sleeper cell) become believable, as I show below, largely through unspoken but nonetheless invoked racial images of Muslim and Arab irrationality, tribalism, and, finally, disease or pathology. These ideas position non-Arabs and non-Muslims, in contrast, as belonging to a society of individuals who are rational and secular. As CSIS reiterates time and time again through the hearings, Arabs and Muslims are not like us. The power of this narrative structure is such that it is virtually impossible to question its coherency by asking, for example, how we come to know about these characteristics. The force of law without law, where questions need not be answered, only entrenches further the narrative of a potentially deadly clash of civilizations.

The Osama bin Laden network is described as an organization set up by Bin Laden after the Soviet pull-out from Afghanistan. Bin Laden created training camps in Afghanistan with the goal of waging a 'jihad' against the United States and Israel. Bin Ladin's 'jihad' is not distinguished in the text from 'jihad' in general as described earlier in the statement as a duty of all Muslims. Importantly, 'Membership in the Bin Ladin network is defined by an adherence to a shared ideology.' It is 'an association of individuals linked by a common past,' a past of anti-Soviet 'jihad.' As the Service elaborates in its summary of the evidence against Hassan Almrei,

> the backbone of the network is the ideological and personal bond among the Arab volunteers who were recruited by Bin Laden in the fight against the Soviet occupation of Afghanistan (1979–1989). As a result, this variety of terrorism transcends national and organizational boundaries which may or may not take the form of a structured, hierarchical organization of militants with pre-determined roles.[55]

Unconventional and unpredictable, Bin Laden's network employs the tactic of 'sleeper cells,' where 'operatives are often established in foreign countries for extended periods of time, up to several years, prior to a given operation being executed. Preceding the activation of the operation, they may live as regular citizens, leading respectable lives, avoiding official attention.'[56] The concept of the sleeper cell, with its biological associations, is one that is central to the state's case, invoking as it has historically, the 'bodily degeneracy' of the marked group as well as the threat of contamination. A 'sleeper cell' provides the possibility of being pathological, yet appearing 'normal': disease deceptively hidden in an otherwise respectable body.[57] Relying on the conceptual tools of Sander Gilman and others, Carmela Murdocca has shown that the notion of a degenerate, disease-ridden body of colour against a healthy bourgeois citizenry has long structured the ideological production of the Canadian nation: 'The use of the discourse of contamination and disease is used to reaffirm colonial ideas about the inferiority and bodily degeneracy of colonized peoples.' The presence of disease, Murdocca points out, requires regulation wherein 'the diseased is represented both as a moral danger and as a bodily danger to otherwise law-abiding, legitimate citizens.'[58] Historically we might recall, as Karen Engle has pointed out, that one further advantage of the sleeper cell as a construct invoking biology is the potential it has to enable us to make the claim that the disease has spread, even to citizen bodies, a logic in operation during the McCarthy period in the United States, when white citizens were considered to have caught the disease of foreignness (communism).[59]

Hassan Almrei is considered to fit the profile of an Al Qaeda sleeper-cell operative to a T. At seventeen, Almrei went to Afghanistan to support the Afghanis in their fight to oppose the Russian invasion. He returned several times over five years, staying in guest houses that the Service alleges were bases for Al Qaeda. While in Saudi Arabia, Hassan Almrei had a small honey business that gave him the opportunity to travel to Pakistan in the 1990s. Citing a *New York Times* article by journalist Judith Miller, the Service maintained that the honey business was a favourite way for Bin Laden's network to acquire money. While his past associations are critical to the case against him, for CSIS Almrei's behaviour in Canada strengthens their belief that he is a member of a terrorist network. Almrei appears to be connected to Nabil Almarabh (he visited him in jail and lent his uncle money), a man the United States once suspected of terrorism but whom it has since cleared. Almrei is said to have behaved 'in a clandestine fashion,' displaying a security consciousness that the Service maintains is 'an important characteristic of the Bin Laden Network.'[60] Almrei also used false passports to come to Canada, and while this is a practice of the vast majority of refugees unable to obtain legal documents,[61] Almrei's culpability becomes more evident when it is discovered that he once gave advice to someone on where to obtain a false passport, information for which he charged a fee. Additional evidence of Almrei's connection to Bin Laden included computer photos that Almrei is said to have accessed from certain websites, including pictures of airplane cockpits, of Bin Laden, and of Ibn Khattab, a now dead Arab man who is thought to have been involved in anti-Russian terrorist activities in Chechnya and with whom Almrei stayed in Afghanistan and Tajikastan.

They Are Who They Are; We Are Who We Are

Signs that Almrei carries the seeds of terrorism within him must tell the whole story of his disloyalty, since no direct evidence of his culpability is available. The first empty space that the signs must fill is the departure of the right to face one's accuser. At the hearing Almrei's lawyer, Barbara Jackman, began by attempting to secure the right to cross-examine CSIS or the RCMP agents who were the authors of the case against Almrei. Denied access to the specific agents involved, in the interests of national security, instead she is only allowed to cross-examine an intelligence analyst, J.P. Since J.P. discusses generalities more than he is able to discuss the specifics of Almrei's case, this decision secures for the profile its privileged place as truth. In cross-examination, J.P. acknowledged that the file of evidence against Almrei included items that may not be directly connected to him, for example, email in which Almrei's name does not appear. He agreed that the Service does not always collect its own evidence, relying instead on media reports. On the issue of the meaning of Almrei's attendance in a training camp in Afghanistan, something Almrei denied on his application for asylum but later admitted, the Service is clear that while everybody who went to Afghanistan to fight the Soviets did not become Al Qaeda operatives, the fact that Almrei went still makes him of interest. The possibility that Almrei was in a training camp run by a group that later became part of the Northern Alliance with whom the West is now allied does not take away the stain of his having been in Afghanistan. Asked about the possibility that Almrei's training was in fact affiliated to factions that ultimately became the Northern Alliance and not Al Qaeda, the CSIS agent replies:

> That doesn't really make a difference, simply because I can't speak to his allegiance to the Northern Alliance today. *All I know is that he has had training as a mujahedin*. I am not aware of the information in the classified SIR.

The classified SIR may be more specific as to where he was training ... The fact is that there is a lot of people who trained in various groups. The essentials are the knowledge that they have acquired and their contacts and activities today and their allegiances today. We have had evidence in the open document that Mr. Almrei has expressed allegiance to Al Qaeda or has expressed support for Osama Bin Ladin and that obviously would negate any support of the Northern Alliance and its fairly secular outlook. It is more of a political and ethnic group. It is largely a Tajik organization. It is not of the same Islamic bent as the Taliban or Al Qaeda.

For all I know, Mr. Almrei could have changed his mind and become more religious. Adhered to a stricter interpretation of Islam. A lot of time has gone by since he last claims to have been in Afghanistan and his world outlook may have changed dramatically. I can't say that Mr. Almrei's training in a Northern Alliance camp, if that occurred would prevent him from being a supporter of Al Qaeda today.'[62] (Emphasis added)

While Almrei's ideological leanings could have been just as easily towards the Northern Alliance as towards Al Qaeda, and he could have just as easily changed his mind and become less religious, it is only the possibility that he may have become more so, a possibility inferred by his presence in Afghanistan, that serves to indict him.

The significance of where and with whom Almrei stayed in Afghanistan and Tajikistan and what he did there are hard to establish. His counsel suggests that one of the guest houses at which Almrei stayed in Afghanistan was run by a man who is now a minister in the government of Afghanistan and who is clearly of the Northern Alliance; she shows that CSIS relied uncritically on right-wing think tanks for some of its information;[63] Almrei's 'military training' consisted in learning how to shoot a rifle; and his 'scouting mission' with the well-known Ibn Khattab amounted to little else than checking out the conditions for establishing a camp. While there is clearly disagreement on these details, they do not form the heart of the case that Almrei presents a security risk to Canada today. Of more concern is his characterization as having been associated with forged passports and with other Arabs. As the CSIS agent insists, it is the fact that Almrei has a profile, the profile of a man of potential use to Al Qaeda, that counts the most.[64]

On cross-examination, the CSIS agent admitted that Almrei was a 'document procurer' and not a passport forger himself, but this fact in and of itself cannot compete with the idea of Almrei's potential use to Al Qaeda. As J.P. contends:

He has access to individuals who can provide the false documents and who are useful resources. I personally don't know anybody I would go to if I needed a false document. An individual like him would go a long way to facilitating anybody's request for such documentation. He has the means of tapping into a local network to obtain false documents, which is not a given skill that one can pick up in an afternoon, especially if you are coming to a country like Canada. You have to have the knowledge of who to go to, where the quality documents are available, how much you should pay for them, and that sort of thing.[65]

If Almrei's knowledge of where to get a false passport indicates he is linked to an international forgery ring, it still needs to be established that this specific ring is connected to Al Qaeda. Where the profile is both the method of establishing the link and the proof itself that a link exists, that connection need not be a direct link but instead an ideo-logical one. In Almrei's case, his father's connections to the Muslim Brotherhood and that organization's ideological connections to Al Qaeda suffice. When questioned about the Service's knowledge of the Muslim Brotherhood, J.P. acknowledges that the Brotherhood may not itself practise violence, but he offers the following assessment of its links to Al Qaeda: 'It [the Brotherhood] supports the notion of the use of violence for obtaining its objectives, yes. Because it doesn't practice it doesn't mean that it doesn't have its ideological repertoire. To my knowledge, it has never denounced the use of violence for their objec-tives or for the pursuit of an Islamic extremist agenda.'[66]

One difficulty with offering as evidence an 'ideological repertoire,' failure to denounce violence, and profiling based on presence in Af-ghanistan is that thousands of young Arab men went to Afghanistan, as Almrei did, and possess the signs of ideology that interests CSIS. J.P. is unfazed by the challenge of establishing who of the 30,000 Arab men who went to Afghanistan are terrorists in the making. The problem of generalizing and stereotyping becomes more intractable, but is still of little interest to J.P. when Almrei's lawyer suggests that many people agree with Bin Laden's critique of America, as Almrei does, without believing in his methods of violence. Confidently declaring himself as someone 'probably using a wide-angled sense of male world view' in asserting that few people could dissociate Bin Laden's views from his violent means, J.P. proudly asserts that his opinion is that of a 'White, anglo-saxon Canadian.' And that, it is implied, is the end of the story. We need know no more about J.P.'s credibility. Just as Almrei's origins and life history indicate his character, so too does J.P.'s. Ideology remains the key marker of Almrei's designation as a security risk. Madame Justice Tremblay-Lamer found the security certificate to be reasonable and declared that the evidence, both openly disclosed and secret, supported 'the view that Mr. Almrei is a member of an international network of extremist individuals who support the Islamic extremist ideals espoused by Osama Bin Laden and that Mr. Almrei is involved in a forgery ring with international connections that produces false documents.'[67]

Al Qaeda–Inspired

When Hassan Almrei had a chance to seek bail in 2005,[68] Madame Justice Layden-Stevenson, in deciding against his bail, focused once again on ideology and specifically on the evidence heard from another senior Middle East analyst of CSIS, named P.G. As he had done in other security cases, P.G. described Al Qaeda as including 'Al Qaeda proper,' 'Al Qaeda associates,' and 'Al Qaeda inspired.'[69] It is the last category that is of most relevance for the court, since 'Al Qaeda inspired' 'refers to individuals or small groups that share the same ideology as Al Qaeda and are as committed to acts of violence and acts of terrorism as are the core and affiliated groups.'[70] Individuals in this group cannot be specifically tied to Al Qaeda, but they are no less contaminated by their association with its ideology. Under this logic, Almrei is diseased by his association with Ibn Khattab, whom the Service now believes is *not* part of the Al Qaeda core (a change from early claims), but who is 'affiliated.' P.G. offers this conclusion, although he admits that he himself cannot claim a knowledge of Chechen affairs.

Still faced with the problem of connecting Almrei's procurement of false documentation to Al Qaeda, P.G. can only maintain, as did J.P. earlier, that Al Qaeda needs false documentation and thus Mr Almrei is useful. By way of evidence, P.G. pointed to Ahmed Ressam, an Algerian Canadian extremist caught at the U.S. border (allegedly on his way to committing a terrorist attack) with a false Quebec birth certificate. Confronted with the possibility that Al Qaeda would have little use for someone as high profile as Hassan Almrei now was, P.G.was adamant: When someone is committed ideologically to Al Qaeda, they remain so no matter what the obstacles.[71] Recalling P.G.'s testimony, Madame Justice Layden-Stevenson accepts that those committed to the cause 'remain committed as long as they live.'[72] In her decision she offers a portrait of individuals who are devoted for life to Al Qaeda. Such individuals travelled to Afghanistan, where they learned the ideology. Some returned from Afghanistan seeking to spread the ideology. Most frightening of all, their continuing ideological activity can be evident in something 'as simple as going onto the internet and reading sources, reading statements, reading papers that explain the ideology, its goals and its intent. It is not possible to define a linear process through which a given individual will commit himself or herself to a movement of Islamic extremism.'[73] Given his travel to Afghanistan and his perusal of websites such as Al Jazeera's, Almrei's fate is sealed. Almrei continues to pose a threat simply because, once infected with this ideology, there is no cure. It is P.G.'s position, Layden-Stevenson writes, that it 'is highly improbable that individuals who have embraced this ideology so fervently would choose at one point to renege or to abandon that philosophy.'[74] Ideology is so crucial that without it neither participation in jihad in Afghanistan nor the document forgery ring would take on the significance it has.[75] Given his infection, Almrei's case cannot be helped by the high-profile support he has attracted to guarantee that he would abide by his bail conditions if released, nor is it helped by testimony that his conditions in detention (segregation) are deplorable.

Jihad

It is the concept of jihad that locks in place the judgment of ideology. Invoking the stereotype of the irrational Arab, the concept jihad is given a composite of details designed to invoke the clash of civilizations. J.P., the CSIS intelligence officer of Almrei's first hearing, had by 2005 become the deputy chief of counterterrorism and counterproliferation in Ottawa. As an analyst intelligence officer his responsibilities included 'processing, corroborating, and packaging information that allows the Government of Canada to be advised on issues of threats to security. ' (In contrast, an investigator intelligence officer is responsible for 'interviewing subjects of interest or members of the public, for recruiting human sources and for running those human sources against mandated targets')[76] J.P.'s testimony in 2005 sheds more light on the key concepts the Service has used to come to establish Almrei's 'stained blood' as a predictor of violence. The first of these is 'jihad,' which J.P. admits (in contrast to the confidence of the 2001 testimony) is a subjective term 'ranging from defining a personal struggle to make one a better individual and a better Muslim and to follow the tenets of Islam all the way to an offensive use of violence in defence of Islam, a holy war in other words.'[77]

Having established the context for their activities through his notion of jihad, J.P. is then able to characterize the activities of Osama bin Laden, and others such as Ibn Khattab with whom Almrei was associated, not solely as part of an anti-Soviet rebellion in Afghanistan, Tajikistan, and Chechnya, but as something much more. These activities indicate a global network of terrorists who, although severely disrupted due to anti-terrorism efforts, have nonetheless reconstituted themselves and adapted, as indeed carcinogenic cells do. Al Qaeda survived, Layden-Stevenson writes, depending on J.P.'s testimony, 'by adopting secretive practices and operational security (operating with individuals in whom it had confidence).'[78] Here 'Al Qaeda-inspired groups are perhaps the most sinister manifestation of Islamic extremism today because they usually consist of small cells of individuals who have no set group affiliation and who come together for a very short period of time in order to mount an operation.' For Madame Justice Stevenson, the London bombings are the most recent example of this pattern of activity.[79]

The journey from jihad to sleeper cells requires heavy reliance on the concept of ideology, an ideology that then has to be emplaced and embodied. The training camps thus become 'a major front in the global jihad at the time that the Soviets were occupying Afghanistan. It is quite significant for an individual to have gone to Afghansitan, to have trained, and to have returned a number of times.'[80] Since going to Afghanistan to a training camp is now the mark of a terrorist, how Mr Almrei fits this profile as an individual hardly matters. Almrei is simply likely to engage in terrorist activities because of his past religious affiliations and geographical history. Unlike the IRA (whose members are characterized as motivated by a political objective), Al Qaeda is a 'religious and ideological movement,' in Layden-Stevenson's words. 'The ultimate goal is the takeover of the world by Islam. While that may sound a little fantastic and hyperbolic, essentially, it does come down to the eradication of the infidel and the creation of a puritan form of Islam for the world.'[81]

In the wake of powerful images of an Islamic takeover, the facts that don't add up hardly matter. Madame Justice Layden-Stevenson accepts that the Service had no specifics connecting Almrei's honey business to Al Qaeda, and that they had relied on a single media article by Judith Miller, a journalist whose 'record of accuracy' has been called into question, a situation of which J.P. was unaware. She also observes that J.P. could offer no direct evidence of Almrei's link to remaining insurgents in Chechnya, especially given Ibn Khattab's death. Similarly, J.P. could not offer proof that Almrei had supplied false documents to Nabil Al Marabh, whom the Service conceded was released by the United States. Clearly short on specifics, the Service is only able to maintain that its basis for the allegation that Almrei supported Islamic extremist ideals is the fact that he lived at a guest house of Ibn Khattab and that there was 'ideological consistency between Khattab and Bin Laden.'[82] J.P. also insists that Almrei's repeated trips to Afghanistan indicate 'a certain level of dedication which is not typical of an individual who is a peaceful member of society.'[83] A notion such as 'ideological consistency' can only assume the weight that it does here if the framework is one of disease spreading.

Faced with the allegation that it is his ideology that primarily counts against him, Hassan Almrei denied his commitment to Osama bin Laden or to his jihad. Clarifying that he believed in the jihad against the Russians for their invasion of Afghanistan, and not in the Bin Laden jihad, Almrei also acknowledges that he respected Ibn Khattab and did not believe that he was connected to Osama bin Laden. He continued to feel that those who died fighting the Russians are martyrs and he kept pictures on his computer of such individuals. His credibility is strained when it is noted that he lied on his first encounters with CSIS, that he received money for passing on a tip about where to get a false passport, and when the Court learned that he assisted one of his restaurant employees to find a husband who could sponsor her, an act for which he was paid.

Madame Justice Layden-Stevenson acknowledges in her decision that Hassan Almrei has been held under conditions that are 'unacceptable and fall far short of what one would accept for Canada.'[84] Since he was held in solitary confinement 'for his own good' for the past four years, it is reasonable to assume that his detention will continue as Canadian courts wrestle with the idea that deportation to face torture is still something that a Canadian court and 'the Canadian conscience' would find unacceptable and contrary to section 1 of the *Charter*.[85] Notwithstanding this situation, the judge is called upon to assess

Almrei as a danger to national security, and it is this issue on which she rules, his jail conditions notwithstanding. As Layden-Stevenson sums up, however, 'Islamic extremist ideology, as noted earlier, is the force that drives the Ministers' case. When reduced to its bare bones, the Ministers' position is founded largely on Mr. Almrei's participation in jihad.'[86] Thus constructed, the primary task is to explore the meaning of Mr. Almrei's participation in jihad in Afghanistan against the Soviets, an assessment that Layden-Stevenson feels must begin with who the commanders of the camps were. Relying on the government's evidence available from a number of websites, she concludes that Abdul Sayyaf and Ibn Khattab 'were hard-line Islamic fundamentalists and were acknowledged as such during the time frame when Mr. Almrei was in attendance at jihad.'[87] Agreeing with J.P. that Mr. Almrei's 'scouting' activities in Tajikstan indicate his military involvement, the judge finds most significant, ultimately, that Almrei returned regularly and consistently to 'jihad' for five years.[88] Further, he must have shared Ibn Khattab's commitment to violence, since Khattab maintained contact with Almrei after returning from Tajikistan, and Almrei continues to think of Khattab as a good man.[89] While these facts do not constitute hard proof, they at least offer evidence that there are reasonable grounds to believe in Almrei's 'Islamic extremism,' an impression that is strengthened by the secret evidence. This, coupled with the 'reasonable suspicion that Mr. Almrei participated in a network involved in forged documentation,'[90] leads the judge to the inescapable conclusion: 'The combination of the factors leads to a situation whereby Mr. Almrei, even if he personally has no intention of committing a direct act of violence in Canada, has the potential to facilitate the movement of others who also harbour such beliefs and ideals and to position them to perpetrate violence on foreign and Canadian soil. This threat is substantial and it is serious.'[91]

That Almrei failed to disclose information because he feared the consequences is not, in the judge's view, credible. Put against P.G.'s testimony that the Service believes that extremists are unlikely to give up their beliefs and practices, something Madame Justice Layden-Stevenson notes 'appears not to have been subjected to empirical analysis,' Almrei nevertheless remains without credibility. He 'exhibits patience, strength, determination, endurance and self-discipline and is not easily diverted from his objectives,' qualities evident in his pursuit of hunger strikes to draw attention to his prison conditions.[92] From her enumeration of these qualities as negatives, we may infer that Layden-

Stevenson is proposing that Almrei's profile might correspond to that of the extremist depicted by the Service. What confirms this assessment, however, is that Mr Almrei has not repented, a finding reached in spite of Almrei's clear denunciation of Osama bin Laden and his indication that he does not support his ideology. As the judge asserts: 'I consider the absence of any expression of renunciation of the fundamentalist ideology from Mr. Almrei to be significant.'[93] We can only speculate that Almrei's failure to renounce refers to his support for a jihad against the Russians in the early 1990s and for his continuing admiration for Ibn Khattab.

Monster Terrorists

When the task is to pin down belief and to extrapolate that beliefs are an indicator of a latent commitment to violence that can never fade, race is an important pivot on which the story must turn. Race makes it possible to accept the outlines of the state's story about ideology because it helps us to believe readily in Muslim irrationality and the monsters it spawns. As Amit Rai discusses, ideas about Muslim irrationality drawn from older Orientalist and colonial discourses now undergird an entire field of knowledge production known as terrorism studies. In terrorism studies, the focus is on the motivations and belief systems of individual terrorists. The psyche is thus the privileged site of investigation and terrorism is explained as a compulsion or psycho-pathology. That is to say, the terrorist is driven to commit acts of violence as a consequence of psychological forces. The terrorist psyche is born in abnormal family dynamics, with the West's own heterosexual family as its point of contrast. Bin Laden, for example, is represented as someone abandoned by a polygamous father whose interests were with his other wives. He was drawn to find substitute father figures in fundamentalist men. Terrorists are depicted as failed heterosexuals who need the promise of virgins in heaven to commit to the cause. Such portraits not only draw on older discourses about the effeminate or sexually dysfunctional Muslim man and the Oriental despot, but they preclude any examination of the socio-political causes of terrorism. Importantly, they are figures that enable the West to feel its own civilizational superiority and to make the case that exceptional violence is required to keep in line those whose uncivilized natures are so much in evidence.[94]

In terrorism studies, particularly scholarship supported by organizations such as the Rand Corporation, Rai shows, the Oriental despot cum terrorist is presented as someone prepared to die for his struggles, someone whose conviction and mindset are described as 'incomprehensible and frightening' and irrevocably pre-modern.[95] For the Canadian context, we can trace the same discourses in popular books such as *National Post* journalist Stewart Bell's *The Martyr's Oath*[96] (assigned as a text in a political science course at the University of Toronto) and the circulation of such narratives about the psyche of terrorists and 'jihad' as his obligation, by web-based, right-wing research institutes such as the Mackenzie Institute, a source cited by CSIS in its testimony.[97]

Where complexity is ruled out, racism can do all the work of providing an interpretive framework. Orientalist notions of monster terrorists also emerge out of what François Debrix describes as 'tabloid realism,' wherein complex geopolitical realities are written about and presented in the media and in scholarship relying on the conventions of tabloid literature. The tabloid medium is one in which 'reality must be described and truth must be revealed in a flashy, surprising, gripping, shocking, often moralising, and sometimes anxiety producing manner.'[98] Focusing on those who write about foreign affairs in the United States, Debrix argues that several influential books have been written in the style of tabloid realism, notably Samuel Huntington's *The Clash of Civilizations* and Robert Kaplan's *The Coming Anarchy: Shattering the Dreams of the Post Cold War*. Such writings are 'made up of short, lapidary sentences, riddled with metaphors that call for the audience to maintain a mostly visual, figurative and imaginary apprehension of the intellectual arguments.'[99] Maps and images (for example, Bell's *The Martyr's Oath* includes several pictures of Canadian 'terrorists' from adolescence to manhood) offer a simplified version of reality, proof, as it were, of a civilized world menaced by a barbarian Other. We might consider here how websites and computer images fulfil the same function in security certificate cases. As Mosse reminds us, one of the main strengths of racism is that it is 'a visual ideology based on stereotypes.'[100] It is not surprising, then, that tabloid realism achieves its coherence through an appeal to the visual.

The tabloid medium 'deploys relatively ahistorical discourses in "contexts" that do not have to abide by rules of temporal and spatial contingency (the realities they describe are at once past, present or future).'[101] The discourses about Islamic extremists and terrorists in security cases are very much in the style of tabloid realism, and the secrecy provisions ensure that this simplified profile cannot be easily challenged. The portrait of the jihadist on which CSIS relies in the hearings has clearly recognizable origins in Orientalist scholarship such as that of Bernard Lewis. Mahmood Mamdani suggests that we locate an earlier and more refined version of the clash of civilizations thesis of Huntington (the West is law and rationality, the East is culture and religion) in the work of Bernard Lewis, for whom the West's distinctive attribute is freedom, in contrast to the Islamic's world fidelity to a world of culture, religion, and community. In the Islamic world, 'an explosive mixture of rage and hatred' lies dormant, ready to erupt at various moments in history.[102] Thus, for Lewis and other Orientalists, the West must constantly protect itself from irrational, pre-modern peoples. Of course, even Lewis argued that there are different versions of Islam and that not all Muslims possess this rage and hatred. This argument, Mamdani observes, anticipates the good Muslim/bad Muslim frame that has so marked discourses of the 'War on Terror.' Good Muslim/Bad Muslim simply sets the stage for the West, as unified, homogeneous, and modern, to sort out good Muslims from bad Muslims. A good Muslim, paradoxically, is a secular Muslim who is influenced by the West, while a bad Muslim remains locked in the pre-modern. The Wahhabi sect of Islam is typically described as the latter, and CSIS agents reportedly spend time looking for its devotees.[103] While good Muslims can be assisted into modernity, bad Muslims, figured as 'anti-modern' and as having 'a profound ability to be destructive,' require incarceration and military action.[104] Complex histories are thus rendered simple by Orientalist scholars' reliance on the idea of good Muslims and bad Muslims. As Ileana Porras has commented, in literature on terrorism, 'religious fanaticism serves the heuristic function of explaining terrorism.'[105]

Where the explanation for violence lies in culture, political details are irrelevant. Hassan Almrei's 'jihad' cannot differ from Bin Laden's if the phenomenon being described is very simply the bad Muslim who possesses a deep rage and hatred towards the West. In the same vein, we need not consider Islamic extremism as anything but an unchanging essence likely to erupt at any moment into violence. Karen Engle has suggested, of the framework good alien/bad alien, that such dichotomies help the United States to make the case for its own tolerance. Profiling confirms the West's civility, since it provides an initial opportunity to sort good from bad aliens. Although Engle acknowledges, relying on Irene Porras, that the 'the trick is to locate [the terrorist] in the category of the most terrifying and traditional enemy, that which the public is accustomed to thinking of as the barbarous and primitive outsider,' she maintains that a number of practices remain in place that are intended to confirm that good Muslims can escape the net.[106] For example, those Muslims who are able to demonstrate their patriotism, and who are careful not to engage in criticism of the state, can escape unscathed. As I show throughout, however, this is not the case. The exits are increasingly closed off for those who are Muslim. If the state is able to preserve an appearance of tolerance at all, it is only able to do so because the collective punishment of all Muslims is understood as reasonable, a necessary move to preserve Western civilization. It is useful to bear in mind both Rai's and Debrix's point that monster terrorists enable us to believe in "democracy in the time of monsters,'[107] a time when we need states of exception and the authority to suspend fundamental rights, invade, and drop bombs on their heads for their own good. Monster figures legitimize new regimes of citizenship and security where we become accustomed to state violence as a warranted part of the social order, the transformation Agamben described as that from the state of exception to the camp. Without monster terrorists, states of exception would not be justified and states would confront the threat of terrorism *within* the law.

Sleeper Cell Logic instead of Law: Harkat, Mahjoub, Jaballah, and Charkaoui

In each of the security-certificate cases considered here, the profiling of the terrorist as a person with the stain of Islamic extremist ideology and his immediate eviction from political community stands in place of solid evidence, knitting together strands of the evidence into a story of the monster terrorist. In the absence of law, an absence indicated by the low threshold of proof that operates throughout the security-certificate hearing and the difficulty of assessing the merits of the available evidence, the profile must do most of the work to convince us that the men are a profound and *self-evident* threat.

This is not to say that their cases contain little that warrants investigation or that they are all innocent. It is clear, however, that in the absence of full legal scrutiny, we can only err on the side of our own ideological leanings. Race, always waiting in the wings, provides the most accessible meaning to events, helping us to find the men not credible and their stories merely confirmations of their associations with terrorism. We do not need proof when we have a racial configuration of signs. The patterns discernable in *Almrei* are evident in the cases of the other four detainees, often with the same testimony from CSIS lending force to the state's case of the profile as fact.

Mohamed Harkat, like Hassan Almrei, has in his profile the three biggest indicators of Islamic extremism.[108] First, Harkat worked in Peshawar, Pakistan, with a Saudi-funded Islamic charity known as the Muslim World League, a charity that is alleged to have links to Osama bin Laden.[109] Second, he had associations with men who themselves have a high profile – for example, he accepted a ride from Toronto to Ottawa with Ahmad Khadr;[110] he was allegedly identified by Abu Zubaida (reportedly Bin Laden's second in command) as a member of Al Qaeda;[111] one of his friends in Peshawar, a banker, may have been involved in financial dealings with Al Qaeda;[112] he is alleged (and he denies) knowing Ibn Khattab;[113] he is alleged to have been a member of a radical Islamic group in Algeria.[114] Finally, Harkat exhibited behaviour that was suspicious: he used a false passport, and while this is common for refugees, he used a fake Saudi passport that CSIS noted was the passport of choice for Al Qaeda members;[115] he used aliases in Pakistan;[116] he did not keep his money in a bank and appeared to have been paid an overly high salary.[117] The credibility of each detainee is of course always strained by any evidence that he has been untruthful. In Harkat's case, he lied to Canadian officials about working for an Islamic relief agency in Pakistan and about using an alias. He also lied about associating with individuals known to be involved with extremist movements.[118] While there is little doubt that lying profoundly affected his credibility,[119] it is also the case that to have admitted any of these facts would have surely altered the success of his asylum claim, and would have ensured that he would become a figure of suspicion. His position, like that of the other detainees, was very much a catch-22. If, for example, travel to Afghanistan virtually guarantees that a man of Middle Eastern origin will come to the attention of the state and a chain of events will be set in motion that has a strong likelihood of leading to a security certificate, lying appears to be a gamble that it might be well worth taking. In a world where a profile is proof, it is unlikely that the context required to understand why someone might use an alias in Peshawar for reasons unconnected to wishing to hide any Al Qaeda connections will easily enter a hearing. In effect, through the operation of a zone of law that contains no law, those who fit the profile are damned if they lie, and damned if they don't.

Each of Harkat's three red flags can be interrogated, but in the interests of national security it became difficult to do so. For example, the first of these flags, the information that Harkat was identified by Abu Zubaida, came from an unnamed source whose identity cannot be revealed in the interests of national security. In the absence of assessments of the merits of each piece of evidence, the case must rest on a thread. Harkat stated that he did not talk much during the van ride to Ottawa with the notorious Khadr, something the court found incredible since it is a five-hour journey from Toronto to Ottawa by car.[120] The allegation that he belonged to a radical Islamic group in Algeria requires considerable history and context, since it is not clear what a radical group committed to violence is and which point in history the assessment considers. Yet CSIS confidently asserted Harkat's membership and there was little to go on besides Harkat's story that when a legal party to which he belonged split into two, with one wing becoming radical, he fled Algeria.[121] If the places (Algeria, Peshawar, and the training camps), the associations he had, and his behaviour cannot entirely bear the weight of the case against him, two contentions enter to take up the slack and to seal his fate. The contention is that Harkat is a member of a sleeper cell, assigned to wait until he is called upon.[122] The second is that those with terrorist associations will never renounce their beliefs and will, if freed, immediately re-establish themselves with their former terrorist connections.[123] As we saw with Almrei, both these contentions cannot be proved (and in fact there is evidence to the contrary), but both invoke and rely on the idea of an irrational figure, defined by culture and religion, a man willing to die for his religious beliefs.

The case of Mohammed Zeki Mahjoub illustrates another way that race steps in to provide ballast to what might be an otherwise weak case. In 2001 Mr Justice Nadon found the security certificate issued for Mahjoub to be reasonable on the grounds that he was a member of the Vanguards of Conquest and/or Al Jihad and was therefore likely to engage in terrorism in the future. As in Almrei's case, Mahjoub's case is particularly marked by the fact that he initially lied at this first certificate hearing about his conviction in Egypt in absentia for his involvement in 'Sunni Islamic terrorism including his role in connection with the U.S. Embassy bombing in Nairobi, Kenya.'[124] Although he 'came clean' before the end of the proceedings, his credibility was certainly not helped by the initial denial. As well, he lied to CSIS about having met Marjouk, a terrorism suspect who is serving a fifteen-year sentence in Egypt for his involvement in the embassy bombings, and about having met Ahmad Said Khadr, whose in-laws he stayed with when he first arrived in Canada. Particularly damning is the fact that Mahjoub worked for Bin Laden in Sudan, where he was supervised by Mubarak Al-Duri, a factor CSIS argued showed that his relationship with Bin Laden was significant.[125]

Mahjoub maintained that the Egyptian conviction began with his wrongful arrest and torture. Similar hearings in absentia have been declared to be fraudulent by Amnesty International, and Britain has recently released a terror suspect with the same profile as Mahjoub who was also sentenced to fifteen years in absentia. Mahjoub's lawyer noted that while CSIS declares Mahjoub to be a high-ranking member of Al Jihad, his name does not appear on a list of its leading members. Once again, it is not possible on the stand to probe the source of CSIS's allegations. J.P. did not seem to be aware of the British cases,[126] of the news reports that the FBI acknowledges that it does not know of any sleeper cells,[127] and of the problems that arise with 'Jane's information service,' a website on which the Canadian Border Service Agency relies in the preparation of its reports on refoulement.[124] Mahjoub's lawyer also raised the issue that J.P. took a course on Islamic terrorism that was coordinated by the Egyptian government. There is just enough showing through these points to suggest that Mahjoub's profile as a high-ranking member of Al Jihad is not something that survives even a cursory questioning on the stand. J.P. does not appear to be a particularly well-informed expert, and if we are to believe that secret evidence would make clear that the Service's allegations are borne out, his limited knowledge of *public* information limits our trust.

Jaballah's case also rests on the allegation that he is a senior member of Al Jihad, an organization 'inspired' by Al Qaeda. He was also indicted based on sleeper-cell logic. As P.G. of CSIS elaborated for the Court, readily invoking the devious, endlessly patient Oriental, Al Qaeda 'has a different sense of time than we do. They will wait for years before they attack.'[129] As in *Almrei*, while not everyone involved in Al Qaeda can be said to be 'personally violent or personally engaged,' those who are are unlikely to give up their dedication to the cause. As P.G. emphasized, 'Violent beliefs of Islamic extremists will not fade with time, rendering these individuals threats to public safety for years to come.'[130] Pressed by defence counsel to explain the risks that someone like Mr Jaballah posed, P.G. relied on the example of Guantanamo Bay. According to a news article, ten people released from Guantanamo re-engaged in terrorist activity. When it was pointed out to him that only 10 of the 250 released re-offended, P.G. was undeterred. Since there is no way to predict which 10 will re-offend, and as long as the risk is not zero, no one should be released.[131] His position was made even clearer when Jaballah's lawyer, John Norris, cited an article from ABC News noting that the United States believes that there are no sleeper cells.[132] Norris also suggested that the Service seems to rely on right wing think tanks. P.G. simply repeated that he had not noticed any political slant to the information the Service relied on and, in any event, a risk is a risk.[133] Again we are more likely to be convinced by the suggestion that detainees invariably pose a security risk if we keep in our heads the idea of irrational men who are always prepared to die for their religion, viewing it all as a sacred duty.

Like Majoub, Mohammed Jaballah was tried in absentia and condemned as a member of Al Jihad, something that CSIS learned on 29 November 1999, after the first security-certificate hearing was quashed.[134] At the second security-certificate hearing, Mr Justice Mackay indicated that new information had been offered, including the evidence of the Egyptian hearing. The Service indicated that it had since learned that Jaballah had spent some time in Afghanistan in 1993–4, although he said that he had never been there. Finally, 'new' related evidence included that Majoub had Jaballah's phone number on his person when he was arrested. The mailbox Jaballah rented, but said he never used to communicate with his brother, was in fact used. Finally, a person arrested in Pakistan and deported to Jordan had a computer disk with Jaballah's mailbox address on it. These three 'new' pieces of evidence were combined with old evidence that, as a member of Al Jihad, Jaballah poses a permanent risk. Jaballah's dangerousness based on this marking is enhanced by these details and furthered confirmed when it is alleged that in the summer of 1998 Jaballah made several calls to the International Office for the Defense of the Egyptian Peoples, an office that CSIS alleged was a cover for Al Jihad and a front for those planning the embassy bombings in Kenya. Jaballah maintained that he was advised by his lawyer to pursue evidence of his refugee claim and that was his reason for calling the office. Finally, the Service made a case that Jaballah had contacts with senior Al Qaeda operatives (Al-Zawaheri in Yemen and Pakistan and Thirwat Salah

Sihata in Yemen). His 'guilt' in this respect appeared sealed when it was revealed that Jaballah made several phone calls to Yemen from Canada, which he initially denied but then said they were made by his wife. Without the full evidence or a chance to determine its value, the Jaballah case must be carried by the logic that the meaning of these actions lie with the idea that once a suspect is stained by terrorist associations (in this case the Egyptian conviction), we need look no further.[135]

Adil Charkaoui is perhaps the best illustration of what it means to be caught in a profile. Charkaoui has four characteristics that bring him to the state's attention. First, he appears to be normal. That is to say, he is married with two children and he was pursuing graduate studies in Montreal. As CSIS testified at his hearing, this very normalcy is what suggested that he was a part of a sleeper cell. The agent clarified at length that a sleeper agent is instructed as follows: 'Go back to your usual life, act as if nothing is happening ... And then one of these days ... you will get a message ... and that's the time to do what you want to do.'[136] On cross-examination, the CSIS officer in question acknowledged that he did not know whether Adil Charkaoui was an Al Qaeda member.[137] To make matters worse, Charkaoui has taken martial arts training, as did one of the September 11 hijackers.[138] Paradoxically, although he is normal, Charkaoui has several of the other elements of the terrorist profile, primarily the geographical profile of an Islamic extremist. First, he is from Morocco and CSIS alleged that he was in fact a member of a radical Islamic group. Second, he is religious, and through going to the mosques in the Montreal area he came into contact with a number of suspicious individuals. Third, Charkaoui travelled to Pakistan in February of 1998 and stayed until July. He maintains that he was undertaking Islamic studies in order to write a book, while CSIS alleges that he attended a training camp in Afghanistan. A key piece of evidence against him are the statements of Abu Zubaida and Ahmed Ressam (which are part of the summary of the evidence previously given to Mr Charkaoui on 26 May, 17 July, and 14 August 2003) identifying Mr Charkaoui, upon presentation of photographs, under the name of Al-Maghrebi and stating that he had been seen by them in Afghanistan in a camp.[139] (Charkaoui argued that the information obtained from Ressam and Abu Zubaida were not credible since they were obtained under torture or, in the case of Mr Ressam, under the pressure of an agreement for clemency or a reduced sentence in connection with his hearing in the United States. Abdurahman Khadr, whose father knew Bin Ladin and was a part of his network, testified that he never saw Mr Charkaoui in Afghanistan.)

There are few details to confirm the allegations. Refusing to testify at his first three hearings since he believed that his testimony would be used to conclude that he was not credible and, in addition, would lend credibility to a legal process that Mr Charkaoui wished to protest, Charkaoui relied on the testimonials of his Montreal university teachers that he is an open minded individual who, while critical of the treatment meted out to Arabs and Muslims in Canada, was nevertheless of the opinion that Muslims could live peacefully with other groups in Quebec.[140] Denying all the allegations, Charkaoui took a polygraph test answering questions concerning whether or not he has been or still was a member of a terrorist group. Although he passed the test, at his bail hearing in 2005 Mr Justice Noel rejected its results on the grounds that the question of travel to Afghanistan was not asked and there were irregularities in how the test was administered.[141]

In the absence in these cases of support for either the state's case or the detainee's, courts – for all the careful legal reasoning of decisions – come ultimately to rely on notions of sleeper cells and indicators of a detainee's commitment to Islamic ideology. When he agreed to testify at his fourth detention review, Adil Charkaoui did not hide his views of 9/11. In his decision to release Charkaoui on bail and to the custody of his family under stringent bail conditions, Mr Justice Noël discussed at length his testimony as to his views on terrorism. He noted that Charkaoui

> found it deplorable that a 'terrorist' [TRANSLATION] prototype had developed over the years, that of a young Arab Muslim male who traveled a lot, and studied languages and martial arts. He said he knew many innocent people who had been suspected of being terrorists, often on account of this prototype. He also told the Court that he found it difficult to understand how anyone 'who was in a medieval country in a cave' [TRANSLATION] (namely, Osama bin Laden in Afghanistan) could have perpetrated an attack on the scale of September 11, 2001 in the U.S. Charkaoui noted that in December 2000 he was searched by the F.B.I. at JFK airport when he was accompanied by his pregnant wife, while nineteen young Arab men were able to board aircraft on September 11, 2001 without difficulty. He found it strange that the 19 passports of these men had been found but the black boxes of the four aircraft were still missing. From his reading, his study on the Internet and the newspapers, Mr.

Charkaoui is not convinced that the attacks were committed by Muslims; he says it is equally likely they were carried out by neo-conservatives and religious authorities in the U.S.[142]

It is difficult to say to what extent Charkaoui's challenge of profiling and of the official story of 9/11 might have influenced the outcome of his case. If it seems unlikely that a devious terrorist would take such a chance, it is of course possible to read his pronouncements as those of a 'fanatic' who is so deeply committed to his cause that he would risk his own freedom to say what he has to say. Race thinking does not have to make sense, since its coherence derives from the force of the narrative line that they are not like us. As in all the detainees' cases, when evidence cannot be corroborated, we can only conclude that the final decision rests on the court's own belief that a religious Arab man who has travelled to the Middle East and who may have associations, albeit distant ones, with other suspects suffices as proof of a threat to national security.

Conclusion

In their book *The Culture of Exception*, Bulent Diken and Carsten Bagge Lausten take care to clarify that their argument that today the exception is the rule is not an argument that 'contemporary society is characterized by the cruelty of the concentration camps, although camp-like structures are spreading quickly.' Instead, they argue that 'the *logic* of the camps tends to be generalized.'[143] It is this logic that we see first in the immigrant and refugee as exceptions in immigration law, and second, as *homo sacer*, in security-certificate hearings since the 'war on terror' began. It is a logic that is first and foremost about the power of the sovereign. The zone of non-law into which refugees are plunged is a legally authorized place in which rights are suspended. Simultaneously in the legal order and outside of it, the refugee confirms the terrible power of the state to determine every aspect of his life.[144] When this terrible power unfolds as bureaucracy, when the life of the refugee can depend on a few whispered words about jihad or training camps, then we too must accept the power of the state.

Race soothes any worries we have about the display of raw power. It invests the proceedings with a kind of coherency that belies the arbitrary nature of what is unfolding. There are monster terrorists, we believe, and the things we must do in order to contain them, things we

would not ordinarily accept, become justified. It is through the powerful evocations of jihad and pitiless, misogynist men in beards that we
come to accept that we do not need due process, that proof does not
matter. We become inured to lawlessness, as long as it remains in the
camps, as long, that is, that it is applied only to certain bodies who live
outside of reason.

The position that all Muslims and Arabs live outside of reason, and
should therefore be cast outside of the law, is not one that is made once
and for all. The story of race in the law is one that is full of internal contradictions: they are secretive and duplicitous yet it is we who rely on
secret evidence; they are irrational yet it is we who depend on wild
assertions about the Muslim fanatic and his counterpart in security
hearings, the Anglo-Saxon man. The story of monster terrorists does
not make sense yet is common sense. As I suggest in chapter 2, it is
useful, as Meyda Yegenoglu suggests, to think of race as 'a historically
specific fantasy,' one in which Western subjects learn to imagine themselves as sovereign only through marking the other as different and
outside reason.[145] The other will not stay fixed and the claim of universality that the Western subject must make requires a continual
engagement with difference, an engagement that the law reveals to be
fraught with desire, fear and anxiety.

2 If It Wasn't for the Sex and the Photos: The Torture of Prisoners at Abu Ghraib

This phenomenon of feeling superior through a sexually reified racism is always sadistic; its purpose is always to hurt.

Andrea Dworkin[1]

The violence inflicted on prisoners at the Abu Ghraib prison in Iraq by both male and female American soldiers was both widespread and very clearly sexualized. A pyramid of naked male prisoners forced to simulate sodomy conveyed graphically that the project of empire – the West's domination of the non-West – required strong infusions of a violent heterosexuality and patriarchy. The image of Private Lyndie England grinning and pointing her finger to the genitals of naked Iraqi prisoners confirmed that participation in sexualized racial violence and humiliation crossed gender lines. The photos, reportedly numbering in the thousands, shocked the white Western public, if not the non-white and non-Western one, the latter having had the advantage of recent and ongoing colonial experience.

As a Canadian, my own response to the violence at Abu Ghraib was one of recognition. Canadians had seen similar photos of grinning soldiers posing behind the tortured bodies of Somalis more than a decade earlier in incidents of peacekeeper violence. The racial and sexualized dimensions of the 'Somalia Affair,' although evident in the photos and videotapes of the soldiers themselves, were nevertheless transformed (in military tribunals and in the press) into the story of war: stressed troops and unscrupulous leaders resorted to violence when confronted by savage, ungrateful Somalis bent on the destruction of those whose civilization they did not appreciate or understand. Peacekeeper violence by Western troops towards the populations they assist shares four characteristics: the violence is collective (many participate, watch, and know of these practices), recorded in photos, videos, and diaries, sexualized (with rape and sodomy occurring), and often committed against defenceless populations, including women and children and prisoners. Notwithstanding these telling features, there is always an attempt to transform military violence into something the troops could not help but commit. Unwittingly revealing the colonial logic that 'they are not like us,' and that the colonies are not like the home country, Canadians largely accepted the official story that the heat and dust of Somalia and the duplicity of the Somalis drove the soldiers to violence. Somalia, it was claimed, was a lawless land, a place where extreme measures were called for. As I have argued, the violence committed by Canadian peacekeepers against Somalis must be understood as a colonial violence, born of the conviction that it is the white man's burden to civilize and keep in line through force racial others awaiting assistance into modernity. The acts of violence committed against Somalis convinced the soldiers of their own masculine, racial, and national superiority.[2]

The parallels between the Somalia Affair and Abu Ghraib are startling. If Somalia was a place where law had to be abandoned in the interest of confronting lawlessness, however, Abu Ghraib was more formally constituted as a state of exception. As several scholars have pointed out, Abu Ghraib was not so much a prison as a concentration camp, where the rule of law simply did not apply.[3] A 'floating colony,' in Amy Kaplan's words, a prison of indeterminate status between domestic and international law, and above all, a camp where nothing had to be justified, Abu Ghraib could be little else than a place of terror.[4] As Avery Gordon observes, prisons where law is suspended have come to be such an everyday feature of the 'war on terror' that we now have an ability to name the locations of what would once have been secretive military prisons.[5] Gordon notes, too, that there is a continuum between U.S. military prisons abroad and territorial U.S. prisons, even to the point of shared personnel (two of the convicted soldiers at Abu Ghraib were former prison guards considered experts in practices of brutality). Today's prisons are sites where an exceptional brutality is normalized. Drawing on Agamben's notion of bare life and Ruth Wilson Gilmore's characterization of the contemporary prison as a 'regime of abandonment' in which surplus and unwanted populations who are mostly of colour are permanently imprisoned and evicted from law, Gordon reminds us that the prisoners of empire are the socially dead. Both the military prison and the domestic prison industrial complex now share the 'organized oblivion' of the concentration camp first identified by Arendt of totalitarian regimes.[6]

If it seems obvious that Abu Ghraib is a camp, a place where the rule of law no longer applies and where, as Agamben observed, nothing committed against the camp's inmates can be considered a crime, it is nevertheless important to examine closely the 'normalcy of exceptional brutality' that Gordon and others associate with both the military prison and the prison industrial complex. As Arendt noted of the Nazi concentration camps, brutality was not simply born of guards who were unusually sadistic or resentful of prisoners who had once been their social superiors. Instead, 'the old spontaneous bestiality gave way to an absolutely cold and systematic destruction of human bodies, calculated to destroy human dignity; death was avoided or postponed indefinitely.'[7] Systematic destruction and systematic abandonment of surplus or unwanted populations is *productive*. When we come face to face with utterly normalized practices of terror, practices that turn prisoners into *homo sacer*, the being who may be killed not sacrificed, it is here that we see the logic of the exception as it is undergirded by race thinking. Racism, Gordon insightfully notes, determines not only who becomes a prisoner but also what the prisoner becomes – 'an inferior race in and of themselves.'[8] By the same token, the guards, and all those who are drawn to participate in their practices, become the superior race. It is these psychic underpinnings of the exception that I suggest are revealed when we consider sexualized racial violence.

The photos from Abu Ghraib depict acts of intimacy, acts requiring a psychic closeness that endangers the barrier between the human and the subhuman even as it creates and affirms it. Totalitarian regimes turn hatred into fantasy, Jacobo Timerman wrote in an account of his own torture in an Argentinian prison, knowing that torture is much more than a physical method of getting prisoners to talk.[9] This chapter explores what we can learn from Abu Ghraib about some of the psychic processes of empire, the terror that moves empire forward, and the individual performance of violence on which empire relies. It charts the realm of fantasy that we can just barely glimpse from the photos, where gleeful torturers seek to emasculate, to turn their prisoners into sexually violated men, and to keep their moment of intimacy and triumph alive through thousands of trophy photos. Empire, it must be hypothesized, comes into existence through multiple systems of domination. In the first section, I discuss visual practices such as photos and their role in the making of racial subjects who understand themselves as members of a superior civilization. In the second section, I consider the violence as a ritual that enables white men to achieve a sense of mastery over the racial other at the same time that it provides a sexualized intimacy forbidden in white supremacy and patriarchy. In the third section, I consider how white women participate in these processes. I argue that it is as members of their race that we can best grasp white women's participation in the violence – a participation that provides the same mastery and gendered intimacy afforded to white men who engage in violence. In the conclusion I consider the regime of racial terror in evidence at Abu Ghraib and other places, focusing on terror as a 'trade in mythologies' that organizes the way that bodies come to express the racial arrangements of empire.

If what we saw at Abu Ghraib was neither the aberrant behaviour of a few soldiers nor an overly aggressive approach to terrorism gone awry, explanations much favoured in the media and by the current American administration, then it is the public participation of ordinary people in racial violence that requires the most explanation. How do race, class, gender, and sexuality underwrite each other in these moments of public racial violence and how do these practices of violence enable men and women to achieve a profound sense of (gendered) racial superiority? These are questions that require an interlocking approach for understanding the violence at Abu Ghraib – an approach that tracks how multiple systems of oppression come into existence through each other.

I use the word interlocking rather than intersecting to describe how the systems of oppression are connected.[10] Intersecting remains a word that describes discrete systems whose paths cross. I suggest that the systems *are* each other and that they give content to each other. While one system (here it is white supremacy) provides the entry point for the discussion (language is, after all, successive), what is immediately evident as one pursues how white supremacy is embodied and enacted in the everyday is that individuals come to know themselves within masculinity and femininity. Put another way, the sense of self that is simultaneously required and produced by empire is a self that is experienced *in relation* to the subordinate other – a relationship that is deeply gendered and sexualized. An interlocking approach requires that we keep several balls in the air at once, striving to overcome the successive process forced upon us by language and focusing on the ways in which bodies express social hierarchies of power.

The problem of language (interlocking versus intersecting) is not simply an academic one. If we view the acts as evidence of the operation of one system that is merely complicated by another, we will end up missing something about the violence and its psychic origins. Jasbir Paur offers an example that illustrates the outcome of analysing one system at the expense of another. Those who viewed the Abu Ghraib photos of Iraqi men forced to simulate having sex with each other as evidence of rampant homophobia (the photos show homosexuality as degradation) missed the bodies of the tortured Iraqis themselves.[11] Paur insists that both gender (Iraqi men are being made to feel like women) and race (Iraqi bodies are the ones marked as degenerate) are effaced if we concentrate on sexuality as a discrete system. In this respect, Paur's argument is in line with scholars of colonialism who trace how colonizers sought to establish their claim to ownership of the land and conquest of its occupants, not only through the rape of women but also through the feminizing of colonial men. As Revathi Krishnaswamy has shown in her study of colonial rule in India, 'the real goal of feminization is effeminization – a process in which colonizing men use women/ womanhood to delegitimize, discredit, and disempower colonized men.'[12] Several systems are in operation in the process of empire and they give content to each other. It is in order to overcome the problem of the discreteness of systems, and the obscuring of the full tangle of oppressive relations, that I propose a focus on the bodies of the torturers rather than those of the tortured – a focus that requires an interlocking, historicized approach. The torturers can surely be seen as seeking to delegitimize and to disempower, processes communicated in the language of patriarchy, but how did those acts produce their own racial sense of identity?

My question concerning how ordinary people come to participate in racial violence is one that has concerned others, among them educators working in critical pedagogy. The question we all have, of course, is what kind of education would it take to interrupt the production of subjects who so easily answer the call to participate in what Robert Fisk ironically called 'the great war for civilization.'[13] In

2004 Henry Giroux published an article entitled 'What Might Education Mean after Abu Ghraib: Revisiting Adorno's Politics of Education.'[14] As I do, Giroux rejects the argument that what went on at Abu
Ghraib was the work of a few bad apples, although he still considers
that special conditions prevailing in Iraq pushed soldiers to the brink
and he believes that the torture is simply culturally specific torture.
Recognizing that the photos reveal something about collective will,
however, Giroux explores where soldiers learned the identities they
enacted at Abu Ghraib. The 'pedagogical conditions' that produced
Abu Ghraib have something to do with 'discourses of privatization,
particularly the contracting of military labor, the intersection of mili-
tarism and the crisis of masculinity, the war on terrorism, and the
racism that makes it so despicable.'[15] Specifically, the media's cele-
bration of violence, hegemonic masculinity with its insistence on
'masculine hardness' against feminine softness, and market fundamentalism all combined in a 'furious jingoistic patriotism' that is
evident in these acts of torture.[16]

   Race is present here as one of many factors, among them gender and
class, but how they come together to produce subjects who engage in
acts of racial violence (which Giroux does not consider Abu Ghraib to
be enacting) remains unclear. This becomes a major failing when
Giroux must consider what kind of education would enable students
to be critical of the ideologies that led to Abu Ghraib. Turning to
Adorno for help (in view of Adorno's identification of the aggressive
nationalism that led to Auschwitz), Giroux proposes a self-reflective
critical education. He remains vague as to what the specific educational practices are that would interrupt the aggressive nationalism
that surrounds us today, remarking only that there is the possibility
that 'inhuman acts of abuse under incredibly nerve-wracking conditions represent a rare outlet for pleasure.'[17] I believe that what an interlocking approach has to offer is an understanding of just such a possibility of race pleasure in violence. If one considers that what happened
at Abu Ghraib had little to do with especially stressful circumstances
and more to do with deeply historical processes through which Americans understand themselves as white, then we can better confront the
educational and political challenges we face in this new world order
by understanding the complex ways in which systems of oppression
(white supremacy, capitalism, and patriarchy) operate on a psychic
level through sexual desire and fear.

1. 'Why Record Evil?'

The photographs did not lie.[18]

'The photographs did not lie' is the line that introduces a book containing the official reports of what has come to be known as the 'shocking prisoner abuse in Iraq.' If the images of American men and women gleefully posing beside a pyramid of naked Iraqi men or giving the thumbs up beside hooded and naked prisoners did not lie, what truth did they tell? There has been remarkable consensus around the answer to this question in the media and in the official reports. As the Fay Inquiry summed up, the soldiers who abused detainees were 'a small group of morally corrupt and unsupervised soldiers and civilians.'[19] Circumstances, however, pushed many of them to the brink: 'The occupiers were overwhelmed.'[20] Inadequately trained, demoralized, fearful, and pressured 'to obtain information that could help save American lives,' they fell into torture and the sexual humiliation of prisoners.[21] Perhaps the only disagreement over this version of events has been over whether or not morally weak, low-ranking soldiers were in fact encouraged by their leaders to 'mistreat' prisoners.

The attempt to contain the violence to a few weak and stressed individuals could not easily stand by itself. The explanation required reinforcement. There were simply too many images and they appeared to the public to depict a sexual depravity, to say nothing of cruelty and brutality. The sex, if not the brutality, seemed to warrant explanation. The theory that went the furthest to provide an explanation of the sex was based on the idea that sexualized torture was simply a culturally specific interrogation method. Fitting in nicely with the 'clash of civilizations' thesis[22] that had come to dominate Western explanations for conflict between West and non-West, and the Islamic world in particular, pyramids of naked men forced to simulate having sex with each other was everywhere to be understood as nothing more than a contemporary form of torture. Few in the media questioned the Orientalist underpinnings of this claim. (Unlike us, they are sexually repressed, homophobic, and misogynist and are likely to crack in sexualized situations, particularly those involving women dominating men or those involving sex between men.) No one asked whether such methods would in fact humiliate men of all cultures both because they are violent and because they target what it means to be a man in patriarchy.

The 'clash of civilizations' approach to torture reinforced the idea of their barbarism at the same time that it enabled the West to remain on moral high ground. Through the idea of cultural difference, sexualized torture became something more generic – torture for the purpose of obtaining information. Sexualized torture, then, was meant simply 'to attack the prisoners' identity and values.'[23] Believing that the fault had to be traced back to the top, Mark Danner declared the photos 'comprehensible' given the cultural characteristics of Arabs *and* the Central Intelligence Agency's manual on interrogations. The photos are 'staged operas of fabricated shame intended to "intensify" the prisoners' guilt feelings, increase his anxiety and his urge to cooperate,' Danner wrote, quoting parts of the CIA's interrogation policy.[24] Photos are a 'shame multiplier,' according to the Red Cross, since they could be distributed to the prisoners' families and used to further humiliate detainees.[25] Second, through the idea of culturally specific interrogation techniques, Americans were marked as modern people who did not subscribe to puritanical notions of sex or to patriarchal notions of women's role in it. The Iraqis, of course, remained forever confined to the pre-modern. When we in the West see photos of prisoner abuse, and when our official inquiries declare without irony that what is depicted amounts simply to a speciality form of torture required in these strange nether regions of the world, we too mark the boundaries between self and other – between here and there. 'More than skin color, and dress, soldiers view mannerisms, cultural beliefs and traditions as the true ground upon which they distinguish themselves as better and thus able to inflict pain and suffering,' speculates one journalist, thereby reducing the encounter in those prison cells to a culture clash.[26]

For many who remained uneasy about pyramids of naked men or women soldiers brushing their bare breasts against prisoners and wearing thongs specifically for interrogations (as they are reputed to have done at Guantanamo), the sex was nevertheless scrupulously avoided. The current American administration's aggressive approach to terrorism helped to fill the silence.[27] Both for those who saw prisoner abuse as the work of a few reservists and those, such as Seymour Hersh, the journalist who broke the story, who concluded that the abuse at Abu Ghraib was 'a fact of army life that the soldiers felt no need to hide,'[28] torture had a political utility. For Hersh, the torture was 'eye-for-eye retribution in fighting terrorism,' something dictated by Donald Rumsfeld, Dick Cheney, and George Bush – payback perhaps for 9/11.[29] Despite determined efforts to view the torture instrumentally – that is as having a *military* function – the sex does not easily go away. Three questions persist about the Abu Ghraib photos, questions that are not answered in the latest findings of Donald Rumsfeld's 'independent' panel of civilian experts (the Schlesinger report), which conclude that 'chaos' and 'sadism' prevailed at Abu Ghraib prison.[30] Why the photos? I have yet to find anyone other than Mark Danner and former Brigadier General Janis Karpinski[31] who believes that the nearly 2000 photos soldiers sent to their families and to each other were really destined for Iraqi prisoners' homes or were meant to hang as a threat over detainees of their continual humiliation.[32] This leaves the compelling question, as one of Canada's national newspapers headlined, 'Why record evil?'[33] Why so many of them? It is the excess of it all that troubles. When you are in the realm of such excess, it is harder to believe official accounts about a few bad apples. Finally, why the sex? (This last question is often connected to the question of women's participation.) There is something too disturbing about the deeply sexualized acts and the grins. There is also something too familiar. Certainly the leash that Lyndie England held to lead around a naked Iraqi man reminded many of pornography, and the black-hooded figure from whose arms electrodes were suspended seemed to one scholar a spectacular and telling inversion of the white hoods of the KKK.[34] The photos hold the key to answering many of these questions.

In her important book *American Archives*, Shawn Michelle Smith argues that visual practices such as photographs have long served as a kind of technology of belonging, expressing the collective will at the same time that they create it. When they were first invented, photos were quickly enlisted 'to establish social hierarchies anchored in new visual truths.'[35] From depictions of the physical attributes of criminals to the middle-class family shot and photos of lynchings, photographs were called upon to tell us something about gender, race, and class hierarchies. In so doing, they not only reflected what was imagined but also actively produced what they declared to exist.[36] Photos helped an emerging middle class to affirm their place in the nineteenth century by marking who was white and middle class and who was criminal and racially other. Building on Smith's insights, we would then have to consider how the photos at Abu Ghraib, which were mailed to family and friends and tacked up on the unit's doors (as they were in Somalia), confirmed an imagined community among Americans – one that is profoundly racially structured since it is achieved through the tortured and humiliated bodies of Iraqis and racialized others.

At the very least, the existence of large numbers of photos indicate something about the widespread nature of these acts of sexualized torture. Of the photo exhibit 'War of Extermination: Crimes of the Wehrmacht, 1942–1944,' which toured Germany and Austria during the late 1990s – an exhibit that contained hundreds of photos mostly taken by the perpetrators of crimes against Jews – Omer Bartov writes: 'What many Germans found hard to take was that the exhibition demonstrated in the most graphic manner the complicity of Wehrmacht soldiers in the Holocaust and other crimes of the region, especially in the occupied parts of the Soviet Union and Yugoslavia.'[37] If the soldiers all knew of these crimes, and close to twenty million soldiers passed through the ranks of the Wehrmacht, then it follows that Germans knew much more about the Holocaust than they were prepared to acknowledge after the war.[38] A debate has long raged among historians about what it took to get so many ordinary Germans to participate in, approve of, or remain indifferent to the Holocaust. The photographs seem to confirm that crimes against Jews had public approval. The record of abuse suggests, too, that there was no fear of reprisal. However, if the public recording of brutal acts reveals widespread approval and thus something of the collective will, it does not in itself tell us what the photographs *do*. The photographs oriented ordinary Germans to where they were (in an Aryan regime) and *who* they were – Aryans who were able to mark the boundary between themselves and non-Aryans.

A spectacular national use of the productive function of visual practices in a context not unlike prisoner abuse in Abu Ghraib was evident in France at the end of the nineteenth century when Alfred Dreyfus, a Jew, was charged (unjustly) with selling military secrets to the Germans. The military faced a terrible problem in that Dreyfus did not look like the prevailing stereotype of the degenerate Jew. How, then, to prove that although Dreyfus looked like a regular Frenchman, a sinister alien lurked below this exterior? The answer was to transform his body into text, offering visual proof of his degeneracy. Ceremonially ripping the military epaulettes from his clothes and photographing Dreyfus in ways that might make him appear non-military and effeminate, Dreyfus's body then served to resolve the French military's own concerns over its virility as well as French anxieties over

Jews, especially those who too easily passed for being French.[39] Photos, then, must be understood, as Shawn Michelle Smith suggests, as 'visual codes of national belonging.' The photos that did this most spectacularly for America were the photographs of lynched African Americans.[40]

2. Rituals of Violence

[Lynching] transform[ed] 'whiteness' into something visible and terribly tangible, into something 'real.' In the gruesome act of dissecting the body of an African American man, white men and women convinced themselves of their own physical superiority.[41]

Writing about these photos and the collective will they reveal, Andrew Austin considers the grins on the faces of the white people in the pictures. He asks how we might understand motive and agency. Why did so many participate so gleefully in these kinds of acts and wished to prolong their joy through recording it? It is remarkable, Austin observes, that one can find many expressions in the crowds of white men, women, and children who watch or who actually do the lynching, but the expression one never sees on anyone's face is horror.[42] Ordinary Americans participated in these crimes, had their photos taken beside lynched bodies, smiled for the camera, and sent postcards of the event in which they circled their own faces and described the 'barbecue.' As I am suggesting for Abu Ghraib, lynching photos were not intended for Blacks but for whites, a tangible and lasting reminder of an important occasion.

Clearly, it was not enough to simply kill Blacks, Austin comments. Instead, 'the killers had to murder Blacks in the most excessive and public way. Afterward, instead of shame and guilt, the perpetrators expressed pride in their actions, taking trophies, fragments of the corpse, selling body parts as souvenirs, and proudly displaying the photographs they had taken in local shop windows.'[43] People walked around town carrying the bones of lynched men. The collective, open aspects of these acts make them hard to grasp. Phillip Dray recounts the story of W.E. Dubois discovering that crowds were excitedly gathering to see the lynching of Sam Hose. Dubois was forced to face the fact that lynching was not the action of a few violent men as he had assumed, but rather a collective expression of hatred and white supremacy. These acts of violence 'made clear to everyone the proper social order of things.'[44] Those in power did not move to stop it and often participated in it. City officials posed for photographs alongside of lynched men without fear of punishment and the United States Senate failed to enact anti-lynching legislation for several decades, a fact for which it has recently apologized.[45] As an expression of a collective will, lynching and the practice of recording it confirmed for white men and women who they were.

Symbolically and materially, lynching may be considered as a publicly shared and approved of practice to create community – white community. Both historians and Black fiction writers describe lynching as a ritual, as Trudier Harris documents. Through the ritual, 'Whites consolidate themselves against all possible encroachments upon their territory by Blacks, whether the encroachments – physical, psychological, or otherwise – are committed wittingly or not. '[46] The title of Harris's book, *Exorcising Blackness*, suggests what she thinks the ritual is intended to do. Harris, who focuses on the pedagogic intent of the lynching ritual, first describes it:

> A crowd of whites, attributing to themselves the sanction over life and death and viewing themselves as good and right, are reduced to the level of savages in their pursuit and apprehending of a presumed black criminal; they usually exhibit a festive atmosphere by singing, donning their Sunday finery, and bringing food to the place of death. A castration or some other mutilation usually accompanies the killing in addition to a gathering of trophies from the charred body. Sometimes the crowd lingers to have its picture taken with the victim.[47]

'The actions of white lynch mobs and the ritualistic nature of their behavior,' she argues, 'cannot be attributed to some strange and foreign beast released at the time of cruelty.'[48] Lynching is not only the work of some exceptionally violent white supremacists. There has to be prior socialization to make lynching acceptable, and each participant in the drama understands what is collectively at stake even at the height of the excitement.

When people participate in this ritual, what are they thinking and feeling? What is personally at stake? Harris writes that white men involved in lynching

> spent an inordinate amount of time examining the genitals of the black men whom they were about to kill. Even as they castrated the black men,

there was a suggestion of fondling, of envious caress. The many emotions involved at that moment perhaps led the white men to slash even more violently at what could not be theirs, but which, at some level, they very much desired (without the apish connotations, of course).[49]

Sexualized racial violence does double duty: it provides the sense of power, control, and mastery and, at the same time, it offers an intimacy to what it is forbidden to desire or to see as human. The 'lynched Black man becomes a source of sexual pleasure to those who kill him,' a receptacle for hate and fears and forbidden feelings.[50]

Let me draw on another scholar of lynching to explore further the identity that is achieved through these rituals of racial violence. Robyn Wiegman has argued that lynching is a symbolic sexual encounter between the white mob and its victim. The castration is meant to evict Black men from the community of men. The threat that Black men represent is the threat of masculine sameness (here we could also say that the threat that the racial other represents is the threat of sameness and common humanity). Sameness must be disavowed and no more so than at the moment when it is too threatening a possibility, when, in other words, the racial hierarchy is revealed as a fiction. Weigman notes, as many other scholars do, that lynching increased and led more often to death when Black people gained more rights. (We might consider that racial violence in the policing or prison encounter in North America is often initiated when the prisoner talks back.) Sexualized violence accomplishes the eviction from humanity, and it does so as an eviction from *masculinity*.

Significantly, it is the white man who descends into savagery in order to establish his own civility – the paradox is mediated through the story of protecting white women from the bestial excess of blackness. With the myth of the Black rapist, Black men were accused of what white men were guilty of – rape. The inversion, the imputation of bestial excess on to Black bodies, makes white violence disappear, leaving in its place only white men. White innocence is secured through the sexual disciplining of the Black body.[51] The miscegenation taboo, as several scholars have argued, where white women are forbidden to Black men, expresses white men's fear of racial difference, and provides an instance of how the circulation of women establishes the relationship of men to each other.[52] Notably, while white men are allowed access to Black women in white supremacy, the offspring of such unions are not entitled to access the power and prestige of their fathers, as many miscegenation laws ensured.

In her study of lynching, Lisa Cardyn catalogues the practices that express the sexual disciplining of Black bodies – practices that were present at Abu Ghraib and in peacekeeper violence. Lynching involved whippings of a 'distinctly sexualized cast'; incidents of young men forced to simulate intercourse; humiliation; stripping of victims; the use of sticks as extended phalluses; sadistic homoerotics; group sex; and men made to kiss another man's bottom. Cardyn concludes that 'in their quest to possess, inscribe, and finally obliterate the bodies of their victims, lynch mobs unwittingly revealed the awful coalescence of sexual rage, desire, frustration, and obsession that constrained them to act as they did.'[53] We must turn to James Baldwin for a literary rendition of the 'awful coalescence' to which historians refer. In his story 'Going to Meet the Man' Baldwin describes a white sheriff who finds himself impotent.[54] Sexual excitement is only possible through blackness, a blackness understood as body and savagery against which must stand the hard erection. The sheriff cannot ask his wife to do what the Black girls he arrests and coerces do, and although the image of a Black girl gives rise to 'a distant excitement,' it is only when the sheriff can summon up the sensations of beating a Black prisoner to a pulp and the memory of being taken to see a lynching when he was a child that he is able to generate sufficient sexual excitement to overcome his impotence. As Baldwin shows, the sheriff experiences himself as drowning in blackness, 'an overwhelming fear, which yet contained a curious and dreadful pleasure.'[55] He is haunted, for instance, by the singing of the Black men and women forming lines and defiantly intending to register to vote. It is a singing that he feels he has been hearing all his life, a sound that 'contained an obscure comfort' as though 'they were singing to God.' Yet he cannot indulge in this positive meaning of the song. What he fears most is that the song is not about 'singing black folks into heaven,' but instead about 'singing white folks into hell.'[56] Faced with this ever-present possibility, there can only be the daily battle against the singing – a battle between the fear of and the desire for oneness with the other that wears him out.

Briefly, and it is only a fleeting sensation in the night, the sheriff wishes that he could be buried inside the warmth and safety of his wife's body and never again have 'to go downtown to face those faces.'[57] However, to fulfil this longing for the feminine, to give himself up to the song, means having to abandon the masculine self that stands as a barrier against blackness. He defends himself against the longing by calling up the sensations of beating the prisoner, a Black man who led the voter registration drive and who, as a ten-year-old child, had once confronted the sheriff. When the prisoner reminds the sheriff of that earlier confrontation, a rage builds in the sheriff. Only the sensation of feeling himself violently stiffen interrupts the beating the rage inspires. As with the lynching that he witnessed as a child, the violence (the castration at the lynching) produces a climax, a moment when 'the blood came roaring down.' It is through the violence, a literal orgasm, that the white man knows himself as master of his own fate, as a man not overcome by the singing or by feminine warmth. The violence, the moment of terrible intimacy when the racial and the feminine threat are both averted, offers the only antidote to fear. It also offers a transfer of sexual power from the Black body to the white man. Inspired by the memory of racial mastery and transformed now by this recalled encounter with the Black body, the sheriff calls to his sleeping wife: 'Come on, sugar, I'm going to do you like a n-----, just like a n----- come on, sugar, and love me just like you'd love a n-----.'[58]

The psychic processes that Baldwin captures so powerfully, and that scholars of lynching theorize, are central for post-colonial theorists who maintain that 'we find an ambivalent driving desire at the heart of racism, a compulsive libidinal attraction disavowed by an equal insistence on repulsion.'[59] Robert Young, considering the 'desire in fantasies of race, and of race in fantasies of desire'[60] that is so evident in English fiction, suggests that colonialism is less about the Manichean categories of colonizer/colonized than it is about 'the intricate processes of cultural contact, intrusion, fusion and dysfunction.'[61] Drawing on Gilles Deleuze and Felix Guattari, Young notes their contention that the 'prime function incumbent on the socius has always been to codify the flows of desire, to inscribe them, to record them, to see to it that no flow exists that is not properly damned up, channeled, regulated.'[62] Capitalism, Deleuze and Guattari theorized, requires the territorializing of desire that Freud assumed was an individual process when he described the Oedipus complex. Paraphrasing them, Young writes:

Oedipus is not simply the normal structure through which all humans travel on the path to mental, sexual and social maturity: it is the means through which the flow of desire is encoded, trapped, inscribed within the artificial reterritorializations of a repressive social structure – the family, the party, the nation, the law, the educational system, the hospital, psychoanalysis itself.[63]

Young utilizes the same analytic to argue that colonialism required similar 'violent physical and ideological procedures' as well as the damming up, diverting, and reterritorialization of desire that Deleuze and Guattari describe for capitalism.[64] The 'endlessly repeated colonial fantasy of the uncontrollable sexual drive of the non-white races and their limitless fertility,' for example, 'only took on significance through its voyeuristic tableau of frenzied interminable coupling, of couplings, fusings, coalescence, *between races*.'[65] Colonialism's endless preoccupations with miscegenation (a preoccupation shared in slave regimes) and the policing of sexual boundaries through violence resolve the ambivalence in the moment, only to have it threaten to overwhelm colonial subjects again and again. It is in this ambivalence, and in the violence that it gives birth to, that we find the tracks for what happens at Abu Ghraib, Guantanamo, and similar settings.

In our own time and referring to pornography, Andrea Dworkin notices the same confluence of race, gender, sexuality, and violence that took place in the colonial context in the making of white men today. She comments: 'I am struck by how hate speech, racist hate speech, becomes more sexually explicit as it becomes more virulent – how its meaning becomes more sexualized, as if the sex is required to carry the hostility.'[66] Following a line that I would very much like to take with respect to the Abu Ghraib photos, Dworkin asks: 'What does that orgasm do? That orgasm says, I am real and the lower creature, that thing, is not, and if the annihilation of that thing brings pleasure, that is the way life should be; *the racist hierarchy becomes a sexually charged idea.* There is a sense of biological inevitability that comes from the intensity of a sexual response derived from contempt.'[67] As Dworkin suggests, 'a sexually reified racism is always sadistic; its purpose is always to hurt.'[68] It is perhaps only through a sexualized violence – one that offers both intimacy and repulsion – that white supremacy can maintain its most central fiction of a permanent difference between the races, a fiction that Deleuze and Guattari suggest is always threatened by desire for the racial and cultural other.[69]

Can we consider the racial hierarchy in Iraq a sexually charged idea? What does the sex do? Certainly sexualized torture evicts Arabs from the community of men, and from a common humanity. As the Dreyfus case has shown, both the acts and the photos transform the body into text, confirming that the Arab is emasculated, body not mind, and that occupation is as necessary as it is dangerous. How else to mark the boundary between them and us, and how else to avoid drowning in blackness, but through violence? The excess (overworked prison guards nevertheless find the time to assemble human pyramids and to take pictures – many other soldiers laugh and join the exhibition) and the sex both tell us of what must be so forcefully and ritualistically disavowed – their humanity, their masculinity, and, above all, the desire for what must not be desired.

3. Where Are the Women?

The women thronged to look but never a one
Showed sorrow in her eyes of steely blue.[70]

When scholars theorize racial violence as a ritual, they stress that it is an 'an affair between men.'[71] As in Baldwin's story, men's disavowal of the maternal, the feminine, and the body, as well as the replacing of the body with the phallus, is required to mark the boundary between whiteness and blackness, producing what William Pinar poetically describes as 'the despair of the loveless.'[72] For Pinar, racial violence cannot be understood unless queered – that is to say, in the words of Frantz Fanon, 'the Negrophobic man is a repressed homosexual.'[73] The problem is that white men are neither permanently white nor permanently men and white heterosexual manhood is constituted by perpetually disavowing homoerotic desire for black men.[74] The issue of racial violence, Trudier Harris agrees, 'really boils down to one between white men and black men and the mythic conception the former have of the latter.'[75] For Robyn Weigman too, the obsession with black men's genitals in lynching reveals desire and a sadistic homoeroticism that is being disavowed. Similarly, Andrea Dworkin maintains: 'The essential sexual antagonism that is basic to racism is expressed as if the possession of women were the issue, but fundamentally the antagonism is homoerotic.'[76]

If we accept these premises, where are the women? In Claude Mackay's poem about lynching, they throng to look, an eager part of the crowd. Women are the bearers of the white phallus's meaning, Weigman explains, and Baldwin makes clear that the sheriff's wife must answer his call. Women express white male power. They are its conduits. Black women must confirm with *their* bodies that it is white women who are the coin of the realm. Optimistically and ahistorically, Pinar opines that the major difference between white men and white women was that the latter did not sexualize race: 'White women were – are – often awful to Black women, but they didn't track them, strip them, sexually torture and mutilate their bodies, keeping parts as souvenirs.'[77] They watched, however, as Black people were lynched in their name, made the picnic baskets, kept the photos and treasured the souvenirs, and, in slavery and its aftermath, developed their own gender-specific cruelties. At Abu Ghraib, they also tortured and sexually humiliated Arab men.

Troubled by the direct participation of women in the abuse at Abu Ghraib, several prominent Western feminists have felt unable to account for such agency. Barbara Ehrenreich, for example, confessed that a certain kind of feminism died within her when she saw the photos – the feminism 'that saw men as perpetual perpetrators' and women as morally superior.[78] For her, then, the participation of women in these acts of torture simply meant that anyone could become a torturer under the right circumstances. The circumstances for Ehrenreich were simply about war – working-class women who wanted an education joined the military and found themselves in the midst of 'our species' tragic propensity for violence.'[79] Thoughtful attempts to explain white women's role remained for the most part attached to this notion that as a subordinate group themselves, women could not participate in any way comparable to men. Zillah Eisenstein argues that women were 'gender decoys,' meant to distract attention from the real empire builders. 'In the case of Abu Ghraib,' she writes, 'racial codings are used to deeply seed gender meanings and their confusion to build empire.'[80] In this view, women are merely dupes, working-class women with little agency and certainly no stake in white supremacy who found themselves in the middle of a man's game. The idea of a decoy makes of white women passive, not active, participants in colonialism, and, indeed, Eisenstein claims that '[f]emales are present to cover over the misogyny of building empire.' In the pursuit of redemption for white women, namely, the drive to show that white women are less culpable than white men and that their violence towards people of colour is somehow a lesser violence, it is easy to recognize the staking of a claim for justice by confining white women to the margins as victims and not as oppressors.[81] The problem posed by women's active participation in racial violence is resolved, however, if we begin with the fact that in empire (which Eisenstein acknowledges exists, while Ehrenreich does not) white women signify principally through their race and not their gender.[82] The call to participate in the practices of empire is a powerful one, as I have argued about men of colour who have participated in peace-keeping violence against Somalis,[83] and answering it brings rewards. White women secure access to citizenship when they participate in the violence of nation, as indeed we all do.

If there is any specific aspect of gender that may be glimpsed in what white women such as Lyndie England did, it is perhaps, as Susan Willis has suggested, in white women enacting desire for Arab men, ostensibly to humiliate them, but accomplishing at the same time a crossing of both racial and gender boundaries. The transgression serves, paradoxically, to remind white men that they are not the only objects of white women's sexual attention. White women at Abu Ghraib might have been, as Willis put it, 'playing their poor Southern white boys against racial others of forbidden desire'[84] and coming as close to miscegenation as white supremacy will allow. Yet the joke, in the end, was on the Arab men, and it is more likely that it is in the spirit of cheering on the lynching and drawing of racial boundaries through hostility and fascination that we can better read the white women's actions. The following newspaper excerpt suggests that race overdetermined what went on:

> Colleen Kesner, a resident from England's hometown, said: 'A lot of people here think they ought to just blow up the whole of Iraq. To the country boys here, if you're a different nationality, a different race, you're sub-human. That's the way that girls like Lynndie England are raised. Tormenting Iraqis, in her mind, would be no different from shooting a turkey. Every season here you're hunting something. Over there they're hunting Iraqis.[85]

Of the women who thronged to watch, then, the white wife in the sheriff's bed and the women soldiers at Abu Ghraib and Guantanamo Bay, we might simply assert that they sought access to racial power – a power perhaps coded by white women's role as the bearer of the phallus's meaning. Certainly, through affirming the power of the phallus and rejecting the feminine (alien other), white women ultimately undermine themselves and in this sense they are dupes. In the meantime, however, through such acts of racial power they have gained membership in a racial regime. One becomes Western, Yegenoglu reminds us, through imagining oneself in the fantasy of Orientalism, a fantasy with material effects: both the European man and the European woman must dream of possession of the Oriental other to secure sovereign status for themselves.[86]

Conclusion: Racial Terror and the Trade in Methodologies

As rituals of lynching suggest, what we euphemistically call 'prisoner abuse' today is not new. Colonial regimes have long been structured by what, borrowing from Michael Taussig, we might more appropriately call racial terror. Taussig reminds us that we would be unwise to ignore the role of terror in securing power. Terror is 'the mediator *par excellence* of colonial hegemony,' Taussig notes, and 'the space of death is one of the crucial spaces where Indian, African, and white gave birth to the New World.'[87] Terror is how we come to know and make known colonial power – how it gets written on our bodies.

> Hated and feared, objects to be despised, yet also of awe, the reified essence of evil in the very being of their bodies, these figures of the Jew, the black, the Indian, and woman herself, are clearly objects of cultural construction, the leaden keel of evil and mystery stabilizing the ship and course that is Western history. With the cold war we add the communist. With the time bomb ticking inside the nuclear family, we add the feminists and the gays. The military and the New Right, like the conquerors of old, discover the evil they have imputed to these aliens, and mimic the savagery they have imputed.[88]

To Taussig's list, we must add the Arab / the Muslim.

Taussig is insistent that 'behind the search for profits, the need to control labor, the need to assuage frustration, and so on, lie intricately construed long-standing cultural logics of meaning – structures of feeling – whose bases lie in a symbolic world and not in one of rationalism.'[89] We have to move through the electrodes and the mutilated human body, and the experience of torture, in order to confront 'the hallucination of the military' (referring to Jacobo Timerman's *Prisoner without a Name*)[90] – in other words, to confront what the savagery is all about. Offering a case example of racial terror, Taussig examines Roger Casement's Putomayo report, which was submitted to the British House of Commons in 1913, based on seven weeks of travel in 1910 through the rubber-gathering regions of the Amazon, specifically along the Putomayo River in Peru. Rubber could not be gathered without the help of the Huitotos Indians. Uncovering tremendous violence, what Casement's report conveyed most of all through all the facts and witness accounts was the ordinariness of the violence. People passed the time by hunting Indians. The torture was too excessive to be explained as simply economically rationalized. Taussig suggests that such terror entailed a trade in mythologies. The narratives of terror that abounded tell us something about the terror itself – they were stories of the savagery of the jungle and the savagery of its inhabitants. The 'wild Indians' could reflect back to the colonizers their reality as civilized and business-like only if they were controlled through acts of savagery. Savages, mythically endowed with great strength, had to be put down. Torture took on a life of its own in this environment, passing from individual acts to an organized culture and mode of life. Taussig makes an eloquent plea for coming to terms with the 'hallucinatory quality' of terror, for understanding what I think of as its deeply psychic structure. 'Fascist poetics succeed where liberal rationalism self-destructs,' he warns, unless we confront the emotions generated by terror.[91]

It is in the interest of confronting a 'fascist poetics,' and out of the need to move beyond the mythologies (of cultural difference) that so easily reconciles the West to the sexualized torture of Arabs and Muslims, that I have pursued an interlocking analysis of prisoner abuse. Drawing on scholarship on lynching, I have been advancing a theoretical framework that suggests how white masculinity is constituted simultaneously against warmth and sensuality as well as against desire for (oneness with) the racial other. To adopt this kind of theoretical framework for contemporary prisoner abuse in Abu Ghraib, Guantanamo, and elsewhere is to insist first and foremost that the new world order is an imperial world. People in the West come to know themselves within the Manichean categories that Fanon rendered so superbly, as gendered beings who must participate in violence against racial others in order to mark the boundary between self and other. Yet they do so out of a deep and threatening ambivalence. Culture has been the language of contemporary narratives of terror. Cultural difference, understood as *their* cannibalism, *their* treatment of women, and *their* homophobia, justifies the savagery that the West metes out. 'The Christian in me says this is wrong,' Charles Graner, one of the soldiers charged with abuse and the alleged ringleader, is reputed to have said, 'but the corrections officer in me can't help making a grown man piss himself.'[92] The West has appointed itself as the corrections officer to the non-West, and Charles Graner should not be understood as a man who has simply taken his duties too far. For what else is a civilized man to do in his encounter with savages but civilize them? Baldwin's sheriff resembles Graner in this respect. As the sheriff's rage builds and climaxes in violence and orgiastic release, he reflects of himself later that night: 'He tried to be a good person and treat everybody right: it wasn't his fault if the n----- had taken it into their heads to fight against God and go against the rules laid down in the Bible for everyone to read! Any preacher will tell you that. He was only doing his duty: protecting white people from the n-----s and the n-----s from themselves.'[93]

The fact that the status of Iraqis is so evidently subhuman, so *culturally different*, and so in need of discipline, crowds our newsreels. Unless we too have become numb to it all, we will need to find an explanation for the sexualized terror and for the ways that ordinary people participate in it. Pyramids of naked men forced to simulate having sex should not baffle us, but neither should we believe that they are trivial or exceptional moments in a giant clash of civilizations. To grasp their import, we will have to attend to prisoner abuse as a publicly enacted, sexualized ritual of racial violence and track the trade in mythologies signalled by our persistent marking of ourselves as modern and the non-West as culturally different.

If ordinary men and women possess even the smallest connection to the structure of feeling I have been sketching for the soldiers at Abu Ghraib, and if they come to know themselves as subjects only through erecting walls between themselves and racial others – a practice that requires violence – critical educators will have to consider more seriously how white supremacy is embodied. We ignore the psychic underpinnings of the exception at our peril, its unconscious structure, but in order to grasp its installation, we will need to consider how race, class, gender, and sexuality give each other meaning, structuring desire and producing men and women whose sense of coherency rests on anxiously marking the line between the civilized and the uncivilized, between those who are to be abandoned and those who are to remain members of political community. As the next three chapters will show, a growing European and North American obsession with the culturally different and their casting out of political community has coalesced not only around the figure of the 'dangerous' Muslim man but also around that of the imperilled Muslim woman. Unveiling her body, insisting that she be made 'modern,' functions not only to discipline the Muslim man, who is considered to be the source of her containment, but also provides the pleasure of colonial mastery and possession.

PART TWO

'Imperilled' Muslim Women

3 Modern Women as Imperialists: Geopolitics, Culture Clash, and Gender after 9/11

Culture clashes were essential to the success of racial myths, for throughout history the foreigner outside the tribe has never been truly welcome.

George L. Mosse[1]

[T]he imperialist feminist desire to emancipate the Muslim woman is part of a system based on the disciplining and normalizing gaze of modern colonial disciplinary power.

Meyda Yegenoglu[2]

The modern woman is first and foremost an imperialist.

Rosemary M. George[3]

The attacks on the World Trade Center and the Pentagon on September 11, 2001 have resulted in 'anti-terrorism' measures that have included surveillance, stigmatization, and the actual incarceration of men considered 'Muslim-looking or Arab-looking.' In this climate, to write about violent Muslim men guarantees royalties and the prestige of being on best-seller lists. When the writing is done by Western feminists, both Muslim and non-Muslim, it provides the 'war on terror' and the American bid for empire with ideological justifications. The post-9/11 climate has also enabled Western feminists to use the Israeli/Palestinian conflict as evidence of the violence of Muslim and Arab men. A steady stream of books and articles announcing that the current Israeli administration is entirely justified in its treatment of Palestinians and that those who criticize Israel are simply being anti-Semitic[4] have come out in recent years. In many of these texts the violence Muslim women endure at the hands of Muslim men becomes a marker of Muslim men's barbarism and a reason why the claims of Palestinians who are mainly Muslims are unacceptable. This logic is available at a glance in subway posters in San Francisco in which a blond woman announces that she has just been to Israel, a land where women have equal rights.

The United State's 'war on terror' and its inextricable links to American support of Israel have converged to produce a particular geopolitical terrain in the post-9/11 period that has enabled blatant racism to be articulated in the name of feminism. As I will show, what binds seemingly disparate strands of this political position together and provides its coherency is the notion of 'culture clash': the West, Jews included, are caught up in a violent clash with the Islamic world; the clash is cultural in origin; Islam is everything the West is not. Furthermore, as fatally pre-modern, tribal, non-democratic, and religious, the barbarism of Islam is principally evident in the treatment of women in Muslim communities. This line of argument is not of course a new one, although gender ebbs and flows within it. As Edward Said pointed out a long time ago in *The Question of Palestine*, the argument that turns colonial dispossession of a people into a story of an empty land awaiting European improvement draws on 'the picture of a handful of European Jews hewing a civilization of sweetness and light out of the Black Islamic sea.'[5] But if the notion of a Black Islamic sea has long been marshalled in support of the West's oppressive policies towards Palestinians, today that approach has gained greater currency and has more ominous consequences.

When we consider the narratives, both feminist and non-feminist, that turn dispossession into a civilizing move, we must do so conscious of empire's culture of exception, whereby whole populations are abandoned as surplus or unwanted. The eviction of groups of people from political community begins with their *difference*, coded as an incomplete modernity that poses a threat to the nation. While nationalism has always demanded the stigmatization of the foreigner, increasingly that stigmatization carries with it the probability that the stigmatized group will be literally expelled (deported), marked permanently as undeserving of the full benefits of citizenship, or abandoned. Stigmatized groups, Balibar observes,

> are *qualitatively* 'deterritorialized,' as Gilles Deleuze would say, in an intensive rather than extensive sense: they 'live' on the edge of the city,

under permanent threat of elimination; but also, conversely, they live and are perceived as 'nomads,' even when they are fixed in their homelands, that is, their mere existence, their quality, their movements, their virtual claims of rights and citizenship are perceived as a threat for 'civilization.'[6]

Going further, Mbembe describes the stigmatized as marked for dying. Noting the extent of *'the generalized instrumentalization of human existence and the material destruction of human bodies and populations,'*[7] Mbembe suggests the contemporary world is marked by 'necropolitics': 'weapons are deployed in the interest of maximum destruction of persons and the creation of *death-worlds,* new and unique forms of social existence in which vast populations are subjected to conditions of life conferring on them the status of the *living dead.'*[8] For Mbembe, the colonial occupation of contemporary Palestine by Israel has created one such death-world.

> As the Palestinian case illustrates, late-modern colonial occupation is a concatenation of multiple powers: disciplinary, biopolitical, and necropolitical. The combination of the three allocates to the colonial power an absolute domination over the inhabitants of the occupied territory. The *state of siege* is itself a military institution. It allows a modality of killing that does not distinguish between the external and the internal enemy. Entire populations are the target of the sovereign. The besieged villages and towns are sealed off and cut off from the world. Daily life is militarized. Freedom is given to local military commanders to use their discretion as to when and whom to shoot. Movement between the territorial cells requires formal permits. Local civil institutions are systematically destroyed. The besieged population is deprived of their means of income. Invisible killing is added to outright executions.[9]

The mark of the foreigner, always a cultural mark that is understood as an immutable difference, carries with it these dire consequences in an empire of camps. When feminists invoke notions of culture clash through appeal to the idea of dangerous Muslim men and imperilled Muslim women, contemporary political conditions ensure that their words will not be taken lightly. The death-worlds of which Mbembe writes, and the recolonization Balibar suggests is occurring for Europe's Muslims, are projects underwritten by the idea that some have to be killed so others can live.[10] Unbridgeable cultural differences become a significant reason to create communities without the right to have rights, communities of abandoned populations marked as outside the racial kin group that is the nation.

Women's bodies have long been the ground on which national difference is constructed. When the Muslim woman's body is constituted as simply a marker of a community's place in modernity and an indicator of who belongs to national community and who does not, the pervasiveness of violence against women in the West is eclipsed. Saving Muslim women from the excesses of their society marks Western women as emancipated. Observing that 'the declaration of an emancipated status for the Western woman is contingent upon the representation of the Oriental woman as her devalued other,' Yegenoglu reminds us that women can only enter the privileged space of the universal through 'a masculine gesture.'[11] Just as men claim the universal for themselves through confining women outside of it as non-rational subjects, so the Western woman requires the culturally different body to make her own claim of universality. Unveiling the Muslim woman, rendering her body visible and hence knowable and available for possession, renders the Western woman as the colonial, observing, possessing subject. Thus, old colonial technologies enjoy renewed vigour at a time when Islam versus the West is the hegemonic framing of the New World Order.

This examination of Western feminism's role in empire today has been prompted in part by my own experiences as a secular feminist with a Muslim name. Whereas this 'marking' that identifies me as Muslim seldom drew attention before, at least not to the extent that Brown skin did, my body, my feminist commitments, and my scholarship became suspect in the post-9/11 environment. In 2002, for instance, I became the target of an email campaign vilifying me for having distributed a petition denouncing the Israeli state's military activities in Jenin. This campaign had the predictable features of threatening, violent, misogynist language of the kind familiar to any woman who takes strong anti-sexist and anti-racist positions. Yet, what was different was that I was now being reminded of the barbarities of Muslim/Arab culture's treatment of women, a culture assumed to be my own. Quite often in these messages 'the oppression of women, religious intolerance, lack of freedoms, lack of democracy, absence of free press and honour killings of family members in the Arab countries' were put against Israel as a 'free country with tolerance of all religions and equality for women.'[12] To criticize Israel, my correspondents insisted, was not only to be anti-Semitic and anti-

American, but also to be on the side of patriarchy. Since these messages were targeting me specifically, I knew that my body had indeed become something of a global sign and that a strange nexus had emerged in contemporary geopolitics between Western feminism and racism.

A similar confluence between Western feminism and racism was taking place in popular culture. In 2002–3, three books appeared that did very well in sales and were almost without exception positively reviewed in the press: Orianna Fallaci's *The Rage and the Pride*; Phyllis Chesler's *The New Anti-Semitism*, and Irshad Manji's *The Trouble with Islam*.[13] Each of these books advances the idea of a culture clash of epic proportions between the West and Islam. They outline the need to defend the West generally, and Israel in particular, from an Islamic threat, a threat reinforced by the idea of misogynist Muslim men. Each book also suggests, either implicitly or explicitly, that to take up a political position that is critical of the current American and Israeli administrations (George W. Bush and Ariel Sharon) was at best being callous towards Muslim women and at worst being supportive of pro-foundly misogynist political regimes.

In this chapter I examine the geopolitical terrain for feminists post 9/11. I do so principally through an examination of Fallaci, Chesler, and Manji and through reflection on the degree to which these three texts were widely and popularly acclaimed in the media. I focus on these books because of their popularity and also because of the ways the racism/feminism nexus is evident in each. While only two of the three authors (Fallaci and Chesler) can be said to have a feminist past, in that their previous publications offered them a public place within feminism, all three marshal feminist ideas in support of their political positions. It is true, of course, that all three also have somewhat of a right-wing reputation and advance neoliberal arguments. However, as I suggest below, these are taken up across the political spectrum *on the basis of their feminist claims*. That these books do well further attests to the fact that, their provocative and polemical nature notwithstanding, they resonate with large numbers of people in the West. My interest, then, is in the popularity of racist arguments that claim the ground of gender equality. I do not make an empirical argument that the three texts I have selected are either the most representative of the logic of empire or the most popular. Rather, I rely on them to demonstrate the connections that are made between feminism, neo-liberalism, and the clash of civilizations. As in other chapters, I examine the racial logic structuring so much of this geopolitical terrain, gesturing to gender as one of its principal technologies, but remaining focused nevertheless on the overall thrust of these books: a message of European superiority in which both the American bid for empire and the contemporary politics of Israeli occupation are defended and legitimized. My aim is simply to stop and to take stock of the geopolitics that have begun to alter so profoundly the conditions under which feminists engage politically, and to sound the alarm that feminist arguments are part of the conceptual arsenal underpinning the permanent stigmatization of Muslim communities and their subsequent eviction from political community. The chapter is divided into three sections. In the first I explore the notion of 'culture clash' to show the modern/pre-modern racial logic that it depends on and the role that gender has played in its construction. In section 2 I focus on Fallaci's book to show how integral the culture-clash argument is to characterizing the Muslim man as a threat to all women. In section 3 I connect the ideas of culture clash and of Muslim male violence to the representations of the Israel/Palestine conflict in the books by Chesler and Manji. The chapter ends by reflecting on how Western feminist responses might transcend culture-clash logic.

1. Culture Clash Logic

Mosse's observation that racial myths depend upon the language of culture (our culture is more developed than theirs) is an important reminder of why it is dangerous to consider culture apart from racism. The close connection between assertions of cultural difference and racism has meant that in white societies the smallest reference to cultural differences between the European majority and Third World peoples (Muslims in particular) triggers an instant chain of associations (the veil, female genital mutilation, arranged marriages) that ends with the declared superiority of European culture, imagined as a homogeneous composite of values including a unique commitment to democracy and human rights, and to the human rights of women in particular. Culture clash, where the West has values and modernity and the non-West has culture, consolidates membership in the dominant group; it provides belonging through enabling dominant groups to imagine that they share something in common, something that marks them as superior.

Today in the West, culture clash as the means of expressing European superiority is often organized around the Muslim Other, whose presence on European and North American soil has been increasing. An Internet search for the phrase 'Muslims and gender equality,' for instance, readily produces this popular articulation of culture clash: 'The newcomer Muslims bring an ancient social structure that is authoritarian and misogynist, where knowledge is an inherited commodity rather than derived through rational inquiry. Western culture, on the other hand, has built upon its Greek, Roman and Renaissance traditions to value *democracy, gender equality, individual rights and rational thought* [italics added].'[14] We have only to examine the premises of Samuel P. Huntington's widely cited book *Clash of Civilizations* to see the importance of the notion of culture clash to the contemporary making of empire.[15] Huntington argued that the primary source of conflict in the world today is the cultural difference between the West and non-West, a culture clash in which Islam figures prominently as the antithesis of Western civilization. People who are alike culturally cooperate with each other; dislike or fear of the foreigner and accompanying feelings of superiority are present in all cultures. From such simple premises, Huntington explains a wide range of complex phenomena such as the Rwandan genocide, the massacre of Muslims in Bosnia, and the triumph of political Islam. Islam has been at war with the West for fourteen hundred years, a conflict that flows from the two civilizations' differences, he declares. For Huntington, cultures are distinct entities with values and practices that form an unchanging essence. Indeed, he explicitly rejects historicizing. 'The causes of this ongoing pattern of conflict lie not in transitory phenomena such as twelfth-century Christian passion or twentieth-century Muslim fundamentalism. They flow from the nature of the two religions and the civilizations based on them.'[16] Today, because of the West's attempts to universalize its own values of democracy and human rights, the West faces considerable challenge from the Islamic world. To add fuel to the fire, large numbers of Muslims now live in close proximity to non-Muslims (Europe being a prime example) and this, Huntington reports, has an innate 'propensity towards violent conflict.'[17]

Critics of Huntington's thesis of a clash of civilizations have all pointed out that the cultural line of argument ignores historical processes and works handily to foster what Said called 'defensive self-pride' and an ensuing 'War of the Worlds.'[18] However, few scholars have expanded on the role that gender plays in culture clash. Huntington himself merely warned cursorily that, under the banner of multiculturalism, Muslims attempt to dislodge American values and that we should be vigilant about calls to respect diverse cultural practices, many of which involve women.[19] Here he sets up a classic dichotomy between multiculturalists who foolishly respect Muslim cultural practices with respect to women and those who understand the menace they pose, a polarization I shall discuss below. Some of Huntington's admirers, however, have had rather more to say about culture clash and gender in the New World Order.

Echoing Huntington, Ronald Inglehart and Pippa Norris have sought to show that a fatal cultural flaw plagues the Muslim world. In their estimation, it is the issue of gender from which the '*True* Clash of Civilizations' (italics added) emerges. Gender is the reason 'freedom' will never grow in the Middle East.[20] Their 2003 book *Rising Tide* argues that regardless of the degree of economic modernization, an Islamic religious heritage remains one of the most powerful barriers to 'self-expression, subjective well-being, and quality of life concerns.'[21] Because the Islamic world lacks the core self-expression values of individual autonomy, tolerance, personal freedom, and interpersonal trust, Muslims exhibit a weak commitment to gender equality and to democracy. The empirical basis of Inglehart's and Norris's claims are data taken from value surveys. For example, the survey includes the question 'Do men make better political leaders than women?' Those who disagreed that men made better political leaders also scored highest on the self-expression scale and came from the most democratic societies.[22] Gender, they conclude, is the site of the single most important value change in post-industrial societies, a marker of whether or not a society has progressed. Islamic societies, then, are clearly still trapped in the pre-modern.

Analyses like Inglehart's and Norris's, in their abstraction of culture from history, depend heavily on the logic of culture clash. The aim is to show that Islam is unchanging and untouched by politics or economics. Patriotism and nationalism are characteristics of traditional societies and not of secular-rational ones such as the United States. The rise of the Christian right and President George W. Bush's repeated reliance on the notion that God is on America's side[23] is not, according to this line of argument, comparable to the religious rhetoric of Al Qaeda. The West's valuing of quality of life is straightforwardly a sign of progress and the mark of a superior civilization, a condition unrelated to the economic coercion required to achieve progress.

Inglehart and Norris anticipate several of the arguments to be found in Fallaci, Chesler, and Manji and by the majority of those who positively reviewed their books. As in *Rising Tide*, these arguments naturalise free market capitalism considering it to be a feature of modern civilizations. Muslims, trapped in the pre-modern, not only fail in the economic realm but remain locked into tribal cultures in which women are treated particularly badly. As with all culture clash explanations, the modern and the pre-modern exist as discrete realms with the latter stuck in culture and the former having progressed to the age of enlightenment.

2. Culture Clash and the Politics of the 'War on Terror': 'On Vile Creatures Who Multiply Like Rats'

The events of September 11, 2001 and the ensuing 'war on terror' have greatly facilitated the widespread dissemination of culture-clash explanations. Oriana Fallaci, a journalist of Italian origin who divides her time between Italy and the United States, describes her 2002 book *The Rage and the Pride* as emerging from the shock of 'the eve of the apocalypse' when, sitting in her New York apartment, she witnessed the destruction of the World Trade Center towers on television and soon thereafter saw the reports of rejoicing on the part not only of Palestinians but also of some Italians. Fallaci writes of the urgency to make clear that the clash between Muslims and the West is a cultural and religious one, a 'Reverse Crusade'[24] and a 'war which is conducted to destroy our civilization, our way of living and dying, of praying or not praying, of eating and drinking and dressing and studying and enjoying life.'[25] Formulated less by a notion of culture clash than by an undisguised belief in Muslim inferiority, Fallaci's text is peppered with portraits of contemporary Muslims who invade Europe and transform beautiful Italian cities into 'filthy Kasbahs.'[26] Muslims grope at her breasts, sell drugs, defecate in beautiful buildings, and infect the local population with AIDS. Gender once again clinches the argument, and Fallaci spares no space to itemize the crimes against women committed in the Islamic world. Equally central is Fallaci's support for Israel and for Ariel Sharon, whom she describes as a 'Shakespearean gentleman' moved to phone her to thank her for her bravery in writing the book.[27]

Despite the book's extremely blatant racism, only one critical review was easily found. In the *Guardian*, Rana Kabbani was alone in pointing out that Fallaci's anti-Muslim hysteria would have been considered hate speech if its targets were any other group than Muslims. Addressing Fallaci's claim that there is a rising anti-Semitism, Kabbani notes that we must also recognize that 'the vast majority of racially motivated maimings and killings across Europe over the past decade have been directed at Muslims – not at the asylum seeking "aliens" shoved into salubrious camps, but against second and third-generation Europeans such as my own children, whose continent this is as surely as it is Oriana Fallaci's.'[28] Kabbani's views were an exception. *The Rage and the Pride* sold an unprecedented 700,000 copies in its first two weeks in Italy, and sales figures that included Europe and North America topped one million.[29] Journalists, undoubtedly finding good copy in Fallaci's pronouncements on 'vile creatures who urinate in baptistries' and 'multiply like rats,' have accepted without question Fallaci's characterization of herself as someone facing constant death threats for her views, and for the most part describe her critics as those who would muzzle free speech.[30] Although several of Fallaci's readers have in fact named the book's virulent racism and its stirring of hatred against Muslims as the reason for their opposition to it, journalists and reviewers gloss over this objection and instead salute Fallaci for daring to speak the truth and 'to shock awake a noble civilization hypnotized by multiculturalist mumbo-jumbo.'[31] For Dreher, the 'few ugly parts of the book could make the whole thing dismissible as a work of frothing paranoid prejudice – if there weren't so much truth beneath the sometimes lurid rhetoric.'[32] Rebuked for her lack of 'good taste' by another reviewer, and for her excesses ('It's quite unnecessary to deny Islamic architecture or poetry to decry Islamic terrorism'), Fallaci is on the whole lauded for her 'greater courage.'[33]

What lies behind the impulse to forgive Fallaci's racist tirades and to salute her for her courage? The eminent Canadian philosopher Charles Taylor, while acknowledging that *The Rage and the Pride* is full of 'more bigotry than I've ever encountered in any other book worth reading,' nonetheless deems it a significant book.[34] Admitting that he feels queasy as he makes his way through the book's innumerable racist characterizations of Muslims (a feature Taylor seems to prefer to call bigotry or xenophobia), Taylor nevertheless argues that Fallaci offers a 'cogent, coherent argument' and 'a bracing response to the moral equivocation, the multicultural political correctness, the minimization and denial of the danger of Islamo-fascism that dogs the response to September 11 and to the ongoing "war on terror."' Taylor (drawing on Christopher Hitchens) is particularly concerned that the Left has engaged in a kind of ridiculous 'moral equivalence' between American acts of dominance and contemporary terrorism and has been so mesmerized by multiculturalism that it will not criticize those cultures that oppose freedom.

Taylor is able to glide smoothly over the racist utterances in Fallaci's text. His own arguments rest on the same characterizations of the Islamic world and of Muslim/racialized communities in the West as Fallaci's. To understand the work that racism does in Taylor's narrative, it is important to track his deployment of the idea of culture clash. The West is up against so great a menace that the ends justify the means. The threat, while named as Islamic fascism, is easily transferred in the entire Islamic world, which stands for everything the Left should despise. An unwavering story of culture clash holds sway where, as one commentator pointed out, September 11 is seen simply as 'the product of an insane, fundamentalist culture and irredeemably evil at heart. '[35] We are invited into this construction of events from the usage of words like 'medievalist' and 'mindset.' The Islamic mindset (something that sounds as immutable as biology), Taylor writes, citing Karen Armstrong and noted Orientalist scholar Bernard Lewis and stressing the treatment of women in Islamic countries, is one prone to barbarism. Islam's alleged lack of separation between religion and community, its roots in 'a semi-nomadic tribal culture,' and the overwhelming poverty of the Middle East, which can only be blamed on the region's 'prohibition against women working and the fundamentalist wish to sever ties with the rest of the world,' all amount to a potent mix. Fallaci's accomplishment, concludes Taylor, is to grasp the magnitude of the threat that the Islamic world poses to the West, and particularly to America, the 'most benevolent superpower' that there has ever been. Fallaci is to be saluted, then, for daring to break two taboos: 'the taboo of one culture criticizing another, and the deeper taboo of criticizing a religion.'

3. Culture Clash and the Politics of Anti-Semitism

The structure of the racial myth of European superiority, sustained by the idea of a clash of civilizations and its corresponding geopolitics, may be grasped in their popular form at a glance in the media interventions of Daniel Pipes. An American professor of Middle Eastern Studies, Pipes has become widely known as much for his hard-line opposition to a just peace between Palestinians and Israelis as he is for his widely disseminated anti-Muslim and anti-Arab pronouncements in the media. Pipes has recommended, for example, that all Muslims should be kept under surveillance. He is the founder of Campus Watch, a website that, among other things, 'invites student complaints of abuse, investigates their claims, and (when warranted) makes these known.'[36] Campus Watch has identified professors who are critical of Israel, posting their names on its web site, a practice some have experienced as a witch hunt or as McCarthy-era persecution. Amid strenuous protest, the White House nominated Pipes to the board of directors of the United States Institute of Peace, a nomination personally endorsed by President Bush.[37]

In an article co-written with Lars Hedegaard in August 2002 and published in the *New York Post*, 'Something Rotten in Denmark,' Pipes turned his attention to the context of Denmark's new asylum and immigration laws and to forced marriages. The authors begin with the announcement that a Muslim group planned to pay a bounty to anyone[38] who murdered prominent Danish Jews (a threat Danish police failed to confirm). Muslim immigrants, who 'show little desire to fit into their adopted country,' are then vilified not only for planning the murder of Jews but for living off welfare; engaging in crime (primarily the rape of non-Muslim Danish women); and importing unacceptable customs such as forced marriage, described in biblical language as 'promising a newborn daughter in Denmark to a male cousin in the home country, then compelling her to marry him, sometimes [on] pain of death.' Making an appeal to almost every possible racist stereotype, Pipes and Hedegaard are able in this short diatribe to identify the Muslim Other as a threat to European Jews as well as to other Europeans, a useful alliance when building political support for Zionist positions such as Pipes's. It goes without saying that there exists a range of Zionist positions. However, those premised on the idea that a Jewish state must be created by force regardless of Palestinian opposition benefits from the companion notion that Palestinians are not entitled to the land by virtue of their refusal to enter modernity. That Jews and other Europeans face a common enemy in the Muslim pre-modern Other is established through an appeal to a more widespread resentment of the foreigner.

A shared Europeanness is made possible principally through gender. Endorsing Pipes's views, for example, Brenda Walker illustrates these connections, arguing that when European generosity towards immigrants and asylum seekers is returned with 'rape, physical attacks, theft, general disrespect and refusal to learn the language, then the public realises that multiculturalism is a philosophy based on falsehood.'[39] The belief that all cultures are equal and should be respected as such, she concludes, has resulted in widespread violence against women and the death of Muslim women themselves at the hands of Muslim men. Women's bodies are marked here as the terrain of struggle, and culture serves to define the conflict as one between Europeans and non-European Others as well as one between those who support multiculturalism and those who do not.

The Muslim man as rapist of white women, a perennial marker of the Other's degeneracy, surfaced in September 2001 (before 9/11) when a Norwegian newspaper reported that 65 per cent of the country's rapes are committed by non-Western immigrants, a category that is primarily Muslim. Once the figure of the Muslim rapist entered into circulation,[40] it was soon taken up as the basis for diatribes against multiculturalism, and against the immigration of non-Europeans altogether. In Canada, columnist Kevin Michael Grace wrote of 'a pro-rape constituency among Pakistanis and other Muslims' in Norway, France, Australia, and Canada, in the case of the latter making an analogy between an apparent code of silence that prevails among Muslim rapists and the same code as it operates among Sikh 'drug killers' in Vancouver, Canada.[41] Displaying a pornographic imagination in his column, Grace linked Muslim rapists to forced marriages, describing Norwegian cases where girls forced into marriage were raped every night. Importantly, his information came from government documentaries made in Norway as part of an educational initiative on the issue of forced marriages in Muslim communities.

'The New Anti-Semitism'

The culture-clash argument annexed to the politics of the Israeli occupation is in evidence in two books by writers who describe themselves as feminists: Phyllis Chesler's *The New Anti-Semitism*, and Canadian journalist Irshad Manji's *The Trouble with Islam*. As Fallaci did, Chesler begins her book with these dramatic words:

> On September 11, 2001, at about 11 A.M., I walked over to my computer and typed the sentence, 'Now we are all Israelis.'

Always it begins with the Jews. Osama Bin Laden called the assault on
America 'blessed attacks' against the 'infidel ... the new Christian-Jewish
crusade.' He explained that the twin towers had fallen because of American support for Israel. Both war – and a new kind of anti-Semitism – had
been declared. I had no choice but to write this book.[42]

From the beginning, a racial line of argument buttresses the book's
central claim that the West is now engaged in an apocalyptic struggle
with Islam. The problem, Chesler asserts, begins with the Jews, an
assertion that locates the events of 9/11 in an unvarying, transhistori-
cal persecution of Jews, the latest manifestation of which is attacks on
Zionism and on Israel. Thus, any criticism of Zionism and Israel (and
we are to understand that terrorist attacks are but one manifestation of
this criticism, while academic criticism of Israel represents another) is
anti-Semitism. In an interview, Chesler clarifies that while many anti-
Semitic ideas are 'native to Islam' and gathered force when Arab
Muslims collaborated with the Nazis, the contemporary tragedy is that
'this hatred has, incredibly, been embraced and romanticized by
Western liberals, public intellectuals, Nobel Prize winners, all manner
of so-called progressives and activists and, to a great extent, the presumably objective media.'[43]

For Chesler, Israel/Palestine has always belonged to Jews, 'the original native Indians of the Middle East,' a people who inhabited the
land for three millennia and who had been dispossessed.[44] When they
'returned' from exile to claim Israel in the 19th century, Jews found
themselves in the first phase of culture clash. Chesler is careful to note
(for the sake of the 'anti-colonial ideologues' she often addresses) that
this nineteenth-century encounter under the watchful eye of the
British may have *looked like* a standard racial/colonial encounter, but
was in fact a cultural one:

When Zionist idealists first returned to Israel-Palestine, what ensued was
not merely a clash between white-skinned Europeans and dark-skinned
Arabs. The clash that ensued – and that continues still – was also between
modernity and a hidebound traditionalism that had not changed for
twelve or thirteen centuries; between active doers and passive survivors;
between secularists and religionists as well as between followers of different extremist religions; between those who wanted to bring modern
medicine, agriculture, industry, government, and jurisprudence to the
region and those who rejected such possibilities.[45]

Similar in structure to claims of *terra nullius* in British colonial law, where the land belonged to Europeans because its original inhabitants were simply not modern enough, Chesler's employment of culture clash provides the foundation for her central argument. To attack Israel, and the twin towers, is to mount 'a direct hit on democracy, modernity, religious pluralism, and women's rights.'[46] Stuck in pre-modernity, Palestinians can have no claim to Palestine. If America supports Israel, it is because Jews and Americans share similar cultural values;[47] both represent the force of modernity and both must confront the menace of Islam.

Excoriating feminists who criticize Israel as an apartheid state, Chesler laments that they are seldom so harsh on Muslim countries for their great crimes against women. Ignoring considerable feminist protest from both within and outside the Arab world on such issues, Chesler sums up her position in an interview: 'Many feminists are totally blind to their own Jew hatred and are now more obsessed with the occupation of disputed lands in the Middle East than they are with the occupation of women's bodies worldwide.'[48] Feminists even opposed the 'liberation' of Afghanistan and Iraq, laments Chesler, so blinded were they by their antipathy to what they imagine to be colonial ventures. For Chesler, passionately endorsing free-market capitalism, America 'may have risen on the backs of others,' but capitalism and colonialism are in the end good things, especially for women. Global capitalism 'exploits and educates, impoverishes and enriches'; colonialism 'sponsored practices such as education (for girls as well as the children of peasants), hygiene, health care, governmental infrastructures, and technology.'[49]

In an article on 'Feminism in the 21st Century,' written with Donna Hughes, Chesler goes to greater lengths to elaborate the feminist and neo-liberal ground on which she stands in making claims about America and Israel. Four arguments are offered in sequence: American women are liberated; Islamic fundamentalism threatens women all over the world; feminists are 'romanticizing and cheering Third World anti-colonialist movements and condemning the U.S. where feminism has triumphed'; accompanying the rise in Islamic fundamentalism is an increase in anti-Semitism and anti-Zionism.[50] A clear us/them distinction infuses this analysis. On the one side, standing with Chesler, are Americans and the conservative and religious right, whom Chesler and Hughes advise might make better allies with feminists than the left. Standing against feminists are Islamic fundamentalists, the liberal left, multiculturalists, and anti-colonialists. In this view, feminism has no room for anti-colonial, multicultural, or Palestinian politics. Instead, using the rhetoric of the Bush administration in the U.S. invasions of Afghanistan and Iraq and the support of 'regime change' in Haiti, Chesler and Hughes assert that feminists should also seek 'regime change' and join with 'pro-democracy forces around the world to liberate humanity from all forms of tyranny and slavery.'[51]

The View from Inside the Harem

Writing as a young, openly lesbian Canadian of Muslim origin, Irshad Manji's book *The Trouble with Islam* soon became a best-seller in Canada. Unlike Chesler and Fallaci, Manji has an insider's perspective. While addressed to 'my fellow Muslims,' however, and ostensibly about calling Muslims to account for their own backwardness, the book is from the beginning an invitation to consider the merits of Jews, Judaism, and the contemporary Israeli regime. The principal means through which we are invited to recognize Israel's claims is once again culture clash, the notion that Islam and the Arabs who practise it are a fatally pre-modern, misogynist, and tribal community whose shortcomings reveal why Jews must occupy the land and must defend themselves against the ever-present barbarism of the Arabs who surround them.

The *Trouble with Islam*, marketed as an insider's view, is the view from inside the harem, one in a long tradition of Western fascination with glimpses into a forbidden world.[52] Manji begins with her childhood and the apocryphal story of her family's flight from Idi Amin's Uganda to the place where Manji was able to learn democratic values. Life in Vancouver is nevertheless bleak and violent. Her father's violence towards her and her mother (graphically conveyed by the story of Manji spending the night on the roof of her family's house in order to avoid his beatings) come to stand in the text for the violence of Islam and the non-West. Her lot, Manji speculates, would have been one of 'unyielding hierarchy' had she remained in Muslim Uganda, and as the rest of the book makes clear, the same would have applied had she not fled home, culture, and community.[53] Hers, Manji declares, calling to mind Samuel Huntington, was a 'personal clash of civilizations.'[54]

The fundamentalist religious schools she is compelled to attend, where Manji learns such truths as that Islam does not permit excessive laughter, and where she never hears stories and histories as she does in the Sunday school she was also permitted to attend because her father saw it as babysitting, provide the basis from which Manji learns that there is trouble with Islam. The trouble does not crystallize until the day that Manji's boss, Moses Znaimer, the owner of an important Toronto television station, demands in a memo to know whether she can reconcile her faith as a Muslim with female genital mutilation or with the public lashing of a seventeen-year-old Nigerian girl who was sexually assaulted by three men but who was punished for having sex outside of marriage. Brushing aside the aggression of the question (could Manji, an employee, have asked her Jewish boss to defend Israeli policies towards Palestinians?), Manji appreciates only what she sees as the reasonableness of the question, and it launches her on a journey to determine if the fault really lies with Islam. She concludes that it does.

'Pick a Muslim country, any Muslim country, and the most brutal humiliations will grab you by the vitals,' humiliations particularly of women and girls.[55] A 'cruel, crude Islam' thrives even in Toronto (where Manji works as a broadcaster), a city where Muslims react to Manji's broadcasts of brutalities by denouncing homosexuals as Jews. You might find Christians and Jews of this ilk, Manji grants (noting that Jews encourage debate in their religion, whereas Muslims rely slavishly on the Quran), but in contemporary Islam, such figures are mainstream. The Quran provides support for fundamentalist views, even as it occasionally supports more liberal positions. As she moves quickly through Spanish Jewish–Christian relations in Moorish Spain to the Taliban, the history of Muslims confirms Manji's hypothesis: Muslim brutalities originate in Islam. If there are no moderate Muslims to be found, it is because so few exist. To historicize, and to suggest for example that U.S. support for the Taliban effectively destroyed any moderate opposition in Afghanistan, is to blame the United States unfairly. Muslims, Manji declares, have to start being self critical, and the first step they must take is to acknowledge that 'being self-critical means coming clear about the nasty side of the Koran, and how it informs terrorism.'[56] Outraged that the Muslims she meets have refused to acknowledge any complicity for the events of 9/11, Manji is insistent that we recognize that Osama bin Laden is 'scripturally supported.'[57]

The Trouble with Islam reaches the heart of its argument when Manji accepts a six-day trip to Israel funded, as she put it, by 'Zionists.' The

Israelis we meet in the second half of the book are self-critical, democratic, and tolerant towards Palestinians. Israel, however, is plagued
by the same sort of Muslims Manji knows from her childhood. She
meets leering fundamentalist Muslim men who insist that she wear a
'girdle' over her outer garments when visiting a sacred Muslim site
and who are unwelcoming and relentlessly misogynist. Palestinians
who are not fundamentalists are welfare cheats. Encountering a Palestinian woman who pleads with her to employ Palestinians as a camera
crew because Palestinians are desperate for work, Manji relates with
pride her blistering response:

> 'But what about all the foreign aid the Palestinian Authority gets from the
> West?' I counter. I don't bother to bring up additional monies from a
> United Nations relief agency that's been devoted to Palestinian refugees
> for three generations now. 'We're talking millions of dollars that can be
> used for labs and hospitals and schools and business enterprise zones.
> Why do you still have refugee camps? Where does all the aid go?'[58]

Chastened, the Palestinian woman has finally to admit that her people
are corrupt and care more for symbolism than they do for their
own.

In the West Bank Manji finds Palestinians who mouth 'the script,'
the line of argument that Israel has occupied Palestine. Recognizing
that this claim requires a complicated historical counter-claim, Manji
offers the same argument as Chesler does. Palestine really belonged to
Jews anyway, and in any event Jews needed a refuge from anti-Semitism. If there are Palestinian refugees, it is only because of the 'dis-
ruptions of war – a conflict initiated by Arab countries that couldn't
accept Israel's existence in their midst.'[59] The United Nations has
deepened the crisis by acknowledging that the descendants of the
originally displaced people are also refugees. Not really refugees to
begin with, Palestinians face the additional disadvantage that their
fellow Arabs will not help them and they themselves keep refusing
reasonable deals. Only Israel has ever been prepared to help Palestinian refugees. Israel, Manji concludes, 'brings more compassion to
"colonization" than its adversaries have ever brought to "liberation."
The Jewish state negotiates tensions openly. That's the stuff of
genuine democracy.'[60]

Lest we are tempted to conflate Israel with the United States, Manji
ends her book with a catalogue of Arab sins in order to make the point

that U.S. power cannot be blamed for most of the world's ills. Instead, it is clear that these may be blamed on Muslims themselves. 'The cancer begins with us,' Manji writes, and not with America, a country that has the courage to acknowledge its own corruption, as it did with Enron! By the end of *The Trouble with Islam*, it is not clear what will redeem Muslims from their fatally pre-modern cultures. Manji has only one small suggestion: 'God-conscious, female-fuelled capitalism.'[61] In line here with *Vogue* magazine's suggestions that beauty schools will save Afghanistan,[62] Manji is hopeful about small income-generating projects for women in Muslim countries. That, and a continued vigilance in the West towards Muslims.

As with Fallaci and Chesler, reviewers of Manji's book, such as Andrew Sullivan of the *New York Times*, quickly bypass the book's evident lack of scholarship, conceding that *The Trouble with Islam* is not the 'most learned or scholarly treatise on the history or theology of Islam' and that Manji is a little 'naive,' 'haphazard in her geopolitics,' and 'a mite attention-seeking.' Nonetheless, Sullivan concludes of the book: 'Its spirit is undeniable, and long, long overdue.'[63] Manji is lauded for bravery in daring to criticize people well known for their murderous tendencies towards critics. Thus Manji, who considers herself one and the same as Salman Rushdie and Taslima Nasreen, is admired for having dared to write a book that apparently endangers her life.[64] Reviewers comment that Manji has installed bullet-proof windows in her home and is accompanied by bodyguards.[65] Itemizing these measures in his review, Daniel Pipes observes: 'And non-Muslims wonder why anti-Islamist Muslims in Western Europe and North America are so quiet.'[66] Not unaware of the currency of these images, on the eve of publication Manji's publishers announced that it was just possible that Manji might be the subject of a fatwa, as Salmon Rushdie had been. They approached the federal solicitor general to grant 'international protected person' status to Manji, a request the Canadian government denied.

Manji, whose reviewers maintain that she is 'fearless and intrepid,'[67] was recognized by *Maclean's*, Canada's national magazine, when it named her a 'Leader for Tomorrow' and by *Ms Magazine* where she was named a 'Feminist for the 21st Century.' She is 'a spiky-haired spitfire,'[68] and the 'smartest, hippest, most eloquent lesbian feminist Muslim you could ever hope to meet.'[69] In its first-ever 'Chutzpah Awards,' given to women who have 'pushed, pulled, prodded, and persevered through thick and thin, poverty and wealth, hope and hopelessness, past naysayers and yes-men,' *O Magazine* saluted Manji for standing up to 'Islamic bullies and terrorists.'[70] These accolades, and the fact that *The Trouble with Islam* has been on the best-seller lists for several months and is being translated into several languages, suggest that the journey thus far has not been, as one reviewer sympathetically predicted 'a rough ride'[71] but, rather, highly rewarded. Only one reviewer, Justin Podur, notices the irony of Manji's claim that she is likely to be targeted by Muslim extremists and to pay dearly for daring to criticize the Islamic world.[72] While Manji styles herself a Muslim refusenik, Podur points out, she profits handsomely from her position, while the real Israeli refuseniks who are conscientious objectors, who refuse to serve in the West Bank and Gaza and whose actions Manji does not mention, are jailed for theirs. Indeed, Podur notes, dissent in the Islamic world or among Palestinians goes entirely unmentioned throughout Manji's book. If the Revolutionary Association of the Women of Afghanistan (RAWA) were actually mentioned, it would be less easy to characterize Afghanistan as filled only with the Taliban and victimized women. For RAWA too is the Islamic world.

Despite its obvious instalment of notions of Western superiority, and also because of it, *The Trouble with Islam* reaches young Muslims in the West, an interest that I can only corroborate through personal conversations. Where Manji succeeds is in giving voice to the exclusion that young Muslims experience from *within*. She confronts head on the fundamentalist turn of political Islam, and even while she offers misleading explanations of the phenomenon, she notes the take-over of Islam by Wahhabi Muslims.[73] All three texts discussed in this article profitably exploit resistance to the very real inroads made by political Islam and the undeniable abrogation of women's rights in Muslim countries and communities. What they offer is a simple way to understand an undeniable scourge, an analysis that easily harnesses real concern with the status of women to racist images of barbaric Muslims. In doing so, these texts draw on a feminist narrative that has come to dominate feminist studies: the story of equality as requiring a journey from pre-modernity to modernity, and from the non-West to the West, the latter understood as a place of universal values. As a place where a single woman can make a difference and a dollar, the West is marked as inherently civilized because free-market capitalism underwrites the freedom to act. It is no accident that Fallaci's, Chesler's, and Manji's 'bravery' rests on ideas about intrepid individuals who make it despite tribe and clan, a capitalist message that depends upon the notion that anyone with defining links to the community simply remains stuck in the pre-modern.

A Conclusion for Feminists

The easy alliances demonstrated in these three books between racism, neo-liberalism, the American politics of empire and Israeli politics of occupation reveal the tie that binds them: a wilful inattention to history. In culture-clash explanations, if fundamentalism has arisen in Muslim parts of the world, it is because that is how they are. We cannot begin to consider, as Yegenoglu does of veiling in *Colonial Fantasies*, how colonial policies in Algeria, for example, so denigrated everything Islamic that anti-colonial movements won popular support by proposing a return to Islamic tradition, a tradition understood largely as the opposite of the foreigners. Within the Manichean world created by colonialism, women's bodies remained the terrain on which men sought to articulate their desires and fears.[74] Moderate Algerians advocating an improvement of women's status (again in the name of strengthening the indigenous) found themselves having to distinguish their political policies from colonial ones. In such an environment, it was far easier for those making the case for a return to indigenous traditions to advocate a kind of 'reverse orientalism.' That is, what the French thought to suppress in the name of penetrating Native culture was the very thing the nationalists would seek to revitalize. Drawing on Marnia Lasreg's conclusion that before colonial conquest the Algerians perceived their Muslimness not very differently from the way the French perceived of themselves as Christians, Yegenoglu reminds us of Gayatri Spivak's observation that the figure of the woman disappears here in 'the violent shuttling' between tradition and modernization.[75] Neither Muslim women nor Muslim men have any history, content, or specificity and all we ever know of them from culture-clash explanations is that they are stuck in pre-history.

Western feminists have relied on culture-clash logic when analysing patriarchy. As illustrated in one recent book, two authors describe how new relations of equality became possible in modernity:

As women became better educated, went out to work and won more rights, as families became smaller and less tied to the land, as information flowed more freely, scientific and technical knowledge became more widely disseminated, and thrones and dynasties crumbled in favor of representative democracy, the natural similarity of the sexes was supposed to stand revealed, making possible new, more equal and companionable relationships between them. The same forces of progress, this view held, would cause organized religion to wither away or at any rate modulate away from dogma and authority and reaction toward a kind of vague, kindly, nondenominational spiritual uplift whose politics, if it had any, would be liberal.[76]

However, while Europe modernized, strangely, the rest of the world did not. Tradition and religion 'tightened its grip' in non-European regions, and a religious fundamentalism took hold that has resulted in tremendous violence against women.

The story that 'we' modernized and 'they' did not sets the stage for a clash between multiculturalism and feminism. Many feminists have understood Western states' reluctance to condemn practices of violence against Muslim women, practices including female genital mutilation, forced marriages, and honour killings, as due to the triumph of multiculturalism over universal values. Simply put, the logic is this: in liberal democracies all citizens are treated equally. This means that minority cultures must be respected (multiculturalism). However, minority cultures include practices that are harmful to women. States often choose to respect culture over respecting women's human rights. As Beckett and Macy put it: 'Multiculturalism does not cause domestic violence but it does facilitate its continuation through its creed of respect for cultural differences, its emphasis on non-interference in minority lifestyles and its insistence on community consultation (with male, self-defined community leaders).'[77] Reinforcing the idea of the West as a realm beyond culture and the place of universal values, some feminists set the stage for the neoliberal world imagined by Fallaci, Chesler, and Manji with its civilized Europeans, imperiled Muslim women, and dangerous Muslim men.

Western women achieve their own subject status through claims that they are the same as, but culturally different from, Muslim women, women who have to be rescued. Gender, unmoored from class, race, and culture, facilitates this imperialist move, as does culture that is equally removed from history and context. As Leila Abu Lughod discovered when she was repeatedly sought out as an anthropologist of women in Muslim societies to provide the cultural explanations that would help Americans to understand the terrorist attacks on the World Trade Center, the turn to culture frozen in time and outside of history helped Americans to feel innocent. As she writes, it was as though

> knowing something about women and Islam or the meaning of a religious ritual would help one understand the tragic attack on New York's World Trade Center and the U.S. Pentagon, or how Afghanistan had come to be ruled by the Taliban, or what interests might have fuelled U.S. and other interventions in the region over the past 25 years, or what the history of American support for conservative groups funded to undermine the Soviets might have been, or why the caves and bunkers out of which Bin Laden was to have been smoked 'dead or alive,' as President Bush announced on television, were paid for and built by the CIA.[78]

Abu Lughod itemizes here what both the cultural and the feminist explanation so neatly dislodge. A cultural framing has 'prevented the serious exploration of the roots and nature of human suffering in this part of the world.' Of the West's insistence that its values represent progress, Abu Lughod insightfully asks: '[M]ight other desires be more meaningful for different groups of people? Living in close families? Living in a godly way? Living without war? Why presume that our way, whatever that is, is best? The historical record of the secular humanist West is far from unblemished, with genocides, colonialism, world wars, slavery, and other forms of inequality deep parts of it.'[79]

Post 9/11, to put both gender and culture back into context, to see Muslim women less as sisters awaiting our help into modernity and more as subjects whose lives are profoundly affected by the West's bid for empire, Western feminists will need to be deeply aware of the historical record. And we will have to refuse to come into being as subjects against women constituted as culturally different. This exploration of the geopolitical terrain in which we find ourselves illustrates the dire need to reject such explanations that locate patriarchy in premodernity and that position Western feminists as poised to help their Muslim sisters into modernity. As we shall see in the next two chapters, Western nations, pressed by feminists, have enthusiastically responded to the call to save Muslim women from their violent families. The enacting of legislation against forced marriages and banning of faith-based arbitration have enabled Western parliaments to claim the high ground as progressive and feminist. At the same time,

Western states win the unqualified right to engage in practices of surveillance of Muslim communities, practices that intensely regulate the
movements of Muslim men. The regular management of immigrant
populations receives a boost in this environment and the way is paved
for the immigrant and the refugee as exceptions, banished to places
beyond full citizenship.

4 Racism in the Name of Feminism: Imperilled Muslim Women in Norway

War makes strange bedfellows. The body of the Muslim woman, a body fixed in the Western imaginary as confined, mutilated, and sometimes murdered in the name of culture, serves to reinforce the threat that the Muslim man is said to pose to the West, and is used to justify the extraordinary measures of violence and surveillance required to discipline him and Muslim communities. Against the hyper-visibility of the Muslim woman's body (customs officers, shop clerks, and restaurant workers now all presume to know how Muslim women are oppressed by their terrible men), it is virtually impossible to name and confront the violence that Muslim women (like all groups of women) experience at the hands of their men and families without providing ideological fuel to the 'war on terror.' The extent to which Western feminists have begun to share conceptual and political terrain with the far right is troubling. Both, for example, have called for stringent border control in the West, feminists in order to root out unassimilable Muslims who have no regard for women, and the far right in order to keep out terrorists and rapacious immigrants and refugees who only want to grab the riches of the West and to plot its destruction. As a feminist, a woman identifiably of Muslim origin, and an immigrant from the South to the North, I find that this current situation leaves me in an impossible bind. How is it possible to acknowledge and confront patriarchal violence within Muslim migrant communities without descending into cultural deficit explanations (they are overly patriarchal and inherently uncivilized) and without inviting extraordinary measures of stigmatization, surveillance, and control? In this chapter I seek a place to stand, one where I accept the legitimacy of neither the bombs falling on Muslims nor a man's fists falling on a woman's face.

Although several European states have sought to regulate the conduct of Muslim migrant communities through laws condemning various practices, including female genital mutilation, the wearing of the veil, and forced marriages, I choose in this chapter to explore recent Norwegian initiatives in the area of forced marriages. Unlike other European countries such as France, Norway does not have a long history of hostile encounters with Muslim populations and appears to be less openly anti-immigrant than are some other countries in the region. Norway provides an interesting context for exploring how notions such as integration and culture clash in fact conceal the same anti-immigrant and anti-Muslim agendas evident in European states considered to be further right and more openly racist. I suggest, then, that although Norway is more moderate than countries such as Denmark, Norwegian responses have been nonetheless racist, 'culturalizing'[1] violence against women as an attribute of Muslim peoples and using the opportunity to justify a number of initiatives that have more to do with teaching 'them' how to behave than having any meaningful anti-violence objective. Unpacking the racist logic that underpins culturalist responses is a necessary first step towards confronting violence against women. When we examine the figures installed by such responses, both in the law and in popular culture, figures I describe as the civilized European, the imperilled Muslim woman, and the 'dangerous' Muslim man, we can pinpoint the erasures and omissions upon which they rely.

Principally, European culturalist responses have depended on the idea that Muslims come to the West drawn to its superior wealth. They bring with them a hopelessly feudal culture and must either be stopped altogether or be forcibly 'deculturalized' before they multiply and contaminate the superior civilization into which they have migrated. Recognizably racist, the figure of the unassimilable and diseased migrant masks the material relations that structure this encounter between the West and non-West, obscuring in particular the West's complicity in placing those populations under siege both before they leave their homelands and once within Europe's borders. Acknowledging little or no responsibility for the conditions in which Muslim migrants in the West live, and indulging in the fantasy of a culturally superior nation who must discipline and instruct culturally inferior peoples, Western states pursue policies of surveillance and control that heighten the level of racism those communities experience and that exacerbate the conditions under which Muslim communities become even more patriarchal and violent towards women.

If women's bodies become the terrain on which Western states manage racial populations, do such measures ultimately create camps of abandoned people without the rights to have rights? Legal measures that limit citizenship rights, for example, the imposition of a higher age of consent for marriage if the intended spouse comes from outside the country (a measure discussed below as one intended to discourage forced marriages between young Muslim girls and men outside Europe), stigmatize certain populations and materially impose a secondary level of citizenship. Such initiatives, when they become part and parcel of an entire corpus of regulations restricting the rights of immigrants, contribute to what Balibar has termed a movement towards European Apartheid. Defending himself from the accusation that the use of a word such as 'apartheid' could only be 'a useless provocation,' Balibar argues that differential levels of citizenship create 'insiders officially considered outsiders,' a designation that paves the way for the kinds of security controls I discuss as part of the 'war on terror.' Few object to the suspension of rights for groups that are already stigmatized as outside the nation. Second, Balibar argues that such practices are inspired by and produce a focus on migrant families (their composition and way of life) that works to sustain the idea that the nation is a racial kin group constituted against aliens.[2] As I have argued in previous chapters, in the fantasy of Orientalism so brilliantly explored by Meyda Yegenoglu, the Western subject becomes a subject only through signifying the Other as different. The body of the Oriental woman, a body that must be consistently unveiled and modernized, confirms the Western subject as a person of knowledge and reason. To unveil, to bring Muslim women into modernity through force, is to 'territorialize' her body, Yegenoglu argues, a process matched by the wider process of territorialization we call imperialism.[3]

In showing the operation of the fantasy of a superior West and an inferior non-West, as it is evident in the law and in arguments made by those supporting racist legal measures, I hope to underline that the only possible route out of the dilemma in which I find myself is to begin with racism itself, tracing the many ways in which it shuts down opportunity for meaningful anti-violence strategies. In sum, you can't fight violence against women with racism because racism is likely to strengthen patriarchal currents in communities under siege. Through their exclusive emphasis on culture as the sole source of patriarchal violence, culturalist approaches obscure the multiple factors that give rise to and sustain the violence. I approach this argument in two sections. In section 1 I discuss two important and influential books written by women who identify their concerns as feminist and who lay out the case for considering the problem of forced marriage as one of controlling fundamentally unassimilable and culturally inferior Muslims. I explore these works as paradigmatic of the culturalizing or culturalist move. In section 2 I review a variety of legal initiatives in Norway, first contextualizing them as part of a larger European venture to control Muslim populations and then examining what they share conceptually with the culturalist approaches discussed in section 1. I end by proposing how we might begin to develop an anti-racist response to the problem of violence against women.

1. Unassimilable Muslims

In November of 2003, Human Rights Service, a Norwegian feminist organization fighting for immigrant women's rights, announced that it had awarded the 'Cow Bell of the Year' to the Danish minister of integration, Bertel Haarder, for his efforts to tighten immigration laws as a means of limiting forced marriages in Denmark. (The logic of such initiatives is that young people, primarily of Muslim origin, are being forced into marriage with spouses from their parents' countries of origin, spouses who then enter Denmark under the policy of family reunification.) The Danish government, Human Rights Service noted, had done more than any other European government to secure women's rights. Interestingly, because Human Rights Service wished to acknowledge the connection between Mr Haarder's efforts in the area of women's rights and the creation of 'a better functioning multi-ethnic society,' the actual award given was not a cow bell but a camel bell, a change meant to signal that Human Rights Service worked in solidarity with Muslim women and wished, perhaps, to be culturally sensitive.[4]

Human Rights Service represents only one feminist voice on the issue of forced marriages and it is certain that their views are contested both within Norway and elsewhere. In March 2004 the organization found itself in a storm of controversy when Muslim girls who had tried to access services accused the organization of having pressured them to take part in a documentary on forced marriage as a condition of getting help. The girls further alleged that Human Rights Service had exaggerated their stories and provided them with the scripts of what to say, as well as sending them on 'missions' to find girls who had stories of forced marriages to tell. A Norwegian journalist formally complained to the Ministry of Children and Family Services, which partially funds H.R.S., that the organization 'lured' Muslim girls by offering them money.[5] Their recently tarnished reputation notwith-standing, a sufficient case can be made that the position the organiza-tion took in awarding the prize to Mr. Haarder, namely that women's rights require a considerable surveillance of immigrant communities and a tightening of Europe's borders, is one that is winning the atten-tion of European lawmakers.

In October 2003 the Parliamentary Assembly of the Council of Europe tabled for discussion a motion signed by twenty-six member countries to encourage European states to tackle the problem of forced marriages. As its rationale, the motion made reference to Hege Storhaug's book *Human Visas: A Report from the Front Lines of Europe's Integration Crisis*, a study of forced marriages based on a report to the Norwegian Parliament submitted by Human Rights Service.[6] The rec-ommendations of Human Rights Service concerning changes to family reunification through marriage requirements (a marriage con-tract will now have to spell out that women have the right of divorce before spouses can enter Norway) has the support of the Norwegian parliament.[7] Even more important, Storhaug's book garnered consid-erable press attention, as did Norwegian anthropologist Unni Wikan's *Generous Betrayal*,[8] although there have also been some critiques of both. The books make the argument that strong immigration controls, among other policies, are necessary in order to protect Muslim girls and women from forced marriages. Human Rights Service, Storhaug, and Wikan cannot be dismissed simply as examples of the far right's perennial calls for immigration controls and increased surveillance of European immigrant communities. Such views are defended as *femi-nist* in that their expressed objective is to respond to a problem of vio-lence against women. In dismissing them too quickly, we run the risk of dismissing the violence itself, and more importantly, we miss how their Orientalist structures limit an understanding of Muslim women's lives. *How* anti-immigrant or racist positions such as Storhaug's and Wikan's limit our capacity to understand and confront patriarchal violence in minority communities are questions that we must all ask.

Human Visas

Human Visas opens with a story of cinematic dimensions. A Norwegian girl of Pakistani descent is lured to Pakistan and, with the intervention of eight male relatives, is forcibly married at gunpoint. She escapes being raped by her new husband by pleading she is menstruating. Soon after she flees and is helped by the Norwegian embassy in Islamabad to escape to Norway. She tells her story to Hege Storhaug, then a journalist and now information director of Human Rights Service, and then goes to court to have her marriage declared invalid. She wins and the Norwegian parliament reacts to her case by passing a law making forced marriage illegal and punishable by a prison term of up to three years. Despite the fact that 'several thousand young Norwegian immigrant men and women' have been forced into marriage, so far no one has been convicted of the crime. The girl's marriage photo, in which she is dressed ornately in Eastern dress and bejewelled, appears on the cover of *Human Visas*. Thus begins a book subtitled *A Report from the Front Lines of Europe's Integration Crisis*. Its publisher, Human Rights Service, is a private Norwegian foundation that describes itself as 'a politically independent think tank' operating both in Norway and internationally.[9]

From the book's beginning, the problem of forced marriage is analysed as essentially one of culture clash between the West and those non-Western societies where feudal values still rein and where 'an individual's worth is entirely dependent on religion, clan, caste, and class.'[10] There has not been open debate about the problems that non-Western immigrants bring to the West because older colonial countries are too guilt-ridden, the book declares. Even Scandinavia, where debate is more open, Storhaug laments, is still polarized for and against immigration. In contrast, Human Rights Service is primarily interested in *integration*. Immigrants are failing to integrate because they marry within their own cultures, often bringing spouses from their countries of origin, and thus perpetuating the feudal cultures from which they come. The book's argument is a simple one: marriage patterns indicate that immigrants marry persons from their homelands. Often such marriages are forced and involve rape. These practices occur because immigrants want to bring their relatives to the West through family reunification, and they occur because such cultures are deeply patriarchal.

The statistics offered are as follows: family reunification accounts for 75 per cent of all immigration to Norway, and those granted residency are for the most part spouses and children. Among all marriages of first-generation immigrant women 75 per cent are with men who share their cultural background, and of these 40 per cent are men from outside Norway.[11] (This leaves, of course, 60 per cent of marriages contracted with partners in Norway, although of the same ethnic group.) Of marriages by first-generation men 90 per cent are with women of their own national background.[12] Turks and Pakistanis are most likely to conform to this pattern. Significantly, the patterns do not change with the second generation. Very few immigrants, either first- or second-generation, marry 'ethnic Norwegians,' that is to say, Norwegians of European origin. Since the underlying problem is that feudal cultures are reproducing on European soil, the book does not concern itself with the pattern among ethnic Norwegians to also marry overwhelmingly within their own racial and cultural group. Importantly, no statistics are offered to support the connection that is made between the pattern of marriage practices and forced marriages. It is simply assumed that many of the marriages contracted with partners of the same ethnic background who live outside Norway *necessarily* entail coercion. Here the practice of arranged marriage is itself proof of coercion.

Lest we think that the problematic breeding of feudal cultures is limited to Norway, *Human Visas* offers statistics on its prevalence elsewhere in Europe, describing for the reader a problem of epidemic proportions. The same marriage patterns are duly noted for Sweden (which is characterized as refusing to see the problem as one endangering the lives of immigrant women and as fearing being considered racist). Denmark is lauded throughout for having recognized that the problem of forced marriages poses an 'integration' problem, and the same statistics are shown for Denmark, dramatized in a sample studied by Eyvind Vesselbo of 145 Turkish men over four generations. Vesselbo's study purportedly demonstrates the reproduction of the original 145 into an astonishing 2813 persons brought to Denmark through family reunification.[13] Adding to this picture, Danish integration minister Bertel Haarder confirms that only one in four Turkish immigrants continues education after primary school, a schooling crisis attributed to girls being taken away to be married. For England, *Human Visas* lays out the case that, in vivid contrast to Muslims living in Britain, Sikhs have been a success largely because they do not marry their cousins and have fewer forced marriages. The integration problems so evident for Pakistanis and Bangladeshis (poor language skills,

dropout, unemployment) are all attributed to the fact that these communities live among themselves, developing, as a British diplomat
informed Human Rights Service, 'a parallel society.'[14] In Germany, the
same trends, observable among Turks, are getting worse: Turks
increasingly do not accept an ethnic German daughter- or son-in-
law.[15] Each country's profile is accompanied by statistics about marriage patterns and descriptions of spectacular cases, such as a killing
described as an 'honour killing' involving a young Turkish man who
killed his wife when she tried to leave him. (The German press is criticized for being too soft on the problem of forced marriages.) A
German ethnic-minority lawyer is quoted as saying that virtually all
brides in forced marriages are raped.[16]

Although forced marriage is the impetus for the book, and the
problem to be solved, it quickly becomes clear that the real problem is
the culture of Muslim migrants itself. There is a slippage in *Human
Visas* between forced and arranged marriages and little effort is
expended to distinguish them.[17] Arranged marriages are declared to
be a patriarchal custom and part of the culture of honour and are practised only in those places where women's status is low.[18] Europe's own
history of arranged marriages for its wealthier classes is acknowledged, but is used to indicate that whereas Europe has freed itself from
its feudal past, Muslim societies have not. That arranged marriages
lead to domestic violence is underlined in the prominence given in the
text to the story of Mina, a story that spans several pages. Mina was a
battered woman who had an arranged marriage. Her husband is
depicted as a man who is bent on using the system to bring more Pakistanis into Norway. He has a brother who is also defrauding immigration. Both men are criminals. The collective history of the family's
reproduction, a history of immigration fraud and arranged marriages,
is graphically presented as a chart of cells multiplying; the comparison
to disease is inescapable.[19]

If arranged marriages lead to immigration fraud and domestic violence, it is also clear that the Muslim family form of extended rather
than nuclear families is itself bad for women. Storhaug contends: 'All
too many large extended families – and smaller families as well – unfor-
tunately have histories much like that of Mina and her family. And it
seems that the larger the family is, the more strongly fortified this negative pattern is. There is probably a connection here with the way in
which the system of the extended family functions, both socially and
legally, in these families' homelands ... The larger the family the more

imprisoning it is.'[20] No greater proof exists that the Muslim family is intrinsically a dangerous place for women than the evidence that marriage of cousins is practised in many Muslim communities. Quoting extensively from a Danish researcher, Anders Hede, on cousin marriage, Storhaug reiterates his central conclusions: '1. cousin marriage largely involves force; 2. rate of cousin marriage is higher among immigrants than in their homelands; 3. cousin marriage is tied to immigration; 4. cousin marriage prevents integration and creates an underclass.' In sum, cousin marriages lead to continual rape and even death, assertions backed up by scant evidence. Cousin marriages produce children with birth defects and give rise to an integration crisis because they prevent Muslim migrant communities from having an opportunity to acquire 'values such as equality, equal rights, religious freedom, and freedom of expression.'[21] Citing a British study of fifty-nine young people, Storhaug points out that when women resist cousin marriage they are punished, a punishment that can go as far as death.[22]

Unassimilable, duplicitous, tribal, and prepared to sell their daughters into marriage and a life of continual rape, Muslim communities require the force of law to bring them into modernity. *Human Visas* has detailed suggestions about how this might proceed. Since forced marriage really entails rape, it should be treated as such in criminal law, the book suggests. A law that recognizes this must also consider that the family is an aggravating factor to the sexual assault and that forced marriage takes place in immigrants' country of origin.[23] Muslim women living in Europe also require that the right of divorce be stipulated in their religious marriage contracts, since 'HRS is not aware of a single Muslim woman in Norway who has married in her country of origin and had the right to divorce included in her marriage contract.'[24] A number of proposals are offered in the realm of cousin marriage, among them one to study such marriages to ascertain whether the children they produce have birth defects and an outright ban on cousin marriages.[25] Finally, a number of restrictions on family reunification are proposed including a higher age of consent and a requirement that parties seeking family reunification together have a longer history of connection to Norway than to any other country, both measures already existing in Danish law.

Rescuing Muslim women from their feudal cultures is also considered an educational issue. Human Rights Service, a staunch advocate of free choice and romantic love (the organization is able to convince a Muslim family to let a love match proceed, educating them in the process on the

virtues of romantic love), undertakes to educate young Muslims on the
dangers their cultures pose for them. To this end, Storhaug has published a self-help guide for immigrants and refugees entitled *Forced Marriages – A Crisis Guide*,[26] in which there is a chapter advising young
Muslim girls about 'the power of honour and decrepitude' and another
bearing the title 'Life Improvement – You Deserve It,' which encourages
them to resist their oppressive families. Assisting the girls into modernity, the guide explains that honour is an ancient idea held by tribal societies that believe in close control of women's sexuality and that arranged
marriages are a practice born of the concept of honour.

Amidst the tribal figures and irrational Muslims, it is difficult to
establish the truth value of the arguments in *Human Visas*. While the
marriage patterns are indisputable – Muslim migrants do marry others
from within their culture and approximately half of such marriages are
contracted with people outside Europe – the meaning of these practices remains contentious and almost certainly various. It is of course
not at all surprising that family reunification might be a compelling
reason for migrant communities to contract marriages outside of
Europe. Many parts of the non-West currently exist in economic and
political peril, and rich countries have by and large closed their doors.
Cousin marriage where one party lives outside Europe solves two
problems at once: the 'problem' of controlling girls' and women's sexuality and the problem of migration.

Human Visas does not offer proof that cousin marriage is the violent
practice described by Anders Hede in his study of cousin marriage.
Instead, the argument hinges entirely on the assertion that women in
the West have more freedom, autonomy, and equality because they are
not generally a part of extended kinship networks and are not subjected to arranged marriages, as are Muslim women. The divide is
between those who live as autonomous individuals and who make
decisions without the influence of kin and community and those who
live their lives within communities, the two sides serving to illustrate
not only the unbridgeable cultural divide between the West and non-
West but the non-West as a place of danger for women. Any factors
that might serve to complicate this picture of autonomously acting
individuals – for example, immigration as a condition that Muslim
communities are compelled to negotiate or the racism that drives communities into themselves – all remain outside the cultural frame. The
problem of violence, and what are viewed here as its repercussions,
such as the creation of an immigrant underclass, originate only in

culture, and Westerners, imagined as living autonomously and outside culture, remain privileged in this formulation.

In *Culture and Imperialism*, Edward Said reminds us what such culture-clash explanations accomplish. Considering Orientalist scholar Bernard Lewis's argument that expanding the Western literature curriculum to include non-Western works would soon take us down the path of slavery, polygamy, and child marriage, Said notes that, their comic dimensions notwithstanding, Lewis's arguments, predicated as they are on 'a highly inflated sense of Western exclusivity in cultural accomplishment,' but also reflecting 'a tremendously limited, almost hysterically antagonistic view of the rest of the world,' foreclose 'the possibility that any advance over tyranny and barbarism could or did occur outside the West.' We end up with 'a murderous imperial contest' that has the effect of driving the non-West 'into a violent rage or, with equally unedifying consequences, into boasting about the achievements of non-Western cultures.'[27] The actual conditions of arranged and cousin marriages, or any other patriarchal practices, remain completely unexamined when we engage in imperial contests. Since 'all roads lead to the bazaar,' then such details are unnecessary.[28]

We should keep in mind the productive power of the idea of the foreigner and the unassimilable minority. As George Mosse has shown, the myth about the 'Wandering Jew,' the eternal foreigner in our midst who clings to his backwardness and who 'would never learn to speak the national language properly or strike roots in the soil,' was a central plank in the ideology of national socialism in Germany.[29] Ordinary Germans held a cultural model of Jewish difference and believed in the fundamental unassimilability of Jews, Daniel Goldhagen argues, a model that made them receptive to the messages of national socialism.[30] The unassimilability of Jews and their cultural inferiority became the proof of the superiority of German culture,[31] a dynamic equally apparent with respect to Muslims in the contemporary European context.

Unni Wikan: The Need for Kindness

The unassimilability of Muslims grounds much of the discussion of forced marriages in another popular Norwegian book, producing not only the barbaric foreigner but also his or her counterpart: the civilized European. The story of the unassimilable, fatally pre-modern Muslim community encountering an advanced civilization is told in anthropologist Unni Wikan's *Generous Betrayal*, a book (along with *Human Visas*) the Danish minister of integration announced constituted his summer 2003 reading.[32] In Wikan's work we can see clearly the contours of culture clash in the plot line. The civilized European feels compelled to be kind to new, culturally different citizens, but his or her civilized impulses fall headlong into the perils of cultural relativism.

The Norwegian government has been too respectful of the cultural practices of Norway's immigrants, Wikan believes, and of its Muslim minorities in particular, and is far too soft overall on its immigrants. Women have paid the price for what Wikan terms the government's 'generous betrayal,' a price that has often included violence against their persons.[33] An anthropologist of Muslim societies, Wikan gained both fame and notoriety for her provocative contentions that culture has been misused in the service of men's domination over women and that 'the government was compromising the welfare of immigrants by practicing a policy of welfare colonialism that undermined people's capacity for self-help.'[34] The Norway that so generously betrayed its immigrants, Wikan suggests, did so because it was 'terrified of doing anything that might elicit accusations of racism.' In making such arguments, Wikan viewed herself as 'breaking the silence' around the destructive repercussions both of respecting Muslim cultures and of state welfare policies.

An overly patriarchal Muslim culture, a generous, misguidedly tolerant and humanitarian Norwegian culture, whites victimized by minorities, and victimized Muslim women all come together in the case of forced marriage. In Wikan's publications, spectacular instances of forced marriages are marshalled in support of the book's main contentions that Norway has been too generous and that Muslim culture oppresses women. *Generous Betrayal*, for example, begins with 'Aisha's story.' (Aisha is a pseudonym but the name has significance to Muslims, for whom Aisha was the prophet's youngest wife, the daughter of Abu Bakr who was to become the first caliph after the prophet's death. Aisha is said to have been only nine when the prophet, then a man of more than fifty, married her, a custom of Islam, Judaism, and Christianity at that time.) Aisha is a fourteen year old whose father was drawn to Norway because he knew he could make 'a career as a social welfare client.' Embodying the stereotype of the duplicitious immigrant bent on betrayal of a generous country, he amasses wealth by investing his welfare benefits in his home country, all the while living in a great apartment in Oslo paid for by the Norwegian government. Aisha disappears one day and is presumed to be the victim of a forced marriage. Earlier, she had attempted to convince Norwegian welfare authorities of what was in store for her. Believing that they would be called racist if they took Aisha away from her family, the authorities decline to intervene: For Wikan the authorities appear not to have known that 'forced marriage is a common sanction against youth, especially girls, of Asian or African descent who rebel against their parents' culture.'[35]

The failure of the authorities to act, apparently out of fear of being labelled racist, explains Wikan, is a particularly Scandinavian vulnerability that is connected to the region's commitment to humanitarianism and gender equality. Norwegians, according to Wikan, experience the national commitment to fairness so intimately that they are shattered when accused of unfairness, experiencing it as a loss of identity:

> 'Racist' has become a 'deadly word' – to borrow a metaphor from Favret-Saada (1980). It pierces the heart of the well-meaning Scandinavian whose cherished identity is that of world champion of all that is kind and good. Norway, the richest of the Scandinavian nations, is the most generous dispenser of aid to the developing world (measured per capita), and its humanitarian organizations have a long and venerable history. These are just some of the indices of an ethos that places a very high value on kindness, goodness, and charity. Add that belief in the equality of all human beings, irrespective of gender, age, and other factors, undergirds Scandinavian societies, and it is more understandable why 'racist' would strike so hard.[36]

Norway, as a country deeply committed to 'kindness,' belongs to a family of civilized nations, Europeans who had good intentions towards immigrants who were often their former colonized subjects. Their intentions were 'to honor the humanity and dignity of previously colonized people by respecting their traditions, customs, and ways of being.' Thus 'culture – which formerly had been used in its adjectival form, 'cultured,' meaning civilized, enlightened, and had been regarded as the hallmark of the colonizers in contradistinction to the colonized – was divested of its elitist notions and given a plural form.'[37] Here respect for the culture of the Other is presented as born out of a European impulse to treat former colonized subjects well, a reading the recipients of such generosity would surely question. Acknowledging that cultural identity became a means of resistance to colonialism, Wikan cites Alain Finkielkraut's articulation of the problem of culture for the colonized Other:

At the very moment the Other got his culture back, he lost his freedom: his personal name disappeared into the name of community; he became an example, nothing more than an interchangeable representative of a particular class of beings. While receiving an unconditional welcome, the Other found that he no longer has any freedom of movement, any means of escape. All originality was taken away from him; he was trapped insidiously in his difference.[38]

Europeans, on the other hand, ranked the individual above everything, giving up their culture to gain rights.[39] And it is this that Wikan wants the law to uphold: respect for the rights of the individual, limits on family reunification, citizenship as a social contract between individuals, and no dual citizenship for places that do not share the same values and practices as Norway. While feminists such as the Southall Black Sisters share her position as I show below, Wikan's views clearly become enmeshed in the story of European superiority. To be Norwegian is to be by definition anti-racist, and Wikan cannot bring herself to acknowledge that racism exists in Norway. What exists instead is a surfeit of kindness, as evidenced by the state's welfare policies.

It is noteworthy that what Wikan is often praised for is her invocation of Europeans' misguided generosity, and specifically her identification of the perils of respecting the cultures of racial Others. One reviewer even speculated that Europeans had a strange fascination for 'primitivism' and 'over there' that probably stemmed from a 'mythic desire to escape from modernity.' Wikan is lauded for warning us just in the nick of time that the Other often 'refuses to melt into the great mass that culture is to become,' that in fact we can take our respect for culture and our romance with the Other too far.[40] What is written out of the story of the overly generous European and recalcitrant and ungrateful Muslims, and what makes it possible for so many people to believe in these figures? In other words, what does the focus on culture displace as well as produce?

A People without a Colonial and Racist Past

The first omission in Wikan's narrative is of course colonization itself. In one fell swoop, Europeans move from being colonizers to becoming people intent on being honourable towards their former subjects. Importantly, the material relationship between colony and metropole is nowhere in this picture, and we could not guess that European generosity might in fact have been underwritten by decolonization itself and the demands of 'restless' natives themselves for recognition. European tolerance arises out of the European character itself, a misplaced tolerance given the natives' failure to be reborn.

The notion that Norway (and the rest of Scandinavia) has a history of generosity towards the Third World is an old one. Norwegians, like Canadians, are often pleased to consider themselves as being without a colonialist past. As I have written elsewhere, Canadian involvement in British colonial projects is obscured in this national remembering, as is internal colonization of Aboriginal peoples.[41] Norway's participation in imperial projects through its union with Denmark and subsequently, following independence, through its affiliation to Great Britain are also elided when Norwegians make the claim of being uninvolved in imperial projects. As Elizabeth Eide traces, following in the path of these older colonial relations, Norway went to India first in missionary projects and later with development aid beginning in 1952. For Norwegians, development projects provided a base from which the country could imagine itself as a member of the family of European nations, sharing in Europe's taking care of the Other. Eide documents the importance of development to Norwegian national mythology and the prominent place such activities have had in the press. As she concludes of Norway's relationship to India, as evidenced in the media, Indians' 'lack or deprivation is constructed as something *we* (i.e. good Norwegians) can help them improve.'[42] Norway's emerging national self, following its independence from Denmark, drew heavily on this notion of goodness to provide the nation with its imagined community. As the relationship between a Third World in need and a generous Norway evolved, three figures featured prominently in Norwegian media: victim heroes, consisting of small children unjustifiably deported from Norway owing to the actions of their parents; Third World women victimized by their cultures; and Third World women willing to speak out against their cultures. These figures easily dominate the news discourse and they offer Norwegians opportunities to imagine themselves as culturally superior as well as generous in saving the Other.[43]

Neo-colonialism: Hosts and Guests

The racial hierarchy evident in *Generous Betrayal* is naturalized through an appeal to a second underlying idea, one that explains immigration as an encounter between hosts and guests and that constitutes immigrants as foreigners against whom emerges what I have elsewhere called 'original citizens' (for the white settler context). Original citizens are those who bear an organic relationship to citizenship and whose claims rest on the basis of their having a natural entitlement (through descent from the 'original citizens') to full citizenship. Immigrants are scripted in this story as guests whose first obligation is gratitude to the hosts. The position is a catch-22. To belong, immigrants must indicate their gratitude and praise of the host culture, but since belonging is premised on membership in the bloodline that shares the nation's history, to be an *innvandrer* or immigrant, as Marianne Gullestad has pointed out, is always to be non-Norwegian, compliance and good behaviour notwithstanding.[44]

The host/guest metaphor is a pernicious one, as Gullestad and others, including myself, have noted: 'A host has the right to control the resources of the home, to decide on the rules of the visit, and, accordingly, to "put the foot down" when the guests do not conform. A guest, on his side has to be grateful for the hospitality received by not provoking the host by calling attention to his own difference from the host.'[45] Gullestad reminds us that when white Norwegians are constituted as hosts and Muslims as guests, the latter permanently extrinsic to the nation and foreign, a moral community is created.[46] Hosts have the moral right to call the shots, an assumption pervading government policies and laws on forced marriages. They have, in other words, a moral basis to instruct and to determine the conditions of daily life, while guests are always in the position of respecting the morality of the household.

It is worth taking the time here to draw out how hosts and guests are racialized categories that depend on specific silences. National mythologies are about an imagined sameness that comes about because a people have made a history together, a history of enterprise and innocence. In Norwegian national mythology, Norwegians courageously resisted the Nazis, something that does not bear up under close historical scrutiny. As a people, Norwegians have built a rich and peaceful land into which newcomers have come only recently. Here, for example, is how Unni Wikan tells the story of immigration to Norway. Immigrants, mainly of Pakistani origin, arrived in Norway in the 1960s, an event explained simply as men seeking a better life, or people were 'invited to Norway as guest workers,' as another Norwegian scholar Thomas Eriksen put it.[47] Guest workers, who are never expected to stay long, soon brought their families and the non-European population grew. In this scenario, Norway does not need the labour of the 'guest workers,' and if it has benefited at all from their presence, this is only coincidence. Norway imposed a ban on immigration in 1975, leaving the doors open only for family reunification and asylum. Here Wikan is only able to see benevolence in Norway's policing of its borders. For example, Norway has a reputation for generosity, which is why asylum seekers, mostly Somalis, Kurds, and Eastern Europeans, come to its doors. The story of generosity makes it possible for Wikan to situate her cast of characters within a fantasy, one I have detailed for the white settler context[48] of greedy migrants who simply want what Norwegians have and kindly original citizens who try at first to meet the needs of non-Europeans who are only out to deceive them.

The story of immigration, told as one of guests and hosts (the former duplicitous, the latter generous), depends upon a profound disavowal of the interconnectedness of the past with the present, of the spaces of wealth with poverty, and of the prosperity of original citizens and the poverty of newcomers. In Wikan's texts, immigrant poverty is born of culture. We might historicize the relationship between hosts and guests beginning with Saskia Sassen's reminder that immigration and ethnicity really describe 'a series of processes having to do with the globalization of economic activity, of cultural activity, of identity formation.'[49] We can make sense of migrations only by understanding 'the ongoing weight of colonialism and postcolonial forms of empire on major processes of globalization today, and specifically those processes binding countries of emigration and immigration.'[50] To name just a few of the processes that go unnamed in the formula of hosts and guests we can draw on Sassen, who notes that in global cities where there is a concentration of international capital and a concomitant class of high wage earners working in finance and technology, there is a corresponding need for low-wage, manual, and service workers, positions filled by immigrants. Those immigrants, in turn, flee the very conditions that have resulted in the concentration of capital in these cities. The growth of export-oriented agriculture, for instance, to service the debt the South owes to the North, effectively destroys the small farmer and the villages around him.[51]

Individualism as Evidence of Civilization

It would be a mistake to dismiss Wikan as simply a right-wing observer whose conservative views of immigrants lead her to understand forced marriage as simply evoking a clash of civilizations. Underpinning the culture clash described in *Generous Betrayal* is a more widespread national and international mythology, one shared even by those who would question Wikan's conservatism and her evident belief in the civilized European. Everyday notions of 'Norwegianness' produce and rely upon the same dichotomy of the civilized citizen and the barbarian Other. Chief among these notions is the idea that Scandinavia in general, and Norway in particular, are societies that have an intrinsic and deep commitment to individualism and to gender equality. When they clash with Muslims, the clash is, then, truly a cultural one in the sense that one cultural characteristic (a commitment to equality and individualism) meets up with another (a commitment to patriarchy, hierarchy, and communalism). As with hosts and guests, it is important to denaturalize these national characteristics.

Norway's cultural superiority lies in understanding that culture and community do not come before the autonomy of the individual. In Wikan's work, the landscape is peopled with tolerant, equality-minded Norwegians and tribal, misogynist Muslims. In a review of 'honour crimes' we meet the young girl who only wants 'to be a girl in a civilized nation,' an 'I' rather than a 'we,' because 'we' means 'fear, resignation, submissiveness, a warm crowd and somebody else deciding your destiny.'[52] Individualism is celebrated even in more critical scholars such as Thomas Eriksen, who acknowledges the presence of racism:

> The practice of arranged marriages in particular has aroused the ire of many Norwegians as it so clearly conflicts with ideals of individuality and equality that the Norwegians hold so dear. Arranged marriages are not forbidden in Norway although forced marriages are. But obviously the Norwegians are unlikely to understand an ideology which puts the interests of the family before those of the individual in a society where many parents, if not most, breathe a sign of relief when sons and daughters finally leave the nest at the age of 19–20.[53]

As a marker of European superiority, individualism works to designate the West as a place without culture but with values, thereby locating Westerners firmly within modernity and on the terrain of the universal. It is not difficult to trace in these formulations of individualism the figure of the citizen of the modern state, the individual who is identified only with the state and who is defined by his capacity to make rational decisions and to pursue his own interests. As David Goldberg has shown, the emergence of the autonomous, rational individual without defining links to community also

> licenses the extension of the rule of self-promoted rationality over the projection of the irrational, rationalizing thus the colonial project as one of modern destiny. So modern states expand their scope of authority, legitimacy, power, wealth, and control not only over citizens – in the name of freedom, autonomy, self-determination, and self-direction – but also over those racially considered incapable or not yet capable of self-rule. The colonial project, necessarily racially configured, is accordingly an expansion of modern state definition.[54]

The deployment of the rational man thus consolidates the exclusion from the state of Muslims on the basis of a fatal incompatibility with modernity. With their eviction from modernity, it now becomes possible to justify a considerable degree of state intervention against Muslims without the inconvenience of showing any direct connection between laws and policies and the harm they are intended to address.

2. The Law

Europe has long had a legal fascination with the Muslim woman's body *as a culturally different body*. Not coincidentally, legal interest intensified when a general tightening of Europe's and North America's borders occurred throughout the 1990s, initiatives often organized under culturalist explanations. As I and others have shown, the 1990s inaugurated a variety of legislative initiatives designed to control the flow of immigrants and refugees to the West (although not to stem the flow altogether, since immigrant labour is so vital) as well as to police those communities already living in the West, initiatives discursively managed through the figure of the illegitimate asylum seeker / immigrant. Most Western states passed laws designed to separate the legitimate from the illegitimate, the latter marked as possessing a cultural capacity for deceit. In Canada, for example, asylum seekers who did not possess identity documents but who were granted asylum were nevertheless denied the full benefits of resident status for five years until we could tell if they were honest and had had time to learn 'our' values.[55] Against the figure of the illegitimate asylum seeker and the bad immigrant, there was also the good immigrant, one for whom we could feel pity and who was deemed assimilable. In the latter category were women fleeing gender-based persecution, women the West was prepared to save providing a case could be made that their own cultures were too patriarchal and their own positions too pitiable to endure the violence.[56] If the majority of immigrants were deemed unassimilable and requiring close surveillance, the West could still preserve its appearance of generosity through saving non-Western women from the perils they faced in their own cultures.

European legal and policy measures that have particular relevance to the lives of Muslim migrant women include prohibitions against wearing the veil in schools,[57] against female genital mutilation,[58] and against forced marriages. For the most part, laws and policies around forced marriages began at the end of the 1990s, but more attention has been devoted to them in the post-9/11 period, when European states began to cooperate with each other on developing legal approaches primarily around family-reunification provisions in immigration law. (It must also be taken into account that the Schengen accords in March 1995 created Europe as a supra-national space and that the Convention on the Elimination of Discrimination Against Women [CEDAW] imposed a reporting requirement on the status of women by states who ratified it.) In the summer of 2003, Great Britain hosted an International Forum on Forced Marriages attended by government representatives and others from several European and Commonwealth countries.[59]

In the area of forced marriages, the remarkably long reach of the law into the lives of Muslim communities in Europe began with press reports of Muslim women being killed for refusing marriage arrangements made on their behalf, murders often described as 'honour killings.' In Sweden, in a case that reverberated throughout Scandinavia, Fadime Sahindal, of Kurdish origin, was killed by her father on the day she planned to move in with her Swedish boyfriend and after she had publicized on Swedish television her plight as a victim of a forced marriage to a cousin in her country of origin.[60] In Norway, Shazia Seleh was reported dead in Pakistan some time after she had sought the help of a Norwegian crisis centre to escape marriage arrangements made by her family. Her death was explored in a series of documentaries made by the Norwegian government, and it sparked an initiative to seek an agreement with Pakistan against forced marriages.[61] Rukhsana Naz, a British citizen and pregnant mother of two, was killed by her mother and brother for having a sexual relationship outside of marriage, a crime for which they were both convicted and sentenced to life imprisonment.[62]

The killing of women who refuse marriage arrangements or who are perceived to have brought shame on their families requires strong social condemnation and there is no doubt that the full force of the law must be brought to bear on the perpetrators of such crimes. While it is difficult to get estimates of the extent of the practice, the very estimates being infused with the moral panic over uncivilized Muslims, the problem clearly exists and is cause for concern. In Britain, conservative estimates are that 1000 women are annually subjected to forced marriages.[63] In France, the minister responsible for the status of women estimated that 70,000 girls between the ages of ten and eighteen are forced into marriage, an extraordinary figure that she bases on discussions with groups working in immigrant communities.[64] Compounding the difficulty of collecting data is the fact that the line between an arranged marriage and a forced one is difficult to draw. It may be useful, as one anthropologist has suggested, to view both types as arranged marriages that fall on a continuum between consent and coercion.[65] Whether the figures are inflated or not, it is difficult to keep in mind their magnitude and to ask at the same time about the social meaning they have been given in Western societies.

A contextualized approach to the problem of forced marriages and honour killings has been singularly lacking in law, where the idea of culture clash has held sway. In their construction as 'honour killings,' such murders are not understood as illustrations of a generic violence against women, a violence that dominant and minority cultures often fail to condemn. Culture, but minority culture only, assumes a pre-eminence that is discernable in the efforts made in legal documents and reports to distinguish honour killings from other instances of violence against women. For example, in her report to the Committee on Equal Opportunities for Women and Men of the Council of Europe, Mrs Cryer of the United Kingdom began by explaining what the concept 'crimes of honour' is meant to capture. A crime of honour is one committed 'as a consequence of the need to defend or protect the honour of the family.'[66] The origins of the crime in community/culture is what distinguishes it from other similar crimes in the West:

'Crimes of honour' should not be confused with the concept of 'crimes of passion.' Whereas the latter is normally limited to a crime that is committed by one partner (or husband and wife) in a relationship on the other as a spontaneous (emotional or passionate) response (often citing a defence of 'sexual provocation'), the former may involve the abuse or murder of (usually) women by one or more close family members (including partners) in the name of individual or family honour.[67]

Presumably, then, when a man kills his wife because he suspects her of infidelity and of bringing shame upon him, this crime cannot be called an honour killing when the man acts as an individual, unconnected to family, community, or culture. It is clear from this tortuous distinction that gender is placed in opposition to race. A crime of honour is a crime originating in culture/race, whereas a crime of passion originates in gender (abstracted from all other considerations). A crime of honour thus involves body, emerging as it does as a cultural tradition, and a crime of gender is mind, a distinctly individualized practice born of deviancy and criminality. The honour/passion distinction not only obscures the cultural and community approval so many crimes against women have in *majority* culture, but it reifies Muslims as stuck in pre-modernity while Westerners have progressed as fully rational subjects with the capacity to choose moral actions, even if the choice is a bad one.

The killing of Muslim women is, in the view of the Council of Europe, a culturally inspired crime 'rooted in a complex code that allows a man to kill or abuse a female relative or partner for suspected or actual immoral behaviour.'[68] The kinds of behaviour for which a woman may be killed include 'marital infidelity, refusing to submit to an arranged marriage, demanding a divorce, flirting with or receiving telephone calls from men, failing to serve a meal on time or "allowing herself" to be raped.'[69] Apart from cases of arranged marriages, this list would be familiar to anyone studying the patterns of domestic violence in the West. Although Mrs Cryer acknowledges the deaths of these Muslim women as due to domestic violence, lodging them in the cultural realm provides an opportunity to warn that they will not be forgiven in the name of cultural respect.[70] She notes that Islamic nations consider themselves targeted as a culture when the West wishes to address the issue of honour crimes, and they accuse the West of being selective in its advocacy of eliminating one type of violence against women and not others.[71] If culture is the overriding problem, however, as Mrs Cryer indicates, then legal solutions have to be crafted with Muslim communities in mind. That is, they have to address the *cultural* context of the crime. The peril of the cultural turn in law is fully evident in the Scandinavian context, where culture clash takes place between the 'Nordic Mind'[72] and Muslims.

Denmark led the way with legal change in July 2002 when a government elected on a strong anti-immigrant platform passed tough new immigration and asylum laws.[73] Included in the package was the provision that no one under the age of twenty-four would be allowed to bring a spouse into the country, an amendment based on the logic that anyone under twenty-four is less able to resist family coercion to enter into marriage. From the age of twenty-four on, in order to bring a spouse into Denmark, an immigrant or a Danish-born applicant must demonstrate that he or she holds stronger ties to Denmark than to any other country.[74] As the Danish government explained in proposing the amendments, '[T]he rules applicable so far for family reunification build on modern West-European standards for family establishment and have regrettably been exploited for immigration purposes through marriages of convenience and arranged marriages with resulting frequent tragedies for young families.'[75] The Danish emphasis on linking forced marriages to immigration is joined to an argument that forced marriages exacerbate problems of integration. The integration argument is bolstered not with statistics on the number of forced marriages or the number of women killed but rather, as in *Living Visas*, with surveys of the marriage patterns of immigrant groups living in Europe. For example, citing the figure that 47 per cent of immigrants married persons who resided abroad, a pattern that did not change from 1994 to 1999, the Danish government justified the need for reform of family reunification policy, adding that integration is particularly difficult for families where one spouse comes from outside Denmark.[76]

The language of integration has been a marked feature of forced-marriage legal debates. Here it is useful to consider that integration can provide a middle position between the extreme right's position that racialized immigrants must be evicted from Europe because they are unassimilable and the left's position on multiculturalism, whereby the rights of minorities must be respected. That is to say, as Miriam Ticktin argues, integration appears to hold out the promise of inclusion, even while it is premised on the notion that there is a national culture and universal values (possessed automatically by all 'original citizens') in which newcomers must be instructed.[77] Integration thus preserves a racial hierarchy even as it appears to dissolve it. The problem of violence encountered by girls and women of immigrant origin is generally attributed to the different value systems of Muslim immigrants and Europeans. Once the situation is constructed in this manner, it is easy to ask, as French media have in connection with the wearing of the veil, whether being Muslim is compatible with being French.[78]

In Great Britain, in November 2001, the Labour government launched a project to eliminate forced marriages in Britain, risking the ire of Asian groups when the Home Secretary characterized the issue as one of teaching immigrants how to be British.[79] Although NGOs and women's groups, as well as the Community Liaison Unit of the Foreign and Commonwealth Office in Britain, seem to have succeeded in keeping educational initiatives focused on women's rights and on getting access to help, and have sought to broaden knowledge of the practice of arranged marriages, the civilizing tone the Home Secretary David Blunkett adopted may well prevail as Britain turns to family-reunification laws for solutions.[80] In Norway, as I describe below, the rhetoric of integration and the idea that Muslim and European values clash has dominated the forced-marriages debate. Once the violence becomes a property of immigrant culture, it cannot easily be uncoupled from debates about how to control foreigners. Most of all, when a practice is condemned so unequivocally as originating in culture, there is little space left to explore how arranged and forced marriages may be understood both as an internal community practice and as a practice profoundly affected by a community's sense of peril.

Norwegian Initiatives against Forced Marriages

Although Norway has not rushed headlong in the legal direction evident in Denmark, and there appears, at least on the scholarly level, to be a much more critical discussion of the place of Muslim immigrants,[81] legal and policy initiatives are nevertheless still organized for the most part within a culturalist frame, wherein the problem of forced marriage is entirely reduced to culture. We can catch a glimpse of the Muslim Other mired in tradition and tribalism and his or her European opposite in some of the legal and policy texts addressing the issue of forced marriages in Norway. These texts are remarkably unselfconscious in their assumption that immigrant communities are to be instructed in matters of citizenship, that is, on how to live in European culture. They are structured by a familiar hierarchy of citizenship: on the one hand, original citizens whose values must be respected (and whose values, it goes without saying, are superior) and, on the other, foreigners whose alien values have the potential to contaminate the body politic and who must be purged. This hierarchical structure of citizenship, underpinned by the notion of culture clash, first emerges in Norway's 1995 'Action Plan against Forced Marriages' and becomes more evident in later texts presenting the government's position. Drafted by the Ministry of Children and Family Affairs, the Action Plan was initially a broader plan dealing with the integration of children and young people from minority backgrounds. The plan took an educational approach to the problem of forced marriages, declaring that its aims were 'to prevent young people from being exposed to forced marriage' and 'to provide better help and support to young people who are, or have been exposed to forced marriage.' (The disease imagery is not, I think, entirely coincidental).[82]

The Action Plan begins tentatively by presenting forced marriage both as a specific custom and as a problem in individual families:

> The principle of voluntary consent is recognized among religious groups in most countries. However, in cases where this principle is not adhered to then specific customs and the practice of the individual family can be the root cause. The possibility of choosing one's own partner acceptable to the parents appears to be increasingly common, especially in towns and cities. However, for those sectors of the population who live as a minority group in other countries, it can be a problem to find candidates who fulfill the traditional requirements for a suitable marriage partner.[83]

Skating delicately around indicting an entire culture and a community, the text makes clear that the government does not oppose arranged marriages per se, but rather those marriages where there has been coercion and where youth may be unable to resist family and community coercion. The Action Plan is forgiving of parents who coerce, believing that such problems arise because minority communities lack information about the laws and values of Norwegian society and assume that their own cultural practices can be followed. Further, the lack of suitable marriage partners makes it difficult for those parents of minority youth who need 'help and/or support in order to resist the wider family's demand that they should follow the tradition of forced or arranged marriage.'[84] Resources should therefore be deployed to make pamphlets and videotapes outlining Norwegian values. Communities would receive state funding to carry out educational initiatives on the issue of forced marriages. As well, parents must be given opportunities for instruction in parenting, while children should receive education in schools. Should education not suffice, however, the plan recommends that legal measures be put in place to ensure communities' compliance with Norway's newly re-instituted law prohibiting forced marriages.

The Action Plan is unabashedly structured around the notion that immigrant youth must be protected from their families and assisted to progress to complete personhood, a personhood defined as autonomy and freedom from tradition, family, and community. An us/them viewpoint saturates the text. They are incompletely modern and shackled by tradition; we are free and able to exercise choice. There is no shared humanity here and no possibility of dialogue. Instead, they must be instructed. As L.H.M. Ling has written, comparing the liberal internationalism of Martha Nussbaum to the overtly racist conservative nationalism of Jorg Haider, both Nussbaum's and Haider's approaches turn on

> a singleminded, unidirectional programme of reform where the Self appropriates the right to instruct Others. Where the Nussbaum-self seeks to empower third-world-women-Others by instructing them in capitalist self-help, the Haider-self aims the same for immigrant-refugee-Others in Austria by returning them to their homelands. Neither wants to engage in a dialogue with Others. Either they have nothing worthwhile to say (Haider's position), or they don't know yet who they are and what they want (Nussbaum's) ... Both stake a claim to modernity through their authority to pass it on to others.[85]

Ling makes the valuable observation that in Nussbaum's vision, tradition is the primary obstacle to complete personhood. The problem lies within Third World communities and cultures. There is no question of economic distributive justice, for instance, because there is no link between them and us. What the location of us in modernity and them in pre-modernity accomplishes is to preclude the possibility that their troubles, as it were, might actually require more understanding on our part. Nussbaum, Ling writes, does not 'consider how we might understand or communicate cross-culturally so that we may have the authority to judge others. She only emphasises the right to judgment.'[86] In the same vein, I suggest that the Action Plan also emphasizes the right to judgment, that is, the right to know what is best for the Other without troubling to establish many of the details. Little need be said about the diversity of views in Muslim communities, the extent of the violence, or its relationship to other factors. A 'right to judgment' framework depends instead upon a fundamental Self/Other dichotomy, one that can lead, as Ling suggests it does with Jorg Haider, to an articulation of a cultural chauvinism. Further, when the Self is constituted in Norway as a white, European nation defending itself against foreign undeveloped Others who have come uninvited into its territory, the path is cleared for the kind of surveillance and stigmatizing activities required to maintain the subordinate citizenship status of Muslims in Europe. For if *they* don't know, then we must not only teach them, but watch them for signs of degeneracy. It seems that Norway has gone in this direction since the Action Plan was first prepared.

Its instructional tone notwithstanding, the 1995 *plan* retains an ambivalence about where to locate blame: all immigrant communities and parents or simply the few individuals who do not know the law and Norwegian values? Seven years later, this ambivalence has disappeared, and there is a hardening of the lines in law. By 2002 the culprit is more confidently identified as culture — the culture of immigrants, and indirectly, because they are the majority group, the culture of Muslim immigrants. For example, in her statement to the UN Commission on the Status of Women on 4 March 2002, the minister of children and family affairs framed the problem of forced marriage more boldly as one of honour killings, a construct associated with Muslim societies: 'the rights of women *that we take for granted* are considered a threat to family honour in some minority groups in our countries' (emphasis added). The government had been 'reluctant to address these issues for fear of criticizing the culture and values of minority groups,' a reluctance that the minister felt had probably given rise to the vagueness of the action plan developed in 1995.[87]

At a Metropolis conference in September 2002, Lise Grette, a senior adviser in the Ministry of Children and Family Affairs, explained the history of Norwegian initiatives since 1995 and the reasons behind the government's earlier tentativeness. Ten years ago, Grette noted, when newspapers revealed that immigrant mothers were arranging marriages for their children to people in the homeland owing to a lack of marriage partners, and that some marriages were forced or arranged between minors, the government was uncertain whether the media had blown the problem out of proportion and stigmatized minorities or many young girls were indeed being forced into marriage. Anja Bredal was hired to explore young minority girls' experiences of marriage arrangements (a study I discuss later). The government 'presupposed that minority communities themselves and their religious leaders would take the responsibility to see that forced marriage did not occur,' and expected 'that all who live in Norway follow Norwegian laws and regulations.' Norwegians were betrayed. By 1999 the government knew from the media and the foreign service that the problem was more widespread than originally thought and was not in fact confined to a few conservative parents. Norway stepped up its educational efforts, as first detailed in the 1995 Action Plan. The biggest difficulty, Grette concluded, was 'the long-term work to change the attitudes of the parental generation.' Although still committed to an educational path ('We must reach out to the mothers'), Grette reported that Norway was now contemplating laws that would penalize religious communities who help with or accept forced marriages. Such communities could have their state subsidies and the right to perform marriages removed. Further, it may be legislated that religious community leaders complete a course in Norwegian language and social studies as a condition for residence permits.[88]

Norway's 'Renewed Initiative against Forced Marriage' includes several of the measures mentioned by Grette.[89] Retaining educational measures (primarily aimed at service providers, who are to be taught how to identify the problem), the new direction is moving towards greater immigration control. The government has announced its intention to impose tougher immigration requirements. As the minister of immigration, Erna Solberg, suggested, Norway now had to consider adopting a provision similar to the Danish law that makes it extremely difficult to obtain family reunification for persons under the age of twenty-three, a proposal Norwegian community groups warn is a violation of basic rights and will not prevent a single forced marriage.[90] Under the new family-reunification provisions, a Norwegian citizen sponsoring a spouse must have an income sufficient to guarantee the spouse's maintenance, a provision that is intended to restrict the marrying off of young girls who are taken to their parents' country of origin during the school vacations.[91] Finally, in the summer of 2003, a proposition was circulated regarding a further amendment to Norway's family-reunification laws that would insert a clause requiring both partners to swear that each is entering into marriage voluntarily and that each party has the equal right to divorce.[92] Here the idea is to signal Norway's non-acceptance of discriminatory Muslim marriage pacts and to encourage women's acquiring of a religious right of divorce, thereby reconciling a cultural practice with public law.

In the summer of 2003 the Norwegian parliament also resolved that a ban on forced marriages should be a part of the Norwegian Criminal Code. It proposed to impose a prison sentence of up to four years on anyone who arranges a marriage with a minor under the age of sixteen. Significantly, as anticipated in the 'Renewed Initiative,' the police and the public prosecutor would have the right to charge a person who forces someone into marriage even when the claimant has not asked for or consented to the prosecution. This latter provision was strongly criticized by the Red Cross, the Norwegian Association of Asylum Seekers, and others as likely to result in fewer youth seeking help for fear that their families will be criminalized. Groups opposed to these measures endorsed preventative strategies and shelters. The proposed law also spells out how force would be understood in the law and included in the definition psychological as well as physical force.[93] Finally, in its 2003–5 action plan for 'Combating Trafficking in Women and Children,' the government raised the possibility that the purpose of some arranged marriages was to bring into the country women who, with their children, were to be forced into prostitution. Contradicting the dominant notion of Muslim communities protecting the 'honour' of their girls and women, this latter suggestion now links Muslim communities to trafficking.[94]

The culturalist narrative discussed in section 1 attributes violence to culture. The exclusive focus on culture means that no consideration is given to social, political, and economic factors that may push immigrant communities to adopt more patriarchal and conservative practices and to become more violent. If the problem is entirely cultural in origin, that is, born out of an inflexible cultural practice to control girls' and women's sexuality and a cultural capacity for duplicity and deceit (revealed in the abuse of immigration), then the appropriate legal response can only be to engage in border control and criminalizing. The legal directions noted above take these two routes. First, they focus on the border, making it harder for family reunification through marriage and, second, they criminalize the practice of forced marriage to the extent that it is unlikely that Muslim youth, fearing the consequences for their families, will seek help. While earlier narratives in the Action Plan make it clear that what the laws and policies imagine is culturalist terrain where new immigrants must be instructed in the values of European civilization, the newer family-reunification and criminal-law provisions consolidate the forced marriage issue as one of an imperial contest between a superior civilization and an inferior one that must be *watched*.

Laws underpinned by notions of European cultural superiority and Muslim cultural inferiority may inadvertently have some positive effect, their paternalism and surveillance features notwithstanding. For example, insisting that women have a right to divorce spelled out in the Muslim marriage contract may well strengthen the position of those who argue, from *within* Muslim communities (as does the group Women Living Under Muslim Laws), that Islam grants the right of divorce. The support requirements in family reunification may also restrict the marrying off of young girls, but it will also stem the flow of many Muslim migrants into Norway altogether. In the end, bearing in mind the enormously productive function of the culturalist narrative, its installation of civilized Europeans who are obliged to instruct and discipline non-European Others, we can best assess the potential of the laws through considering both what they produce and what they foreclose.

Producing a civilized Europe and a stigmatized and closely watched non-West, these laws and policies foreclose a consideration of other factors that operate in the lives of Muslim youth. For example, they do not foster a positive climate in which Muslim youth and more progressive Muslims can internally contest patriarchal narratives. Instead, they polarize. Like Storhaug's handbook for Muslim girls on the perils of their culture, they do not imagine what an educational approach that promoted more positive ideas of Islam might actually accomplish. Instead of considering school dropout among young Muslims as a clear indicator of Muslim cultural deficit, we might consider, as so much schooling literature has shown, that schools in fact fail racial minorities through an inattention to their specific educational needs, and through a school climate of racial hostility.[95] Teaching young Muslims about the superiority of European culture increases this racial divide and does not respond to educational needs more directly connected to their mastery of the curriculum and to the hostility of the school environment. It may well be that laws and policies such as those currently being considered stigmatize and exacerbate tensions within communities more than they actually give rise to the conditions under which less violence might occur. It is at least clear that they are so firmly located in the realm of an imperial contest that their potential to respond to such violence is limited at best.

Conclusion

How can we avoid feeding culture clash, and re-installing European superiority, when we name and confront violent practices? Culture clash works so handily to secure racial myths precisely because there are cultural differences that everyone can point to. As Mosse noted, racial myths of Blacks and Jews in the European context that depend on the notion of cultural differences 'proved so blinding because [they were] based partly on legitimate anthropology and partly upon the obvious differences between the majority Europeans and the Jewish and Black communities. Blacks did have a different skin color and a different culture; and while Jews had the same skin color, they at first did have a different language, dress, and appearance.'[96] Forced marriages and 'honour killings' are specific to certain communities, and we would need to pay attention to their cultural, material, political, and historical contexts even as we bear in mind comparable violence in European communities, for example, women killed by their husbands and boyfriends when they attempt to leave abusive relationships. Researchers on women in Muslim communities have suggested, for example, that Muslim women do find ways to create 'third spaces' between the patriarchy they encounter within and the racism outside.[97]

Until we can actually see Muslim communities in all their complexities, we have little chance of making these spaces less violent. What do we know about arranged and forced marriages in Muslim communities in Europe? I rely here on two studies in order to suggest a more complex approach to strategies for change: a Norwegian study by researcher Anja Bredal (which builds on her doctoral work), who was asked by the Norwegian government to explore the responses of youth to forced marriages, and a British study conducted by two professors from the University of Birmingham, Yunas Samad and John Eade, for the Community Liaison Unit of the Foreign and Commonwealth Office. Starting with the Norwegian context, I turn to work completed by Anja Bredal.

In her PhD research, Bredal begins by declaring the concerns she brought to her study of young racial minority youth and their attitudes to marriage. Chief among them is her observation that in Norway forced marriage has been the focus of a polemic between those who claim that we ignore the violence of honour killings in the interests of respecting cultural diversity, and out of fear of being called racist (the Unni Wikan position), and those who say that the incidence of honour killings is greatly exaggerated and that the issue is used to stigmatize minorities, primarily Muslims. Underpinning the polarity is the idea that the individual stands opposed to the collective. Individuals give up the right to be individuals (the right to exercise free will) in the interests of the collective's need to reproduce kin and caste networks through marriage. As Bredal saw, this approach pits the autonomous individual against the collective and leaves no room for the complicated issue of who an individual is.

In interviews with young Norwegians from immigrant families (the majority of her interviewees were Muslim), a more nuanced and complex picture emerged. Bredal's interviewees described the racism in their lives in a context in which perfect strangers stop immigrant girls on the street and ask them anxiously if they are being forced into marriage. Racism of this kind isolates young people, leaving them caught between a hostile society and parents and communities with whom there is intergenerational conflict. They are left with little room 'to air their insecurities, their indecisiveness and fears, without setting off a whole rescue team in a process beyond their control.'[98] Bredal concludes that, in such a context, there is little communication between parents and children, and when conflict erupts, it does so dramatically.

If we pay attention to young people's narratives of cultural survival, as Bredal does, we find them understanding forced marriages as the response of parents seeking to provide them with cultural community and continuity but going about it in unrealistic ways. When parents turn to their communities of origin for marriage partners for their Norwegian-raised children, Bredal suggests, the risks are high that marriages really will involve men who are simply seeking a residence permit. As young people fear, their own happiness is imperilled under these conditions. While young people fear the outcome of marriages arranged by their parents with partners in their countries of origins, they do not automatically endorse 'free will.' Their position on arranged marriages, if a collective one is even possible, is summed up by Bredal as two messages: '[To majority culture]: What our parents are doing is not right, or even the real, version of our culture – our difference. To the parents: what you are doing is neither true to our culture nor is it sensible if you want our culture to survive.'[99] Young people find a number of covert ways to convey their positions, Bredal suggests. For example, they circulate stories of divorce, and of young people driven to desperate measures in order to escape unhappy marriages. These convey their sense of peril and their critique. Above all, minority youth *negotiate* their lives within culture and community, and do not inhabit, as majority Norwegians often imagine, an unproblematic position as victims of their families and communities, although it is certain that there are also victims.

A very similar portrait of responses to the role of marriage in Muslim immigrant communities emerges in a British study of community perceptions of forced marriage.[100] In their study of Pakistani and Bangladeshi communities in Bradford and Tower Hamlets, Samad and Eade adopt an approach that begins by contextualizing the two communities within a history of colonialism and migration, something I showed was entirely missing in accounts such as Wikan's, where Muslim communities were more or less reduced to their culture. Both communities are rural in origin, working class, possessing low human capital, and a substantially young population. They came to be in Britain through a process of chain migration, after the first immigrants came to supply cheap labour to the wool and garment industries. Their presence can be traced directly to old colonial arrangements. For example, most of the Pakistanis studied were Azad Kasmiris from what is now the Indian state of Jammu and Kashmir. They worked in the engine rooms of the British merchant navy and were encouraged to migrate to Britain to fill the labour shortages of the post-war period. Chain migration accelerated when the construction of the Mangla Dam produced people who were displaced but who had received a small compensation from the World Bank. These migrants (one third of a million) settled in Britain and sent remittances back home.[101] The British labour market contracted during the eighties and nineties and unemployment for this group rose to 35 per cent, three times the national average. Unemployment was even higher for women. The end result was a very young, unemployed population with exceedingly poor educational levels owing, among other things, to the state of schools in their communities. A similar portrait of the Bangladeshi community emerges, except that they came to work in the garment industry, which declined rapidly and was replaced by projects that required skilled workers.

Marriage is used in these two communities to reinforce kinship and job networks, although people marry from a wider pool than they normally would in their communities of origin. Marrying into the right family brings respect and status in the community as well as economic connections. Various forms of arranged marriages exist, but in general the less educated the family, the more traditional the practice. Families arranged transcontinental marriages because of the limited pool of marriage partners. In Bradford, for example, 50 per cent of the marriages were transcontinental ones, a figure that rose to 71 per cent in Oxford.[102] The researchers estimate, drawing on police data and on the Southall Black Sisters, that there are two hundred cases a year of forced marriage. Significantly, 'liaisons with the opposite sex are an important trigger for instigating the process of forced marriage.'[103] That is, families sought to push through arranged marriages without the consent of their children whenever they feared they would lose control of girls and women's sexuality. Immigration was not an important factor in these arrangements.

In focus-group interviews with both young people and elders, researchers documented a general consensus in these communities that forcing young people into marriage was unacceptable, although the use of emotional and psychological pressure was. Women were very active enforcers of patriarchal norms. As well, the older generation saw transcontinental marriage as cultural rejuvenation, but increasingly recognized that arranged marriages without the full consent of their children were risky and unlikely to last. Although young people preferred linguistic and cultural compatibility, and wanted to marry someone from Britain rather than from their parents' countries of origin, they identified increasingly as Muslim in terms of a social identity and did not express a position of wanting to stand outside of community, or outside of arranged marriages altogether. For both generations, the increasing racism directed at Muslims was an important factor in how they understood membership in community. Indeed, the researchers were openly confronted by their research subjects about the issue of arranged marriages being used to denigrate Muslim communities.

I draw a few conclusions from these studies of community perceptions that have a bearing on how we might approach and understand the legal regulation of forced marriages. There is little doubt that both arranged and forced marriages spring from an impulse to control women's sexuality, and that such controls are exercised more vigorously when communities feel themselves to be losing control. In other words, the patriarchal features of the practice cannot be denied. To consider this particular patriarchal practice, we need to see migrant Muslim communities in context. First, instead of seeing them as composed of foreign newcomers and uninvited guests, we might view them as populations displaced by colonialism and now under siege in late capitalism. As communities, they struggle for survival in an increasingly racist context. Members of these communities understand themselves within community, rather than as being victimized by it, although community practices are vigorously contested internally. Communities' capacity to become more reflective and self-critical, their ability to thrive without limiting the lives of their most vulnerable members, young women, is limited by racism, although it is equally clear that patriarchy shapes how communities are organized in the first place. How do these more nuanced portraits of Muslim immigrant communities help us to consider the regulation of forced marriages? To flesh out this answer, I turn to the positions articulated by the Southall Black Sisters, a British feminist organization with a long-term involvement in fighting violence against racial-minority women.

In keeping with what we know to be the factors contributing to forced marriage, the Southall Black Sisters clearly state the role that racism has played in solutions. For example, turning to control of immigration as a solution to the problem of forced marriage is denounced in no uncertain terms:

> In the final analysis, the aim of the Government is to keep black and migrant people out of Britain – through strict racist immigration and asylum laws and policies – not to protect women and others from human rights violations. If this were not the case, then *liberalising* the immigration laws would in fact indicate a greater willingness on the part of the government to prevent forced marriage. If there are no immigration rules to by-pass, then what need is there to force a woman into marriage in order to enter the country?[104]

If immigration is clearly not the problem, and control of immigration not part of the solution, what then are solutions to the problem identified as arising through men's and communities' power over women? For SBS, the answer lies in strengthening women's position through providing them with more options to flee their communities: better services (for example, shelters) and more available housing (achievable through a reform to the housing act), as well as better-trained police and service providers who can more quickly spot instances of forced marriages.

It is on the issue of service provision that it becomes crucial to identify what factors limit the help Muslim women get when they attempt
to flee. For the Southall Black Sisters, a principal reason why Muslim
women do not get the help they need to flee violence is multiculturalism. SBS argues that an important factor contributing to violence
against women and girls in situations of forced marriage are 'agencies
and policy makers [who] refuse to intervene in minority communities
on the grounds of respecting cultural difference and on the assumption
that minority communities are self-governing. This is based on notions
of multiculturalism, or cultural relativism, where different cultures
and religions are tolerated and respected. However, while multiculturalism aims to promote racial harmony *between* communities, it fails
to deal with problems *within* communities.'[105] In sum, powerful patriarchs control communities and this is a problem multiculturalists refuse to recognize. Repeating the sentiment expressed by Unni Wikan,
an inset box in the SBS document presenting their position quotes a
survivor of a forced marriage: 'They are afraid of interfering in the
culture and being called racist.'[106] For SBS the multiculturalists treat
racial-minority women in a way that they would not treat white
women, that is, ignoring the violence directed against them in the
interest of respecting culture. Multiculturalism is also blamed for the
support given by the Home Office to the idea of mediation for women
in forced marriages, an option SBS categorically rejects and which
prompted the resignation of its representative Hannah Siddiqui from
the Home Office Working Group.

As I argued earlier, when multiculturalism (in the form of respect for
cultural differences) is identified as the reason why so little is done
about forced marriage, we can become less attentive to how racism
shapes service provision and how racism often masquerades as respect
for culture.[107] Racism complicates a long-standing sexism whereby
violence against women is condoned because women are regarded as
the property of their men and families. If minority women fail to get
the services they need, it is in the first instance because there are so few
of them, and in the second instance because service providers *naturalize* violence against Muslim women, viewing it as simply a condition
of belonging to their oppressive families and communities. It is simply
the way *they* are. A similar response, and one that I shall insist is racist
rather than multicultural or born out of a desire to respect culture, is
evident in the context of Aboriginal women accessing services when
they encounter violence. Police often respond to Aboriginal women's

calls (when they respond at all) by blaming the victim herself and considering that the violence is deserved because it is simply a part of what they assume to be Aboriginal life (drinking and prostitution and everyday sexual violence).[108] I suggest that something along the lines of culturalization occurs where violence is assumed to be a natural aspect of life, and therefore not something it is worth doing anything about. My suspicion is that South Asian women are met with a similar culturalization. If racism and not cultural respect is the problem, then a critical issue is how to train police and service providers who are racist, something feminists have paid little attention to. Instead, we have sometimes contributed to re-installing the myth of the civilized European.

In the realm of prevention, SBS does not devote as much attention to education as we see in the approaches taken by Scandinavian countries, perhaps having less zeal for the colonial instruction and surveillance of minority communities that such strategies depend on. But in their emphasis on women fleeing their communities, and diminished attention to lives lived in community, there is an implicit endorsement of the notion that a woman is someone who lives outside race and community. The idea of the individual living free of the ties of community and family, and with ties only to the state, is one that has not resulted in less violence against women. Indeed, Norway itself reported to the UN Commission on Equality that 5 per cent of Norwegian women were raped by someone other than a partner, while 10 per cent reported being raped by a partner.[109] If we consider spousal homicide, for instance, in a country such as Canada, we see that for the year 2001, sixty-seven women were killed by their partners or ex-partners and seventeen of these women were killed after they tried to leave their abusive partners.[110] We do not, in these instances, refer to culture as the root cause of the problem, although the violence is directed at women who refuse to stay in their marriages and relationships on account of violence.

If we did not think of hosts and guests, and of culturally advanced versus primitive cultures, of free will versus oppressive communities, how would this change our strategies in the context of legally addressing the problem of forced marriages? I think we would as feminists abandon our focus on multiculturalism and pay renewed attention to racism, and specifically to how cultural racism works. This would enable us to identify strategies that are merely punitive (immigration), to gauge more accurately what we are up against when we think of what service providers need to know, and to think about strategies outside community (the provision of safe spaces for women) as well as within communities (how to foster a feminist critical reflection and how to ensure that young people in Muslim communities have access to education and to work). Our chances to do any of things, I am convinced, are severely restricted if we shift our gaze away from the crucial ways in which the Muslim woman's body is used to articulate European superiority. We cannot forget for an instant the usefulness of her body in the contemporary making of white nations and citizens. Her imperilled body has provided a rationale for engaging in the surveillance and disciplining of the Muslim man and of Muslim communities. Indeed, such force has been unleashed in her name that it is difficult for Muslim women to have open discussions about the patriarchal violence directed at them. It is instructive that it is only the violence emerging from forced marriages, veiling practices, and female genital mutilation that Europe has been concerned about, and not the violence of poor educational and job access or the dislocation and forced migration of large numbers of Muslims through war. If culture clash ensures the success of the racial myth of European superiority, as feminists we need to identify how it operates to restrict our understanding of forced marriage and of anti-violence solutions. It is clear, as Abdullahi An-Naim has suggested writing on forced marriages, that communities under siege are 'most likely to turn inward and reinforce the very practices that those on the outside are seeking to change.'[111] Thus far, the feminists and lawmakers considered here have contributed to the siege rather than worked towards dismantling it.

In his perceptive article 'Culturalism as Ideology,' in which he explores the way in which French medical practitioners culturalize the realities of HIV-positive African women living in France, Didier Fassin advises that since culturalism provides such a sense of superiority to French medical practitioners and since it works handily to obscure the social conditions that so obviously influence why African women living in France make the choices they do, we should perhaps turn to culture as the *last* reason for behaviour.[112] This advice is useful for those considering violence against Muslim women.

5 The Muslims Are Coming:
The 'Sharia Debate' in Canada

What politics are promoted by the notion that the world is *not* divided into modern and non-modern, into West and non-West?

Talal Asad[1]

Entry Point: Dead Bodies and Dead Subjects

In June 2004 I attended a keynote lecture in Toronto on honour killings in Europe by Unni Wikan, a Norwegian anthropologist who specializes in Muslim cultures. I was interested in Wikan because she had had an impact on the debates concerning Muslim women in Norway, as I discussed in chapter 4. Professor Wikan was introduced as someone who had rescued people in great need, particularly young Muslim girls. I learned that she had just received a free-speech award for showing great courage in working for social justice. Her courage in this case was in daring to speak up against Muslim cultures and on the evils of both multiculturalism and a too-soft approach to immigrants.

Wikan's presentation began with Power Point slides of the funeral of Fadime Sahindal, a Kurdish woman murdered by her father (an immigrant to Sweden) when she decided to leave home to live with a non-Kurdish man. Sahindal received a state funeral in Sweden, broadcast live on Swedish television. She had expressed a wish to be buried in a church, and Wikan showed slides of the bishop, who called her a martyr, and the six women who carried her coffin, a practice Wikan speculated that the Muslim men in her community agreed to 'probably because they realised they didn't have a choice.'[2] The keynote presentation continued with many pictures of the beautiful

Sahindal, her long, curly hair flowing. There were even pictures of her grave.

Throughout this somewhat macabre visual journey, I wondered why Fadime Sahindal's dead body had to be so prominently displayed for the benefit of the three hundred or so, mostly white, Western academics attending a conference of the Jean Piaget Society. My discomfort reached an apex in the question period that followed, when members of the audience, some of the women on the verge of tears and with voices quivering with anger, expressed their outrage at the barbarous Muslim men to whom Wikan often referred. A palpable warmth and white group solidarity suffused the audience as they collectively contemplated what might be done to save the Muslim woman and to keep the 'dangerous' Muslim man in line. I was reminded of the regenerative properties of unveiling the Muslim woman, that is to say, of its power to give birth to the European.

On this June morning, the productive power of the ideas of the imperilled Muslim woman and the 'dangerous' Muslim man, ideas that instal the civilized European and enable practices of surveillance and regulation, was not the only thing to worry about. Fadime Sahindal was murdered by her father. How do we keep her murder in mind at the same time that we remember what it can mean to those who are anxious to draw a line in the sand between barbaric Muslims and civilized Europeans? As I have written elsewhere, strategies to confront violence against women, of the kind Fadime Sahindal died from, fail if they mostly work to instal the colour line between modern white subjects and pre-modern non-white subjects, between those who help and those who require assistance. Strategies born of such evangelical impulses seldom undermine the structures and practices that both give rise to and sustain violence against women for the simple reason that such structures are not even acknowledged. If the violence Sahindal experienced is thought to come out of her culture, pure and simple, then there is little chance to confront the multiplicity of factors that have produced and sustained it.[3]

The eternal triangle of the imperilled Muslim woman, the 'dangerous' Muslim man, and the civilized European is fully in evidence in the context that is the topic of this chapter: Canadian feminist and state responses to the prospect of the introduction of Sharia law as an option for Muslims settling disputes in family law. In the French-speaking province of Quebec, faith-based legal options in the realm of family law have been rejected outright. In the English-speaking province of

Ontario an option had long existed through the *Arbitration Act* that enabled individuals to hire third parties to privately adjudicate their conflicts using any agreed-upon rules or laws.[4] This option was mostly used to settle commercial disputes, although Jewish groups had used it in matters of divorce. When a Muslim group proposed to use the *Arbitration Act* to settle disputes in the family-law arena using Islamic principles (which they described as the application of Sharia law), feminists expressed a vociferous opposition to faith-based arbitration. Despite feminist protest, and following an inquiry, the government initially found no compelling reason to deny faith-based arbitration in the settlement of family disputes to Muslims while Jews and indeed all other groups retained the right under the *Arbitration Act*. However, a few short months later, after intense public debate, the government reversed its position, announcing on 11 September 2005 that it intended to introduce legislation that would eliminate all faith-based arbitration.[5] The debate about faith-based arbitration in Ontario, a public discussion that took place for most of 2004–5, is the focus of this chapter.

As this debate progressed, I was sometimes asked by concerned Muslim feminists if I had anything useful to contribute to the 'Sharia debate,' as faith-based arbitration came to be called. Like the women who approached me, I worried deeply about the rise in fundamentalism worldwide and felt sure that Sharia law through the *Arbitration Act* was not a good idea for women. At the same time, I had grave misgivings about how feminists had so far responded to the threat of Sharia, reinstalling the modernity/pre-modernity distinction apparently without hesitation. I considered it risky for feminists to work with ideas of the secular over the religious, the modern and the pre-modern, in short with strategies that deployed the three figures I had come to know so well from the European context. Such constructs fit so neatly into the contemporary Western project to mark Muslims as suspect bodies and to limit their citizenship rights that it seemed to me that a considerable amount of caution was in order. On the other hand, it also seemed likely that those feminists who took an anti-Sharia position did so out of the conviction that Muslim women were at risk of losing their rights under faith-based arbitration, particularly if conservative Muslim interpretations of women's rights in Islam were to prevail. Feminists were concerned that private dispute mechanisms were unlikely to operate in women's interests and that Muslim women could be pressured into accepting faith-based arbitration. The 'Sharia debate' highlighted the fact that Muslim women were caught between the proverbial rock (a state likely to use their rights as a means to police Muslim populations) and a hard place (patriarchal and conservative religious forces within their own communities).

I argue below that in their concern to curtail conservative and patriarchal forces within the Muslim community, Canadian feminists (both Muslim and non-Muslim) utilized frameworks that installed a secular/religious divide that functions as a colour line, marking the difference between the white, modern, enlightened West and people of colour, in particular, Muslims. This colour line is an especially pernicious one in a post-9/11 world when, in the name of anti-terrorism, Western states have won support for a variety of punitive and stigmatizing measures against Muslims and other groups of colour. Such measures are often defended as civilizing measures, necessary in order to bring democracy, human rights, and women's rights to Muslim countries. I suggest that feminist responses have helped to sustain a form of governmentality, one in which the productive power of the imperilled Muslim woman functions to keep in line Muslim communities at the same time that it defuses more radical feminist and anti-racist critique of conservative religious forces. Drawing from Talal Asad's idea that secularism is one way in which the modern state secures its own power and actively produces the citizen whose loyalty is first and foremost to the state, I explore below how ideas about women's rights and secularism are part of the neo-liberal management of racial-minority populations who are scripted as pre-modern and requiring considerable regulation and surveillance. Secularism as a policy regulating the conduct of citizens requires and produces a normative citizen who is unconnected to community, a figure who achieves definition only in comparison to racial Others, the latter presumed to be trapped in the pre-modern by virtue of their particularist tendencies.

We are in a historical moment in which feminism can be easily annexed to the project of empire. As I and others have shown, it is often through the language of human rights and gender equality that empire is accomplished today.[6] The West is understood as culturally committed to the values of the Enlightenment, while the non-West remains incompletely modern at best, or hostile to modernity at worst. Within this conceptual framework, one often described as a clash of civilizations, it is the duty of modern peoples to bring pre-modern peoples in line. When the occupation of Afghanistan by American forces can be justified as necessary in order to save Afghan women from the Taliban, feminists must necessarily pay attention to how their demands serve the interests of imperialism and white supremacy. As Inderpal Grewal has persuasively argued, human-rights discourses, including those regarding women's rights as human rights, are productive discourses. They instal 'free subjects who can save those suffering from human rights abuses' and sustain 'rescue from culture' as the main rationality.[7] What do discourses of rescue erase and what do they produce?

Such considerable legal and social interest in Muslims may seem at first blush obvious if one accepts that the 'war on terror' has brought with it an intensification of race thinking and the marking of the 'culturally different' as aliens outside the polity. It may also seem obvious when viewed as part of the ongoing management of racial populations, especially if one considers that Muslims constitute a majority of Europe's immigrants. In Canada, however, Muslims do not constitute the largest group of migrants. The sensation, therefore, that the civilized world is being overrun by Muslims derives less from the actual numbers and more from a circulating global narrative of the 'war on terror.' This is nowhere more evident than when, in February 2007, the small town of Hérouxville, Quebec, a town with no foreign-born or Muslim residents at all, felt compelled to announce that it prohibits the stoning of women. As the town's city councillors explained to the Muslim women who met with them to discuss the need for such a formal declaration, they were worried that a Sharia law might be implemented provincially. For these councillors, it was necessary to act quickly, pre-empting the threat before it materialized.[8] If, as I suggest, these are moral panics over Muslims even where there are none, we must in the end return to the productive function of the three figures who people the pages of the newspapers: the 'dangerous' Muslim man, the imperilled Muslim woman, and the civilized European.

1. The 'Sharia Debate' in Ontario: 'From Britannia to Sharia'

The Ontario 'Sharia debate' began life as a moral panic. That is to say, a small event came to stand in for a crisis of giant proportions, one on to which was projected social anxieties about Muslim bodies. Parenthetically, it is noteworthy that such media-orchestrated panics are traceable in every Western country since 2001. For example, widespread condemnation of bodies marked as 'Muslim,' and heightened support for punitive measures against them, followed the media-foregrounded gang rape of a white Australian woman by Lebanese males in Sydney, Australia. As Binoy Kampmark has shown, the rape case became a point of departure for public commentary on the dangers of multiculturalism and on the evil Islam posed for the West, in spite of the fact that the rapists were Christians.[9] We can see the same kind of media spectacle around the banning of the hijab in various countries, notably France, a context to which many Canadian social commentators referred when discussing faith-based arbitration. In each of these 'panics,' Muslim women's bodies become the ground on which nations and citizens are established as civilized and modern, while Muslims and immigrants remain trapped in the pre-modern, a process not unlike the one I described with respect to Fadime Sahindal. The polarization successfully pre-empts examining how the state and its institutions are implicated both in the marginalization of communities of colour and in the oppression of women. Not insignificantly, media panics also afford an opportunity for the race pleasure Anthony Farley describes as a pleasure in one's own superiority and the other's abjection.

In late November of 2003, Syed Mumtaz Ali, a retired lawyer, announced to the media that a new organization, the Islamic Institute of Civil Justice, had been established. The organization planned to apply Islamic principles of family and inheritance law to resolve family law and inheritance disputes within the Muslim community in Canada, services he described as the application of Sharia law. (Sharia Law is not a codified set of laws but rather a framework for interpreting laws based on the Qu'ran and the Hadith.) The *Arbitration Act* already permitted the resolution of private disputes in this way and had done so for a decade, but Ali's announcement created the impression that something had changed in law that now made it easier to apply Sharia. The panic that ensued, from the fear that Sharia law (with its associated images of women being stoned to death) had now come to Canadian shores, was of such a magnitude that the federal government, pressed to set up an inquiry into the *Arbitration Act*, was ultimately obliged to clarify that it had not changed the law and that it had not collaborated with the newly formed Islamic Institute.[10]

The tracks for making Syed Ali's announcement into a moral panic were well worn. Headlines on the barbarism of Sharia itself were appearing as early as 2001, and media reports of the story of Amina Lawal, the Nigerian woman sentenced to death by stoning, prepared the ground for the now familiar theme of a 'Clash of Civilizations' between Islam and the West. The events of September 11, 2001 simply escalated the clash. The November 2003 headlines on Sharia that announced the Islamic Institute's plans alerted Canadians that they were on the brink of their own fateful encounter between Islam and the West, a swift descent from the ideals of the British Empire to a barbaric multicultural present, in short, from 'Britannia to Sharia.'[11] The headlines warned of 'legal apartheid,'[12] and suggested ominously that 'religious law undermines loyalty to Canada.'[13] Sharia was above all 'un-Canadian.'[14]

Canadian feminists believed there was a great deal to fear from Mumtaz Ali and his small group. The Canadian Council of Muslim Women met with the government to discuss their concerns. An International Campaign Against Sharia, headed by a Canadian of Iranian origin, was formed. Various feminist organizations, among them the Women's Legal Education and Action Fund (LEAF), the National Association of Women and the Law (NAWL), the Metropolitan Toronto Action Committee on Violence Against Women (METRAC), and the National Council of University Women, added their voices to the general feminist alarm. Feminist lobbying succeeded to the extent that the Ontario government responded by appointing a Member of Parliament, Marion Boyd, a long-time feminist who was well respected by feminists in the mainstream anti-violence movement, to explore the 'use of private arbitration to resolve family and inheritance cases, and the impact that using arbitration may have on vulnerable people.'[15] Boyd met with over fifty individuals and organizations from July to September 2004, releasing a report that left feminists dismayed by her recommendation that the *Arbitration Act* remain unchanged. Boyd also concluded that the safeguards recommended by feminists worried about vulnerable Muslim women were not necessary.

Canadian Feminist Positions

The figure of the imperilled Muslim woman stood at the core of feminist responses to the idea of faith-based arbitration advanced by Ali and the Islamic Institute. As they sought to make clear to the government, extremely vulnerable and at risk in family and community, Muslim women were best protected by the state, a protection achieved through the absolute separation of religion and law. The Canadian Council of Muslim Women, for example, armed with statistics from the 2001 census, declared that even though Muslim women were among the most highly educated in the country, they tended to work part-time and in low-paying jobs. Quoting statistics indicating that fewer separated Muslim women sought divorce than did separated women in the Canadian population, and that marriage breakdown for Muslim women between the ages of eighteen and twenty-four is higher than for other women of the same age group, the Council opined that these patterns could be attributed to higher than usual 'cultural and economic pressures.'[16] Muslim women may in fact be persuaded to agree to arbitration under pressure, and the *Arbitration Act* did not contain safeguards to protect them from their families and communities. Rejecting outright any position that would involve strengthening women's position *within* faith-based arbitration (the government had proposed education materials informing women of their rights under religious and family law), the Council insisted that since there was no consensus about Sharia, and no accountability for how it was interpreted, conservative and patriarchal interpretations were likely to prevail. The answer, then, had to lie in secular law. Without it, women would be left at the mercy of their communities.[17]

If secularism offered women shelter from community, however, then the state became women's chief protector, an entity conceptualized as a neutral power, uncontaminated by conflicting loyalties to kin or community, and offering equal protection to all its citizens regardless of race or gender. Feminists appealed to the state on the basis of its universalism. The Canadian Council of Muslim Women received strong support from the international group Women Living Under Muslim Laws. Echoing the sentiment that family and community were dangerous places for women, and that a fully secular state was women's best protector, WLUML warned that the proposal on the part of the Islamic Institute amounted to 'the political manipulation of culture and identity.' Such moves were global, suggested WLUML, and had already jeopardized women's autonomy in France and the United Kingdom. WLUML described the European situation as

an unholy alliance between some progressives and the fundamentalists who then sought to take advantage of state policies of multiculturalism and the realities of continuing racial discrimination to demand special rights for the 'Muslim community.' But these special rights inevitably involve anti-women practices and highly regressive interpretations of Islam. They also unquestioningly presume that all migrants from Muslim contexts identify with 'Muslim.'[18]

Concluding that 'any victory for conservative forces among communities in Europe and North America will in this globalized world automatically reinforce fundamentalist groups in Muslim countries and elsewhere,' and reminding Canadians that giving power to conservative movements will not address the problems Muslim communities have in Europe and North America, the organization stated its views boldly: 'Obscurantist men' cannot speak for Muslim women.[19] Linking the rise in fundamentalism elsewhere to the Canadian situation both provided Mumtaz Ali and his small group with a profile and power they did not seem to possess and sustained the idea that the state remained beyond reproach as the protector of women. If the community could be kept from contaminating the state through such policies as multiculturalism, then women's rights would remain secure.

In installing an opposition between multiculturalism and women's rights, WLUML repeats an argument that has raged in Western feminist circles for some time. Its academic form, for instance, is discernable in the positions taken by Susan Moller Okin, that multiculturalism is bad for women, and by her critics, who suggest that once feminism is put in opposition to multiculturalism, racism quickly pervades what becomes efforts to save non-Western women from their cultures. Many scholars have pointed out these dilemmas and suggested the issues are more complicated than the simple assertion that multiculturalism is good or bad.[20] As Floya Anthias suggests, to navigate between the poles of feminism and multiculturalism two things must be borne in mind: relationships between dominant and subordinate groups and 'the need to attack this unequal relationship at national and global levels' and similar relationships of inequality within groups.[21] Key to keeping these things in mind is remembering that women are agents with multilayered identities who need to resist class exploitation and racial domination and be free from violence and gender inequality. Anthias stresses that we must avoid homogenizing and totalizing cultures, just as we must avoid treating gender as a unitary category that stands apart from all other things. Further, all 'practices that serve to subordinate and oppress are to be attacked and these practices are tied to a range of structural processes which include the State apparatus, the socio-legal framework and the dominance of Western capitalist and cultural forms.'[22] Similarly, in *Dislocating Culture*, Uma Narayan has argued that feminists must 'insist that there are many ways to inhabit nations and cultures critically and creatively,' pushing for a more historical and political understanding of tradition.[23]

Following the line of argument expressed by WLUML, some Canadian feminists opposed to faith-based arbitration articulated a fervent belief in secularism and a commitment to the position that multiculturalism was bad for women. For instance, they spoke glowingly of the French context, where the hijab, or headscarf, was recently banned in schools. (The presence of French-speaking feminists in some of the more vocal feminist organizations may have accounted for the multiple references to the French context.) Secularism in France was represented as historical progress, the triumph of universalism over class and religious conflict. In a research report for the Canadian Council of Muslim Women, Pascale Fournier wrote admiringly of the French decision to ban the hijab and connected it to France's revolutionary tradition.

The most important feature of current French politics is its neo-republican discourse of French identity, in which membership in the national community involves an absolute commitment to the Republic and to its core values of égalité (equality) and laïcité (the separation of state and religion). This republican model was forged in the context of the 1789 French Revolution, as a direct reaction to the historical French struggle against its own monarchy, ruling aristocracy and religious establishment.[24]

Sharing this faith in secularism, the National Association of Women and the Law elaborated that if faith-based arbitration were allowed, 'freely chosen' arbitrators will be the new judges of women, imposing their own principles as the law of the land. While arbitrators chosen by Muslim communities could not be trusted, judges were deemed a better option for women. In view of the likelihood that judges would be of European origin, NAWL proposed cultural-sensitivity training to augment the latter's capacity to protect Muslim women from their cultures and communities.

Only one feminist organization, the Women's Legal Education and Action Fund (LEAF), initially supported the use of religious principles when they do not conflict with Canadian law. LEAF acknowledged that the use of arbitration was attractive because it was an alternate and cheaper form of dispute resolution. Further, they noted that some Muslim women were in favour of using Sharia. Believing that there was contemporary 'negative stereotyping of Muslims,' but seeking as well to heed women who were concerned about conservative religious influences, the organization recommended that a number of safeguards be built into the *Arbitration Act* to protect women from being coerced into arbitration. LEAF later reversed its position, announcing that it now believed that the government should prohibit the use of the *Arbitration Act* to protect women from being coerced into settling their disputes in accordance with religious law. It is possible that this reversal emerged from the realization that the government refused to consider building in safeguards into the act.[25] On the whole, then, although Canadian feminist organizations did not all adopt the dramatic tones of Homa Arjomand of the International Campaign to End Sharia that Sharia was a 'barbaric act' and that permitting the use of the *Arbitration Act* to settle family law disputes would 'escalate all the slavish obligations of the wife towards the husband under the Islamic Laws and ancient traditions,' feminist organizations remained opposed categorically to religious legal options.

Feminist rejection of faith-based arbitration left no room to stand for women seeking to live a faith-based life, a schism that was clearly in evidence at a community forum to discuss Sharia. At a public meeting sponsored by Arjomand and the International Campaign to End Sharia, a group of young veiled women from a Somali youth group repeatedly asked questions relating to the need for religious tolerance, arguing that their Muslim faith and their Muslim youth group was a refuge from the racism they experienced in high school. Speaking of teacher and principal surveillance, police surveillance, and the media demonizing of Muslims, the young women argued that Sharia would be more applicable in their lives should they choose to use it for family issues. Most of their remarks were dismissed by the speakers on the platform on the basis that the young women did not know how fundamentalism operated. Dismissed as naive, and told that they had been coerced into wearing the veil, some of the young women chose to leave the meeting.[26]

It is not surprising that at least initially the government refused to endorse a staunch secularist position. To do so would have meant, in the first instance, treating Muslims differently from other groups, most notably Jews. The Boyd report also quickly zeroed in on the weaknesses in feminist arguments, exploiting these to defend its position that faith-based arbitration should continue. Noting that feminists and others appeared to be misinformed as to the extent to which such arbitrations could contravene Canadian law, the report made clear that if the principal objection to faith-based arbitration had to do with the specific vulnerabilities of Muslim women, then one option was to educate this group about their religious and secular options (the former suggestion was roundly rejected by the Canadian Council of Muslim Women). Responding to the repeated feminist argument that family and community were particularly perilous places for Muslim women, and for women at risk of domestic violence in particular, the Boyd report quotes a critical feminist scholar, Liisa Hajjar, who holds that a more complex assessment of women's lives was 'an important rejoinder to cultural stereotypes that Muslim women are uniquely or exceptionally vulnerable.'[27] Rebuking feminists in this way for offering an overly simplistic analysis of vulnerable women and dangerous men, the Boyd report also suggested that opposing minority rights (under multiculturalism) to individual rights was an equally simplistic way of describing what was at issue.[28] Thus, feminist criticisms, including important arguments for inserting safeguards into the *Arbitration Act*, were, in the end, dismissed.

The government's reversal of its position in support of faith-based arbitration came several months after the Boyd report. The reversal was greeted in the press by an even more solidly entrenched set of dualisms involving the secular progressive West and brutal Islam. Journalists such as the *Toronto Star*'s Rosie Dimanno reminded Canadians that the ' time has come for Canadians to be weaned off the teat of multiculturalism as a primary source of sustenance and self-identity.' Adding that we should not be labelled racist for 'daring to champion the secular over the infantalizing religious,' she noted that the government's move is clearly aimed at 'circumscribing Islamic authority.'[29] Others were more subtle, defending the women who had opposed Sharia as women who were in a position to know its dangers.[30] Only Haroon Siddiqui, a journalist at the *Toronto Star*, suggested what the long-term impact of the decision to abolish faith-based arbitration might be, writing that the government had 'bought into fear-mongering that Muslim barbarians are knocking on the gates of Ontario' and was 'engendering an atmosphere of fear and mutual hostility.'[31]

2. Towards Rupturing the Dichotomy

When gender is placed in opposition to culture, and women's status becomes linked to the triumph of the individual over the group, two categories of women are brought into existence: those who have successfully made it out of community and culture and others who are to be assisted into modernity. We are, once again, on the emotional terrain I introduced with the Unni Wikan story, where community stands in the way of women's entrance into modernity, and where civilized Europeans must discipline non-Europeans in order to secure the modern state.

Women who tell a narrative of rescue can forget their own class position and histories and secure their own innocence, a politics many scholars have shown. For example, in her critique of the liberal feminist internationalism of Martha Nussbaum, Sangeeta Ray draws on an article by Anupama Rao on elite Indian feminist responses to Dalit women.[32] Upper-caste feminists understood patriarchy in Dalit women's lives in a way that enabled them to inhabit a non-caste position, Rao showed. The forgetting of their own caste dominance was enabled by an exclusive focus on what Dalit men did to Dalit women. Understanding the complex ways in which Dalit women's oppression is structured requires more critical self-reflection than is evident in Nussbaum and other liberals, Ray argues, and it will require something other than positivist methodology, in which we simply ask Indian women how they feel and either take the words at face value (as Nussbaum does when she asks Indian feminists and Dalit women how they feel) or accuse them of false consciousness or immaturity, as Arjomand does. Addressing the same issues as Ray, Carol Quillen commented:

> If we really want to further the cause of justice, we need to understand how discursive and material structures – race, capitalism, nation-states, orientalism, family, and liberalism itself – shape our very emergence as differentiated 'human' by establishing and then occluding hierarchical relations among us. We need, in other words, a view of the human that focuses on the social and psychological processes of self-formation in a

context that acknowledges, as Chow states, how we can be 'at the mercy' of broad ideological and social structures that in many ways 'speak and act' us.[33]

What do these 'discursive and material structures' look like in the context of the Canadian Sharia debate and how were feminists at the mercy of 'broad ideological and social structures,' as Chow suggests? Certainly ideological and social structures 'speak' us as though we are autonomous individuals who simply contract with each other. If, as Inderpal Grewal reminds us, feminist activism constructs a variety of gendered subjects,[34] how might feminists have avoided being drawn into the framework of superior, secular women, saving their less-enlightened and more-imperilled sisters from religion and community, and still responded to the dangers at hand? Finally, what should feminist politics look like in the Canadian context given the dangers of both white supremacy and patriarchy and the exigencies of a post-9/11 world as they operate in the West?

Feminists who have considered the discursive and material structures operating in the lives of women who find themselves confronting the forces of Muslim fundamentalism in the Middle East (or, more properly, Islamization) have sometimes concluded that women do indeed need to turn to the state as arbiter and to stake their claims on universalist ground, as Canadian feminists did. For example, attempting to move beyond the tradition-modernity divide and to pay attention to the ways that ideological and social structures 'speak' us, Amina Jamal explores how Pakistani feminists in the late 1980s and 1990s resorted to liberal notions of citizenship and gender-neutral notions about rights and the universalism of the public sphere to defend women's rights within a context of an intense Islamization and a corresponding oppression of women.[35] Jamal argues that the perils of liberalism notwithstanding, for Pakistani women confronted by the Islamic state's proposal to change the laws of evidence so that two male witnesses would be required for every crime, or the government's disregard for the murders of women accused of sullying the honour of their communities, it made eminent political sense to insist that the state act as a neutral arbiter over various tribal customs and that it respect fundamental human rights. Simultaneously, women's groups also argued their position from within Islam, maintaining that the proposed law of evidence, for example, was both discriminatory and anti-Islam. It is, however, principally in their appeal to the idea of a 'transcendent citizen-subject' that Jamal finds the counter-hegemonic potential of Pakistani feminist strategies against the evidence rule and the state's tepid response to 'honour' killings.[36] She identifies one central rhetorical strategy of Pakistani feminists, whereby rather than stress that women were particularly vulnerable, they stressed women's rights as citizens, underlining that what was at issue was the meaning of citizenship itself.

Jamal is very careful to assess the social and political context of feminist activism that makes Pakistani feminist political choices comprehensible. She notes, for instance, the rising power during this period of religious parties, which stepped in to fill the void left by the mainstream parties' oscillation between a pro-U.S. position, with its promises of membership in the world community, and an anti-imperialist position that often translates locally as pro-Islamic militancy. Allied sometimes to the military government of General Musharraf, and sometimes opposing it, the religious parties' strength, coupled with Musharraf's attention to U.S. security concerns at the expense of democratization, have been bad news for women's rights. Reminding us that Islamists are not fundamentalists with a fixed set of beliefs but rather individuals engaged in a political project with a particular vision, and noting their practice of deriding critics as 'Westernized' and as 'Westernized women' disloyal to the nation, Jamal suggests that we understand the feminist struggle in Pakistan as one between two competing versions of modernity, and between two competing sections of the middle class. Feminists, she maintains, simply had no other choice but to frame their responses in liberal terms, and we must understand their appropriation of modernity as a strategy. Their approach was not without its perils. To argue, as Pakistani feminists did, for the separation of religion and state was to engage in a battle over the meaning of secularism. As in the Canadian context, where Mumtaz Ali and the Islamic Council insisted that the only true Muslim was one who opted for Sharia law, Pakistani feminists found themselves having to defend themselves as still pro-Islam, and insisting that there were other ways of being Muslim. The call for secularism can mean many things, Jamal insists, including a separation of religion and state or a regulation of religious options within the state. In choosing the options they did, Pakistani feminists simply calculated the odds, understanding what they were up against as the eviction of women from citizenship.

I want to suggest that, differently from the Pakistani context, the appeal to the idea of a transcendent citizen subject carries with it some risks that are specific to the local and global context of white nations in the post-9/11 world. As Jamal herself sees, Pakistani feminists opposing Islamic law do so from a context where such laws affect everyone. Canadian feminists rejecting faith-based arbitration do so in a white settler state, one anxious to control its minority populations and to gain membership in the fraternity of white nations. Being tough on Muslims, as many European scholars have observed, is one significant way in which contemporary Western governments secure both their own domestic base (through appealing to the right and consolidating the idea that there is one white national culture) and their international stature (through appearing to be active participants of the 'war on terror'). To consider the material and discursive structures in our own context, Canadian feminists had to be worried by the growing resonance of the idea of a clash of civilizations and the intense regulation in the West of those scripted on the Muslim side of the divide. When feminist strategies unhesitatingly invoked the idea that Islam and Muslim men were intrinsically threatening, and a secular state was the only way to safeguard women's rights, they provided grist for an already powerful mill: as the antithesis of Western civilization, Muslim populations in the West have to be watched and regulated, a surveillance that begins at the border. The companion idea installed by the notion that a secular state provides the best protection is the idea that the normative citizen is one without group-based loyalties, a figure for whom communitarian identities are best kept at home. This 'unbiased liberal subject,' as Gokariksel and Mitchell argue, is extremely important for neo-liberal state formation and economic development, effects Canadian feminists needed to consider more seriously than was evident during the 'Sharia debate' in Ontario.[37] That the unbiased liberal subject achieves definition through comparison to the racialized subject (viewed as communitarian, hence biased) should give us greater pause when we invoke the idea of a free-floating citizen.

Secularism as a Form of Governmentality

In the West, feminist faith in the state and in secularism sits uneasily alongside current legislative and policy moves to restrict the rights of immigrants and racial minorities in the name of anti-terrorism and the protection of Western civilization as secular and modern. As discussed in chapter 1, the *Anti-Terrorism Act*, with its suspension of fundamental rights, for instance, has created a perilous situation for Muslims or those who are taken to be Muslims, a situation often defended as the West's need to protect itself from a barbaric Islam. For another instance, the use of security certificates (discussed in chapter 1) under the *Immigration and Refugee Protection Act* to detain Muslim men who are not citizens, and to deport them after a secret trial in which they are not allowed to hear the evidence against them, suggests that the post-9/11 era has not offered much evidence of Western states' commitment to universalism. How might we reconcile the actions of a state prepared to deprive Muslims of the right of habeas corpus and to hold them in solitary confinement for years without due process with the same state's protection of Muslim women from the men of their communities?

The state's central conceptual tool in suspending the rights of those suspected of involvement in terrorism or considered to have the potential to be terrorists has been the idea that Islam breeds a particular pre-modern subject, one who possesses a violent hatred of the West and who is not committed to the rule of law, respect for human rights and women's rights, or democracy.[38] The Western subject, in contrast, is one who has progressed into modernity, a progression marked principally by his entrance into the secular, the religious leanings of leaders such as George W. Bush notwithstanding. Thus, one might begin to delineate the conditions under which Canadian feminists engaged in the debate over faith-based arbitration by considering how modern states secure their power through the idea of secularism.

Secularism is popularly understood in the way that the philosopher Charles Taylor describes its origins. As Talal Asad discusses in his book *Formations of the Secular*, Taylor argues that the modern state has to make citizenship the primary principle of identity because this is the only way that it can transcend the conflicts that emerge from different identities. But secularism does not simply provide peace and toleration, as Taylor imagines. Secularism secures the power of the state as neutral arbiter. For Taylor, the state resolves the quarrels among different groups through persuasion and negotiation. Asad sees a less benign state that exercises force to guarantee the social arrangements it wants. At its inception in Europe, secularism as political doctrine guaranteed the peace between warring religious factions by shifting the site of violence from within Europe to outside of it. Secularism's triumph as political doctrine is closely connected to colonialism and to the rise of a system of capitalist nation-states. Of all the things that secularism can mean, it has not always meant tolerance. Those who do not fit the public personality of the state are simply defined as religious minorities and find themselves in a defensive position. Asad's arguments suggest that we examine what contemporary notions of secularism secure for Western states and that we abandon the romantic idea that secularism simply represents progress from the pre-modern to the modern.

Asad's comments on the hijab affair in France are perhaps most pertinent here.[39] As in the Sharia debate in Ontario, the vast majority of French intellectuals of both the left and the right felt that 'the secular character of the Republic is under threat because of Islam, which they see as being symbolized by the headscarf.' In France the secular character of the Republic is captured in the concept of *laicité* which most people trace to the end of the nineteenth century. Asad reminds us of its earlier foundation. In the sixteenth-century wars of religion, European Christian states adopted the principle that the religion of the ruler is the religion of the state. What is significant here is that a political principle replaced a religious one and 'transcendent power and authority were now given to the state to decide not only on who was deserving of religious tolerance but on what precisely religious tolerance was.' In Europe we then see French Protestants getting the right to practise their religion in Catholic France at the same time that Spain is expelling its Muslim converts. By the time of the French revolution, when religion comes largely to mean personal belief and the church simply appears as a rival for political power, there is bitter conflict between church and state, a conflict that the state wins in the name of the revolution's ideals of humanity and progress.

Public schools at the end of the nineteenth century became a way in which the state schooled its citizens to take on their new role as secular citizens without conflicting loyalties. A significant amount of France's imperial conquests took place at this time. 'Anti-clerical schooling at home, unequal agreements with the Church, and imperial expansion abroad were the pillars on which *laicité* was established under the Third Republic.' Asad advances the interesting argument that today in France the sixteenth-century political rule (that the religion of the ruler is the religion of the state) is still the operating principle, and what continues to be significant is 'not the maintenance or interdiction of a particular religion by the state ... but the installation

of a single power drawn from a single source and facing a single political task: the worldly care of its population regardless of its beliefs.'
The state takes it upon itself to determine signs of religion's presence
(rather than who is and is not of the religion of the ruler), and in this
way manages various populations through its activities, populations
marked as 'religious' *for one reason or another*. One way to regulate
Muslim populations in France is to mark them formally as populations that must be forcibly brought into the modern through secularism. So seductive is this vision of a modern people civilizing a pre-
modern one that few have considered what else has been achieved by
the banning of headscarves and how the power of the state and its
management of a subordinate population is manifested in the French
context.

I would offer the French rather than the Pakistani situation as the
one that Canadian feminists should consider for lessons in how secularism operates as the management of the conduct of racialized immigrant populations in the West today. As Asad clarifies, the 'headscarf
worn by Muslim women was held to be a religious sign conflicting
with the state's secular personality.'[40] The Stasi commission appointed
to investigate headscarves in schooling interpreted the wearing of
headscarves as the 'will to display' Muslim identity.[41] Since the state
was owed exclusive loyalty in the public sphere, the wearing of headscarves had to be banned. Both the interpretation of what the headscarf means to its wearers and the state's decision to insist that citizens
have a public identity that is exclusive must be understood within a
context of profound suspicion of Muslims.

Asad concludes that important questions were not asked about the
state's reasons for finding the headscarf in schools incompatible with
the practice of French citizenship. First, everyone who lives in France
is not equal before the law. A number of Muslims from France's former
colonies live, work, and pay taxes in France but do not enjoy full citizenship rights. A focus on the veil as a practice antithetical to citizenship marks Muslims as undeserving of full citizenship rights (as
incompletely modern peoples) and it obscures the legitimate griev-
ances that French Muslims have concerning their unequal treatment.
Second, the French state is ceding some of its national autonomy to the
European Union as a result of the exigencies of a global economy. The
control of migrant populations is a central aspect of these largely
hidden manoeuvres, as is the installation of a citizen subject who is
autonomous and without group loyalties or claims. Finally, the circu-

lation of media images and narratives across borders profoundly shape 'the direction of fears, longings, resentments towards peoples and places.'[42] These factors suggest that we are a long way from the uncomplicated idea of a majority of citizens deciding that the social contract requires the banning of the wearing of headscarfs. If these unasked questions were engaged with, we would have to consider how the public sphere might be negotiated creatively given citizens' transnational loyalties and the fact that they do not live their lives in a strict separation of politics and religion, nor are they autonomous subjects freely contracting with each other.

Why is it important to deconstruct the secular and inquire into its productive function? Here again, Asad is clear that the important point is to ask what the secular/religious, modernity/pre-modernity distinction secures.

> Modernity is a *project* – or rather, a series of interlinked projects – that certain people in power seek to achieve. The project aims at institutionalizing a number of (sometimes conflicting, often evolving) principles: constitutionalism, moral autonomy, democracy, human rights, civil equality, industry, consumerism, freedom of the market – and secularism. It employs proliferating technologies (of production, warfare, travel, entertainment, medicine) that generate new experiences of space and time, of cruelty and health, of consumption and knowledge. The notion that these experiences constitute 'disenchantment' – implying a direct access to reality, a stripping away of myth, magic, and the sacred – is a salient feature of the modern epoch.[43]

The categories of secular and religious are the 'terms on which modern living is required to take place, and nonmodern peoples are invited to assess their adequacy. For representations of "the secular" and the "religious" in modern and modernizing states mediate people's identities, help shape their sensibilities, and guarantee their experiences.'[44] As Étienne Balibar has shown,

> individuality itself is always an institution, it has to be represented and acknowledged, which can be reached only if the individual is released from strict membership or a 'fusion' within his (her) Gemeinschaft, thus becoming able to adopt various social roles, to 'play on several memberships,' or to 'shift identity' in order to perform different social functions, while remaining a member of a superior community or a 'subject.' It has

problematic prerequisites, however, because it is connected with the imposition of normality, a normal or standard way of life and a set of beliefs (a 'dominant' practical ideology), which has to be maintained for successive generations, at least for the overwhelming majority, or the 'mainstream,' across class and other barriers.[45]

The implications of taking these ideas seriously are, I believe, that feminists can no longer simplistically assume that the secular is a haven for women, and religion a dangerous place. Lest the point about how the power of the state is mediated be missed, it should be abundantly clear that a reversal strategy, where religion is safe for women and the state is not, would interrupt neither empire nor patriarchy. Instead, keeping a steady eye on their productive function, we, as feminists, would have to consider what we achieve and what we sustain by our strategies as they feed into the state's personality and its particular version of the secular and the religious, as well as into the specific patriarchies of Muslims and non-Muslims in Canada. We should remember that patriarchies themselves are not only cultural practices but systems interlocked with capitalism and white supremacy.[46] Finally, we need to keep our eye on the transnational effects of our strategies, something those against faith-based arbitration understood clearly but only in the context of the spread of fundamentalisms and not in the context of a global white supremacy manifesting as the American bid for empire. Canadian feminists did not consider fundamentalism's mirror image, the spread of the idea that a family of white nations must wage war on terror and religion through the institution of Western law and secularism.

The Neoliberal Subject

Gokariksel and Mitchell have usefully clarified how secularism produces the neoliberal subject. Understanding global neoliberalism as 'a political philosophy of governance that upholds an active achievement of a *laissez-faire* economic system,' they note:

> The concept of neo-liberal governance concerns the ways in which individual 'subjects' are regulated and disciplined through various institutions and processes in society so that they come to understand their own positions and personhood in ways that are compatible with neo-liberal trends towards individual autonomy and entrepreneurship and away

from a more social understanding of the world and of the relationship between the state and its citizens.[47]

The idea of a monocultural, secular state works to consolidate who is understood to be the ideal citizen. Since the ideal citizen is an individual without any sort of group-based identity, a non-citizen is someone who remains trapped within group-based identities. The terrible danger of the autonomous individual as citizen is the closing down of the possibility of acknowledging group-based harm, as well as group-based privilege. If, as Lauren Berlant has shown, property, privacy, and individuality become 'the only ground for the true practice of nationhood' and the ideal citizen is unanchored in history and concrete social relations, then specific harms such as colonialism and racism cannot be acknowledged. Conversely, the specific entitlements enjoyed by colonizers (in this case, the right to be seen as normative citizens) become invisible.[48] Reparations or strategies designed for specific groups come to seem like 'catering to the unique sensitivity of a small group' and not as part of an answer to a highly structured inequality.[49] It is this logic that enables so many to easily dismiss Black-focused schools and affirmative action as encouraging narrow tribal identities rather than the redressing of contemporary and historical injustice. Why don't we all just assimilate is the plaintive response to historical injustice increasingly heard whenever racial minorities press their claims for justice.

The call for assimilation and the idea that the nation must be a single, unified, homogeneous body is one that is highly compatible with a white-supremacist agenda and with the surveillance of Muslims. The Stasi commission, as Ezekiel observed, believed that the 'concern with oneness prevails over all expression of difference, perceived as a threat.'[50] If Muslims are unassimilable, then the state is justified in keeping them out or limiting their citizenship rights. Monoculture readily collapses into anti-immigrant sentiment, as Sivanandan argues, referring to the British context. Assimilationist discourses are not only the basis to anti-immigrant positions but are eminently productive for the 'war on terror.' Multiculturalism, the argument goes, 'has been instrumental in breeding terrorists by steeping them in their own culture and so alienating them from British society.'[51] The best anti-terrorist move, then, is to forcibly integrate citizens, a logic that conveniently ignores the role that injustice, military occupations, and racism play in producing terrorists.

As Liz Fekete documents, the citizen subject without ties to community is the conceptual underpinning for a number of repressive measures across Europe:

> Assimilation is being forced through by the adoption of a number of measures, which include the recasting of citizenship laws according to security considerations; the introduction of compulsory language and civics tests for citizenship applicants; codes of conduct for the trustees of mosques; [and] a cultural code of conduct for Muslim girls and women who, in some areas of Europe, will be forbidden to wear the hijab in state institutions.[52]

It is impossible, Fekete concludes, to divorce the current debate on a single, unified national culture from the 'war on terror.' Fekete asks where the ban on the headscarf will end, noting that in France the government is considering extending its ban to other public spaces and producing in the process a stigmatized and humiliated Muslim population. The French public has already understood the banning of the hijab as licence to do just that, as Ezekiel reports. Although the ban applies to schools, Muslim women wearing headscarfs have found themselves being prevented from doing a wide number of things (working, volunteering, receiving medical services, registering for a marriage, etc.) as citizens take it into their own hands to manage public space, as Ghassan Hage insightfully shows for the Australian context as well.[53] The banning of the hijab made clear who rightfully belongs in public space. The banning of faith-based arbitration in Ontario, coming as it did with all the attendant discourses about modernity and pre-modernity and the normative citizen as someone without ties to community, may well have the same effect.

In Canada, it was quickly evident that the categories of the secular and the religious as oppositions were enabled by, and simultaneously productive of, the idea of a world of civilized Canadians at risk from Muslim terrorists and unassimilable immigrants. Sharia law became an issue of the importation of immigrants' feudal and pre-modern values into a civilized land. Quebec's international-relations minister expressed this view succinctly: 'We must rework the social contract (for immigrants) so that the people, Muslims who want to come to Quebec and who do not respect women's rights, or rights, whatever they may be, in our civil code, at that moment, then they stay in their country and do not come to Quebec, because it's unacceptable.'[54]

The real threat, however, lay not with the importation of feudal values but, more directly, in the presence of dangerous Muslims. A journalist spelled out these connections in a popular women's magazine by writing about Mumtaz Syed Ali that the retired Toronto lawyer was 'linked to a "self-described fundamentalist" who is the cleric at a mosque attended by the grandparents of a young man who has admitted his connections to Al Qaeda.'[55] Terrorist by association (and a long one at that), to stop Syed Mumtaz Ali and the Islamic Institute was to take on terrorism itself. Ariane Brunet of the human-rights organization Rights and Democracy chided Canadians that a civilized nation with a well-known commitment to peace could not possibly tolerate Sharia: 'Here is Canada, the peacemaker, the mediator. We have an image here. And here we're adopting the Sharia law.'[56] In Canada the state seeks to show its membership in the family of civilized nations through its participation in 'anti-terrorism' activities. Through peacekeeping, as I have argued elsewhere, Canada secures its reputation as a nation that is not implicated in the crises that befall the Third World. Rather, our role is simply one of mediator, assisting the Third World out of the morass into which it has mysteriously fallen. Feminist narratives about saving Muslim women through the imposition of secularism rely on the same omissions that underpin the national narrative of a peacekeeping nation. That is, they obscure how the state manages its minority populations and produces neoliberal subjects, sustaining the very conditions in which fundamentalisms thrive – conditions of social and economic marginality.

To avoid sustaining the colour line between tribal Muslims and a modern state, feminists must complicate the simple frames available for understanding how and where patriarchy operates. While for Nobel Prize–winner Shirin Ebadi it may be understandable to consider secularism the only appropriate response to the idea of Islamic tribunals,[57] from the perspective of a state where fundamentalists have *not* achieved anything like the power they achieved in Iran or Pakistan, and in view of the state's compelling interest in marking Muslims and indeed all Third World immigrants as pre-modern and confined to the realm of the culturally marked, perhaps the best response to Syed Ali and his small group might well have been to flood the market with alternative stories of culture, rather than to grant the conservative religious narrative the legitimacy it won by feminists opposing it outright in the name of secularism. It is by no means evident that this strategy would have ruptured the secular/religious, modern/pre-modern divide, but an equal possibility exists that by re-inscribing so completely these dualisms, feminist gains were made at too great an expense.

Conclusion

Azizah Al-Hibri once warned: 'If Western feminists are now vying for control of the lives of immigrant women by justifying coercive state action, then, these women have not learned the lessons of history, be it colonialism, imperialism or even fascism.[58] Making another related point, Abdullahi An-Na'im noted that a human-rights strategy based on gender alone is disastrous. Such a strategy inevitably depends upon, even as it sustains, the idea that 'unmarked' cultures and people (dominant groups are thought to have values while subordinate groups have culture) are already in the modern, while 'marked' groups remain in pre-modernity. As An-Na'im put it, the minority culture is required to clean up its gender act, while the majority culture can take all the time it wants. The argument for gender equality, he insisted, has to be made within culture, and the polarity of gender versus culture has to be undermined. What might Canadian feminists have done to mitigate the power of the state to use feminist concerns to stigmatize and police Muslims and to produce the normative citizen as unconnected to community? How could arguments for gender equality have been made within culture rather than in opposition to it?

The 'Sharia law' debate quickly developed into a spectacle. Those advocating the use of Sharia garnered attention, which only grew as more feminists came on board to denounce them. Here we might consider strategy. Knowing that a full-scale moral panic is entirely likely given today's geopolitics, did feminist groups sufficiently consider the conditions of communication as they immediately embraced the position of the secular over the religious? I wonder what would have been the outcome had Muslim feminists in particular, regardless of their own misgivings, expended more energy on the question, What is needed to safeguard faith-based arbitration for women? The Council of Muslim Women did in fact consider this question, inviting those in favour of faith-based arbitration to a discussion. In the end, however, the dangers posed by faith-based arbitration were considered too great to risk pursuing faith-based alternatives. This was perhaps a strategic error. It might have been possible to get more safeguards within the

Arbitration Act to protect Muslim women who use it, or who are coerced into using it, although the government seemed unwilling to consider this option, as the Boyd report demonstrated. At the very least, the circulation of ideas about alternative ways to be Muslim might have tempered the production of the neoliberal subject as citizen.

It is easy in hindsight to see how there could have been more discussion about the racist dangers present in a modernity/pre-modernity distinction. For example, there could have been a feminist conference on what post-9/11 conditions have meant for Muslim communities. In other words, could the power of conservative Muslims have been diffused through rhetorical strategies that emphasized that there were other ways of being Muslim? And other dangers? To point out that Syed Mumtaz Ali and his new organization had not consulted widely in Muslim communities and to emphasize his group's limited base of support might not have worked as a strategy, however, given the dominant group's investment in the idea that Muslims are an undifferentiated pre-modern people. As Sivanandan and Ezekiel both point out, Western states have been willing to foster separatist religious enclaves providing such groups restrict their claims to culture. In Britain, the anti-racist basis to multiculturalism (responding to specific group claims of injustice) lost ground as the state became willing to respond more to cultural demands for separate spaces than to demands that required redistribution.[59] In France, the French government concurred with the creation of the French Muslim Council, made up of representatives of mosques: the larger the mosque (measured in square footage), the greater the number of representatives, a regulation that facilitated the domination of mosques funded by the Gulf states. Muslim women have little chance of being heard either within community or outside of it as conservative men become the legitimized representatives of community.[60] Finally, in Canada, the Ontario government has resisted the demand for Black-focused schools, a measure intended to counter the drop-out rate of African Canadians, a national commitment to multiculturalism notwithstanding. Under these conditions, it would not have been easy for Muslim women to contest the meaning of what it means to be a Muslim and a citizen of a modern state. If feminists had few tools with which to confront the strategies of governance in neoliberal and white-supremacist states, however, at the very least we could have refrained from deliberately invoking the spectre of a clash of civilizations and the necessity of keeping pre-modern peoples in line.

I do not have answers for negotiating the currents of contemporary neoliberalism and empire, only suggested strategies to interrupt the powerful deployment of the imperilled Muslim woman as the means to draw a colour line between the modern and the pre-modern. My suggestions concern subjecting the state to as much scrutiny as we do conservative religious groups. Where I run aground, however, is in the perception of risk. Many of my good friends breathed a sigh of relief when Premier McGuinty announced the end of faith-based arbitration. These are friends who know the power of fundamentalism and how much it oppresses women. They are women who insist that Sharia always works in favour of men and that for it to work otherwise requires considerable resources that Canadian Muslim women do not have. Making equality arguments within Islam certainly requires a long-term strategy.

As things stand, Canadian Muslim communities will continue to use Islamic principles informally and women remain unprotected in this arena. However, should a woman be able to turn to common law, something that requires resources and a willingness to live without community, the possibility exists that she may be able to secure her rights under Western law. But here too, we must note that Muslim women's experiences of Canadian law have not been entirely positive and that our secular state is a racist state, complete with patriarchal and racist judges. At the end of the day, something positive may have been achieved in that the plans of a small conservative religious faction may have been upset, but it has been achieved through reinforcing some rather terrible dualisms (women's rights versus multiculturalism; West versus Muslims; enlightened Western feminists versus imperilled Muslim women) that, in a post-9/11 era, has tremendous utility for states seeking to regulate Muslim populations. Was it worth it? Only time will tell, but my guess is that the way is paved, if it was not before, for the kinds of laws we are seeing in Europe, which are enacted in the name of protecting Muslim women but are thinly disguised methods of putting Muslim populations under heavy surveillance while relieving the state of scrutiny about its practices towards both Muslims and all women. As in the narratives of rescue with which I began, it seems likely that Muslim women won some protection, but only at the cost of increasing anti-Muslim/anti-immigrant racism and consolidating the idea of civilized Europeans. When the 'war on terror' in the West requires imperilled Muslim women and dangerous Muslim men as a central part of its conceptual apparatus, we become obligated as anti-imperial feminists to pursue anti-patriarchal strategies within, rather than outside, our communities, the difficulties of doing so notwithstanding.

Conclusion: Casting Out

The chapters of this book were initially written as separate projects, and so it was only at the end that I discovered I had written a book about Muslims and the law in the post-9/11 period. I had began the initial project with a broad concern about the culturalization of racism. As I explored in *Looking White People in the Eye: Gender, Race, and Culture in Courtrooms and Classrooms*,[1] a central way in which racism is organized in contemporary society is through a language of culture. Although racialized groups are no longer widely portrayed as biologically inferior (as a cruder version of racism would have it), dominant groups often perceive subordinate groups as possessing *cultures* that are inferior and overly patriarchal, a move described as the culturalization of racism. I set out to explore whether the prevalence of the culturalization of racism shaped the perception and practice of legal and medical professionals who wanted to consider cultural differences. Specifically, what analytical frameworks would enable professionals to assess the meaning and relevance of cultural differences without ranking cultures and inadvertently making legal and medical decisions based on the de-valorizing of non-white cultures? Was culture talk inevitably race talk? It wasn't long, however, before I discovered that discussions about culture in the post-9/11 period disproportionately focused on Muslims. It became clear that these responses to Muslims were organized around the idea of a clash of civilizations, and more significantly around the notion that Muslims posed a threat to Western civilization. When people I interviewed expressed these views, they often drew on global discourses and spoke about the law. Canadians began to express views about Muslims that had been more common in Europe, where Muslims constitute the largest group of migrants. For example, in the past, Canadians have had relatively little trouble with the idea of schoolgirls wearing the hijab or with prayer rooms for Muslims and other groups. In the post-9/11 period, however, this apparently greater ease with different religions and cultures began to disappear. This book emerged as an attempt to understand what all the anxiety I observed in my research project and in my daily life was about.

Race informs everything concerning how I have come to think about Muslims in today's world. As I have shown, Muslims are stigmatized, put under surveillance, denied full citizenship rights, and detained in camps on the basis that they are a pre-modern people located outside of reason, a people against whom a secular, modern people must protect themselves. Once confined outside modernity, evicted as it were to the uncivilized side of things, Muslims are also evicted from the law. The law, it has long been held, does not apply to barbarians, and the West has often denied the benefits of modernity to those it considers outside of it. My insistence on the racial underpinnings of empire offers, I believe, a direction to those of us seeking to dismantle it. If we consider the evictions from law described in this book as racial processes, we can begin to challenge the idea of the modern itself, and find the courage to imagine a better world. If, however, we miss how race structures modernity, we are likely to get caught up in the powerful fiction that what is principally wrong with the world is that some people have mysteriously failed to progress into modernity while others excel at it. As I noted in my introduction, this kind of thinking is only another way of saying that some groups are inherently more rational than others.

How have the events of 9/11 influenced the perceptions and the treatment of Muslims? While the attacks on the World Trade Center and the Pentagon, events that triggered what came to be called the 'war on terror,' caused the deaths of three thousand people, some believe the loss of lives in North America and Europe through terrorism since 9/11 must be put along side the massacres, slower deaths, and daily suffering caused by the collective imperialism of the West. It is believed that close to a million Iraqis have died since the occupation, for instance, and in the decade before, the thousands of children who died as a direct result of Western sanctions against Iraq have yet to be counted as casualties.[2] Few Westerners think that we are implicated in the violence of our world. Instead, we are now much more likely to believe in what I have identified as a contemporary form of race thinking, namely, the story that we are under siege by Muslims and that our governments must save us from this threat. We agree for the most part that stern measures must be taken against 'those who do not share our values.' In every Western country, laws are enacted that suspend due-process rights for terror suspects, enable states to detain indefinitely, permit the 'rendition' of suspects to places where they can be tortured with impunity, limit the citizenship rights of those considered not to share in the values of Western civilization, and cast out Muslims from political community. Enacted in the name of national emergency, these laws announce a clash of civilizations between the West and Islam and the urgent need for the West to defend itself against Islam. Muslims have in this way been evicted from the rule of law and from moder-nity. This is not at all to imply that what happens to Muslims is excep-tional, in the sense normally attached to the word. On the contrary, I locate the eviction of Muslims from the law within a culture of excep-tion, wherein states increasingly exercise the sovereign right to exclude and to abandon populations in the interests of governance.

In *The Colonial Present*, Derek Gregory describes three strategic moves made by administrations in Washington and Tel Aviv in the shadow of the attacks on the World Trade Center and the Pentagon: locating, opposing, and casting out. Locating refers to the way in which those to be obliterated are reduced to objects in a visual field, coordinates on a grid, or letters on a map. Targets are destroyed but not people. Opposing refers to the strategy of reducing antagonism to a conflict between 'a unitary Civilization and multiple barbarisms.' Barbarians are to be 'summarily dispatched.' Finally, casting out mobi-lizes 'a largely political-juridical register, in which not only armed opponents – al-Qaeda terrorists, Taliban troops, Palestinian fighters, Iraqi soldiers – but also civilians and refugees were reduced to the status of *homines sacri*.'[3] Referring here to Agamben's concept of bare life, those who 'may be killed yet not sacrificed,' Gregory calls atten-tion to what may be described as a hallmark of our age: the confine-ment of large numbers of people to camps, people who can be reduced to bare life on the basis of religion, race, and ethnic origin. Agamben suggests that a camp is created every time a structure gives rise to a place where the rule of law does not operate. Bodies become camps when they are cast into a state of indeterminacy that is simultaneously inside and outside the law. For such bodies, judicial protection no longer applies, as the law itself determines that they are to be deprived of fundamental rights.[4]

In using the term 'casting out' for the title of this book, I wish to underline that the eviction of Muslims from political community is a racial *process* that begins with Muslims being marked as a different level of humanity and being assigned a separate and unequal place in the law. Evictions and the camps they create do not all resemble the classic concentration camp. Gregory's emphasis on the multiple practices of empire captures the many ways in which evictions happen. Race thinking structures the exception since it is invoked as a measure of self-defence against those whose inherent difference threatens the nation. From this perspective, whenever the exception is invoked, we can expect to see that it is undergirded by the notion that there are two levels of humanity. We must also consider the inverse as true: when the notion of two levels of humanity is invoked, the legal exception is not far behind.

If it is hard to distinguish contemporary state-of-exception measures from the ongoing management of racial populations, this is only because the exception inheres in several legal and bureaucratic structures. The immigrant and refugee, for example, have long been considered exceptions in the eyes of the law, and the legal and administrative mechanisms that limit their rights have been used to great advantage since the 'war on terror' began. The people who are evicted from political community who are discussed in this book include non-citizens detained indefinitely under security certificates, prisoners tortured at Abu Ghraib prison in Iraq, Palestinians, and Muslim migrants to Europe and North America whose citizenship rights are limited and who are stigmatized and put under surveillance. While a qualitative difference between the regular management of racial populations and contemporary practices of the exception may not be discernable in every instance, I have argued that it is important to take notice of the *increasing* number of people who are evicted from the law, and thus from political community, abandoned outright in camps or stigmatized *as the culturally different*, and thus undeserving of membership in the polity. Violence is easily authorized against those who do not belong.

In this book I have examined the legal and bureaucratic processes of casting out through which we accomplish the eviction of Muslims and Arabs from political community. Race thinking, in particular the melding of race and bureaucracy, render these evictions invisible or as instances of mere fidelity to the rule of law and a legitimate defence of civilization in response to the threat from those who do not share its values. We imagine that people are 'security risks,' not persons who 'disappear,' who are simply deported. Through appeal to the idea of a clash of civilizations, evictions become defensible. A pitiless secularism and monoculture is enforced in the name of modernity and not in the name of capital, invasions, occupations, and the structures of unequal citizenship they sustain. I have shown that if we reject the introduction of 'sharia' into the law, for example, it is easy to make the claim that we only do so because we are committed to secularism and not because a marking of Muslims as pre-modern serves the interests of empire. Similarly, who could be against the introduction of laws designed to prohibit the forced marriages of young Muslim girls to men outside Europe and to safeguard the right to make one's own choices about marriage? One does not have to be a committed feminist to wish for the end of the Taliban and their relentless and punishing misogyny.

What I have tried to make clear, to repeat Talal Asad's point discussed in chapter 5, is that modernity is a project that certain people in power seek to achieve. Freedom of the market, freedom of choice, secularism, individualism, and gender equality are ideas *harnessed* to the project of empire. They are made to function as a kind of dividing line between those who are modern and those who are not. What is so terrible about this? I contend that this framing of what is wrong with the world leaves no room for interrogating the more insidious ways in which modern states secure their power, the economic, social, and political arrangements on which human rights, individualism, and gender equality rest, arrangements that have required the domination of the North over the South and the eviction of large numbers of people from political community. Meaningful gender-equality strategies elude us when we isolate the problem as one of culture and fail to consider the social, economic, and political conditions under which equality thrives. Afghan women today are free of Taliban rule, but their lives have remained relatively unchanged in the ways that count the most; their personal security and that of their families are not assured.

The insistence that modernity is an idea and not a project has left in place a conception of the ideal citizen as someone unanchored in history and concrete social relations. Such a sovereign subject knows himself or herself as autonomous only through comparison to an Other, considered to be less advanced and still mired in community. Muslim men's and women's bodies become the ground on which we construct ourselves as modern and as sovereign. I have described this identity-making process as a structure of feeling, and as participation in a collective fantasy about being members of a superior civilization. Individuals come to understand their place in the world as dependent on such practices as freeing the Muslim woman and confining the Muslim man, ridding the world of all that is pre-modern and dangerous.

Of course it can be claimed that as the Western world achieves some distance from the events of 9/11, fewer and fewer people are drawn into a collective fantasy about the Orient. Indeed, as the *Toronto Star* reported, a British Broadcasting Corporation World Poll of twenty-seven countries released on 19 February 2007 concluded that 'in spite of a climate of anxiety, 56 per cent believe common ground can be found between Muslims and the West and only 26 per cent feel fundamental cultural differences are to blame for tensions between them.'[5] It is certainly possible that cooler heads have prevailed, but the evidence mounts that ordinary people continue to imagine themselves besieged by men in beards and women in veils, and their imaginings are collective ones that are taken seriously politically. The grip that the fantasy has on ordinary people even extends to their perception of Muslim children. When even children are considered threats, we can surmise that there is even greater anxiety and fear concerning adults.

What are we to make of an eleven-year-old girl being sent off the soccer field for wearing a hijab? The referee, himself a Muslim, ruled that the headscarf posed a risk of accidental strangulation. The premier of the province of Quebec, Jean Charest, supported the referee's decision.[6] The board of the International Football Association, to whom the Quebec Soccer Federation appealed, upheld the ban, announcing categorically: 'It's absolutely right to be sensitive to people's thoughts and philosophies, but equally there has to be a set of laws that are adhered to, and we favour Law 4 [outlining the basic equipment required in soccer] being adhered to.'[7] The preoccupation with the Muslim woman's body, and with the veil specifically, is becoming as intense as it was in colonial Algeria, an indicator, surely, of the resurgence of old colonial relationships and the structures of feeling on which they rely. It is not insignificant, too, that soccer officials turned to 'their' law and put their faith in Law 4 of the soccer rule book. Their response must be situated within a broader context where multiculturalism is under attack (we are too generous to minorities and they abuse our trust by refusing to leave their pre-modern practices behind) and it is permissible to express openly anti-immigrant sentiments. Law, with its insistence on abstract individuals who exist outside history, secures the dividing line between the modern and the pre-modern. In modernity, individuals cannot have loyalties to anyone but the state. In Balibar's words, we 'administer the universal by subjecting individuals to it (the school, judiciary, public health and other systems),' a process that 'has gone hand in hand with a vast system of social exclusions that appear as the counterpoint of the normalization and socialization of anthropological differences.'[8]

If eleven-year-old girls wearing the hijab haunt our imaginations and provoke an anxious expulsion, other eleven year olds held in detention camps merit less attention. Around the same time that Asmahan Mansour was being ordered off the soccer field, giving rise to a mad scramble among officials for their laws and regulation books, another Canadian Muslim child, detained with his Iranian parents at a Texas detention centre for illegal immigrants, a place activists describe as a dismal prison unsuitable for children, occasioned much less interest.[9] Had there been such a scramble in the case of this child, it is possible that no law would be found to secure his release. Instead, anyone wishing to protest this child's and his parents' detention would run headlong into the exception – the placing of immigrants and refugees beyond the reach of the law. While the family's Canadian lawyer ultimately succeeded in securing their release to Canadian authorities, U.S. authorities are acting within the law in holding an eleven year old in the detention facility.[10]

Race thinking has made it possible to reconcile what is done to each of these children. Each is expelled from full humanity as deserving subjects. In Mansour's case, there is no pretense of exploring reasonable accommodation of a religious practice. Her status as a member of a stigmatized population stalls any thinking about accommodation, even though this option may still be available to her under the Charter of Rights and Freedoms. Hers is a case of a social rather than a fully legally authorized expulsion. The full weight of the law may not be far behind, however, as was the case for girls prohibited from wearing the hijab in public schools in France. In the case of the child in detention, I have argued in this book that we come to accept the eviction of immigrants and refugees from the law through race thinking, the belief that there are two levels of humanity and two corresponding legal regimes. Citizens sharing territory and the right to punish strangers may not seem like ideas that are automatically embedded in race thinking. Modern nations have long preserved spaces for non-citizens that might be characterized as the antecedents to the camp, spaces of indefinite detention where, as Bauman describes for today's refugees, 'time is suspended; it is time but not history.'[11] If we, those of us marked as normative citizens, are able to accept, and even more, to derive comfort from the fact that non-citizens have fewer rights, if, as Mosse shows, 'the foreigner outside the tribe has never been welcome,'[12] it is only because we require the distinction between those inside and outside the tribe to mark our own belonging. In this project of modernity, like all such projects, race has a stellar role to play.

Notes

Introduction

1 Achille Mbembe, 'Necropolitics,'trans. Libby Meintjes, *Public Culture* 15, no. 1 (2003): 24.

2 Giorgio Agamben, *State of Exception*, trans. Kevin Attell (Chicago: University of Chicago Press, 2005), 39.

3 Canadian Press, 'U.S. Security Rules Force Quebec Plant to Shuffle Staff,' *Toronto Star*, 12 January 2007, A8.

4 Tara Perkins, 'Royal Bank Caught by American Sanctions,' *Toronto Star*, 17 January 2007, F1.

5 Dene Moore, 'Quebec Town Bans Kirpans, Stoning Women,' *Globe and Mail*, 30 January 2007, A12.

6 Sean Gordon, 'Quebec Town Spawns Uneasy Debate,' *Toronto Star*, 5 February 2007, A1, A4.

7 Trevor Wilhelm and Dalson Chen, *Windsor Star*, 13 January 2007, http://www.canada.com/windsorstar/news/story.html?id=465428a2 -657b-4732-b12f-e07548dda592.

8 Mbebe, 'Necropolitics'; Avery Gordon, 'Abu Ghraib: Imprisonment and the War on Terror,' *Race & Class* 48, no.1 (2006): 42–59.

9 Hannah Arendt, *On the Origins of Totalitarianism* (New York: Harcourt, Brace, Jovanovich Publishers, 1973), 296–7.

10 Thomas Blom Hansen and Finn Stepputat, 'Introduction,' in *Sovereign Bodies: Citizens, Migrants, and States in the Postcolonial World*, ed. Hansen and Stepputat (Princeton: Princeton University Press, 2005), 17.

11 Irene M. Silverblatt, *Modern Inquisition: Peru and the Colonial Origins of the Civilized World* (Durham: Duke University Press, 2005), 17–18.

12 Ibid., 17.

13 David Goldberg, *Racist Culture: Philosophy and the Politics of Meaning* (Cambridge, MA: Blackwell, 1993), 63.

14 Rudyard Kipling, quoted in Carl Berger, 'The True North Strong and Free,' in *Nationalism in Canada*, ed. Peter Russell (Toronto: McGraw Hill, 1966), 18.

15 Eric Voegelin, 'The Growth of the Race Idea,' *Review of Politics* 2, no. 3 (July 1940): 283–317.

16 Arendt, *On the Origins of Totalitarianism*, 159.

17 Ibid., 186.

18 George L. Mosse, *Toward the Final Solution: A History of European Racism* (Madison, WI: University of Wisconsin Press, 1978, 1985), 234.

19 Bulent Diken and Carsten Bagge Lausten, quoting Sorkin (1999) in 'Zones of Indistinction: Security, Terror, and Bare Life,' *Space & Culture* 5, no. 3 (August 2002): 290–307, 300.

20 *Modern Inquisition*, 3 (discussing Arendt).

21 For a discussion in the Canadian context of the concept of original citizens as the descendants of Europeans, Aboriginal peoples as dead or dying, and racialized immigrants as latecomers, see Sherene Razack, 'When Place Becomes Race,' in *Race, Space and the Law: Unmapping a White Settler Society* (Toronto: Between the Lines, 2002), 1–6.

22 Michel Foucault, 'Society Must Be Defended,' in *Lectures at the College de France 1975–1976*, ed. Mauro Bertani and Alessandro Fontana, trans. David Macey (New York: Picador, 2003), 256.

23 Mosse, *Toward the Final Solution*, ix.

24 Ibid., xxvi.

25 Ibid.

26 Ibid., 216.

27 Étienne Balibar, *We, The People of Europe? Reflections on Transnational Citizenship*, trans. James Swenson (Princeton: Princeton University Press, 2004), 35.

28 Aihwa Ong, *Neoliberalism as Exception: Mutations in Citizenship and Sovereignty* (Durham: Duke University Press, 2006).

29 Michael Ratner and Ellen Ray, *Guantanamo: What the World Should Know* (White River Junction, VT: Chelsea Green Publishing Co., 2004), xv.

30 Zygmunt Bauman, *Life in Fragments: Essays in Postmodern Morality* (Oxford: Blackwell, 1995), 205.

31 Giorgio Agamben, *Homo Sacer: Sovereign Power and Bare Life,* trans. Daniel Heller-Roazen (Stanford: Stanford University Press, 1998), 174.

32 Bulent Diken and Carsten Bagge Laustsen, *The Culture of Exception: Sociology Facing the Camp* (London and New York: Routledge, 2005).

33 Michael Hardt and Antonio Negri, *Empire* (London and Cambridge: Harvard University Press, 2000), 10.
34 Ibid., 16.
35 Paul Gilroy, *Between Camps: Race, Identity and Nationalism* (London: The Penguin Press, 2000), 84.
36 Ong, *Neoliberalism as Exception*, 7.
37 Agamben, *Homo Sacer*, 2.
38 Ibid., 3.
39 Ibid., 3–4.
40 Gilroy, *Between Camps*, 60.
41 Hansen and Stepputat, 'Introduction,' in *Sovereign Bodies*, 24.
42 Edward W. Said, *Culture and Imperialism* (New York: Alfred A. Knopf, 1993), xi.
43 Nasser Hussain, *The Jurisprudence of Emergency: Colonialism and the Rule of Law* (Ann Arbor: University of Michigan Press, 2003), 29.
44 Achille Mbembe, *On the Postcolony* (Berkeley: University of California Press, 2001), 28–9.
45 Dyer, quoted in Nasser Hussain, 'Towards a Jurisprudence of Emergency: Colonialism and the Rule of Law,' *Law and Critique* 10 (1999): 95.
46 Ibid.
47 Ibid., 100.
48 Hansen and Stepputat, 'Introduction,' *Sovereign Bodies*, 3.
49 Ibid., 8.
50 Ibid., 4.
51 Gilroy, *Between Camps*, 62.
52 Ibid., 68.
53 Balibar, *We, the people of Europe?*, 36.
54 Ibid., 60.
55 Hardt and Negri, *Empire*, 192–3.
56 See, for example, Meyda Yegenoglu, *Colonial Fantasies: Towards a Feminist Reading of Orientalism* (Cambridge: Cambridge University Press, 1998).
57 Ibid., 11.
58 Achille Mbembe articulates a similar list in *On the Postcolony* (Berkeley: University of California Press, 2001).

Chapter 1 'Your client has a profile'

1 Giorgio Agamben, *Homo Sacer: Sovereign Power and Bare Life*, trans. D. Heller-Roazen (Stanford: Stanford University Press, 1998), 170.
2 *Immigration and Refugee Protection Act*, S.C. 2001, c. 27.

3 *Almrei v. Canada*, FCA, *Applicant's Application Record*, vol. 3, 727–8. Federal Court of Canada Trial Division, Hassan Almrei and the Minister of Citizenship and Immigration and Solicitor General of Canada, heard before the Honourable Mr Justice Blanchard, 27 November 2003.

4 Stephen H. Legomsky, 'The Ethnic and Religious Profiling of Noncitizens: National Security and International Human Rights,' *Boston College Third World Law Journal* 25 (2005): 161.

5 Barbara Jackman, 'One Measure of Justice in Canada: Judicial Protection for Non-Citizens,' paper presented at the Canadian Bar Association annual conference, Banff, Alberta, 2005.

6 *Immigration and Refugee Protection Act*, available at http://www.laws .justice.gc.ca/en/1-2.5/index.html. Fewer than 30 certificates have been issued since 1991. See Inter-American Commission on Human Rights, *Report on the Situation of Human Rights of Asylum Seekers within the Canadian Refugee Determination System* (28 February 2000) at 143–57, available at http://www.cidh.org/countryrep/canada2000en/table-of-contents .htm (accessed 16 March 2006). See also Sharyrn Aiken, 'From Slavery to Expulsion: Racism, Canadian Immigration Law and the Unfulfilled Promise of Modern Constitutionalism' (forthcoming) and Jackman, 'One Measure of Justice in Canada.'

7 In 2002 the Supreme Court of Canada determined that a sixth man of Sri Lankan origin, Manickavasagam Suresh, held on a security certificate should not be removed without a careful review of the risk of torture he might face upon his return to Sri Lanka. Released from detention, Suresh remains under a security certificate. *Suresh v. Canada (Minister of Citizenship and Immigration)*, [2002] 1 S.C.R. 3. As Aiken has analysed, while the ruling was a court victory for Suresh, the court made clear that 'heightened due process was required only in cases where there is a "*prima facie* risk" of torture.' Further, the minister retains the discretion to deport a refugee to face torture in 'exceptional circumstances.' Aiken, 'From Slavery to Expulsion,' 111. The federal court reached the opposite conclusion on 16 March 2006, when Mr Justice Andrew Mackay ruled as lawful the minister's delegate's report that Mahmoud Jaballah should be deported regardless of the possibility of torture or the death penalty upon his return to Egypt. Should his security certificate be upheld at a hearing in the spring of 2006, the path is now cleared for Mr Jaballah to be deported to Egypt. http://www.macleans.ca/topstories/politics/ news/shownews.jsp?content=n031643A, 16 March 2006.

   On 7 March 2007, the *Toronto Star* reported that during a detention review hearing, Federal Court Justice Carole Layden-Stevenson made a surprise announcement that Mr Jaballah would be released on strict bail conditions. At the time of writing, Jaballah remains under a security certificate. Michelle Shephard, 'Man Held without Charges Granted Bail,' *Toronto Star*, 7 March 2007, A1, A17.

8 *Almrei v. Canada (Minister of Citizenship and Immigration)*, [2005] F.C.J. 1994; *Almrei v. Canada (Minister of Citizenship and Immigration)*, [2004] F.C.J. 509; *Almrei v. Canada (Minister of Citizenship and Immigration)*, (F.C.) [2004] 4 F.C.R. 327, [2004] F.C.J. 509; *Almrei v. Canada (Minister of Citizenship and Immigration)*, [2005] F.C.J. 437; *Almrei v. Canada (Minister of Citizenship and Immigration)*, [2005] F.C.J. 213; *Almrei v. Canada (Minister of Citizenship and Immigration)*, (F.C.A.) [2005] 3 F.C.R. 142, [2005] F.C.J. 213; *Almrei v. Canada (Attorney General)*, [2003] O.J. 5198; *Almrei (Re)*, [2001] A.C.F. no 1772.

9 *Canada (Minister of Citizenship and Immigration) v. Mahjoub* (F.C.), [2004] 1 F.C.R. 493, [2003] F.C.J. 1183; *Mahjoub v. Canada (Minister of Citizenship and Immigration)*, [2005] F.C.J. 173; *Mahjoub v. Canada (Minister of Citizenship and Immigration)*, [2004] F.C.J. 1335; *Canada (Minister of Citizenship and Immigration) v. Mahjoub*, [2001] S.C.C.A. 151; *Canada (Minister of Citizenship and Immigration) v. Mahjoub*, [2004] F.C.J. 448; *Canada (Minister of Citizenship and Immigration) v. Mahjoub*, [2001] F.C.J. 79; *Canada (Minister of Citizenship and Immigration) v. Mahjoub*, (T.D.), [2001] 4 F.C. 644, [2001] F.C.J. 1483.

10 *Canada (Minister of Citizenship and Immigration) v. Jaballah*, [1999] F.C.J. 1681; *Jaballah v. Canada (Minister of Citizenship and Immigration)*, [2000] F.C.J. 1577; *Jaballah (Re)*, [2001] F.C.J. 1748; *Canada (Minister of Citizenship and Immigration) v. Jaballah*, [2003] F.C.J. 1274; *Jaballah v. Canada (Minister of Citizenship and Immigration)*, [2003] F.C.J. 1495; *Jaballah (Re) (T.D.)*, [2003] 4 F.C. 345; *Jaballah v. Canada (Minister of Citizenship and Immigration)*, [2003] F.C.J. 420; *Jaballah (Re) (T.D.)*, [2004] F.C.J. 1199; *Jaballah (Re)*, [2005] F.C.J. 500; *Jaballah v. Canada (Attorney General)*, [2005] O.J. 3681; *Jaballah (Re) (F.C.A.)*, [2005] 1 F.C.R. 560.

11 *Harkat (Re)*, [2005] F.C.J. 481; *Harkat v. Canada (Minister of Citizenship and Immigration*, [2005] F.C.J. 2149; *Harkat (Re) (F.C.)*, [2005] 2 F.C.R. 416, [2004] F.C.J. 2101; *Harkat (Re)*, [2004] F.C.J. 2101; *Harkat (Re) (C.F.)*, [2005] 2 R.C.F. 416, [2004] A.C.F. no 2101; *Harkat (Re)*, [2005] F.C.J. 1467; *Harkat v. Canada (Minister of Citizenship and Immigration)*, [2004] F.C.J. 1104.

12 *Charkaoui (Re)*, [2003] F.C.J. 1815; *Charkaoui (Re)*, [2003] F.C.J. 2060; *Charkaoui (Re)*, [2004] F.C.J. 1922; *Charkaoui (Re)*, [2004] F.C.J. 1686; *Charkaoui (Re)*, [2004] F.C.J. 1549; *Charkaoui (Re)*, [2004] F.C.J. 1548; *Charkaoui (Re)*, [2004] F.C.J. 1236; *Charkaoui (Re)*, [2004] F.C.J. 338;

Charkaoui v. Canada (Minister of Citizenship and Immigration), [2004] F.C.J. 1571; *Charkaoui (Re)*, [2004] F.C.J. 757; *Charkaoui (Re)*, [2004] F.C.J. 1090; *Charkaoui (Re)*, [2004] F.C.J. 405; *Charkaoui (Re)*, [2004] F.C.J. 78; *Charkaoui (Re)* (F.C.), [2004] 1 F.C.R. 528; *Charkaoui v. Canada (Minister of Citizenship and Immigration)*, [2004] 1 F.C.R. 451; *Charkaoui (Re)* (F.C.), [2004] 3 F.C.R. 32; *Charkaoui (Re)*, [2005] F.C.J. 139; *Charkaoui (Re)*, [2005] F.C.J. 269; *Charkaoui (Re)* (F.C.A.), [2005] 2 F.C.R.

13 Supreme Court of Canada, *Charkaoui v. Canada (Minister of Citizenship and Immigration)*, 2007 SCC 9, 23 February.

14 Kent Roach, 'Cool Heads Needed on Anti-Terror Law,' *Toronto Star*, 27 February 2007. http://www.thestar.com/article/185887.

15 Angelina Snodgrass Godoy, 'Converging on the Poles: Contemporary Punishment and Democracy in Hemispheric Perspective,' *Law and Social Inquiry* 30 (2005): 522.

16 Amit S. Rai, 'Of Monsters: Biopower, Terrorism and Excess in Genealogies of Monstrosity,' *Cultural Studies* 18, no. 4 (July 2004): 538–70. Ileana M. Porras, 'On Terrorism: Reflections on Violence and the Outlaw,' in *After Identity: A Reader on Law and Culture*, ed. Dan Danielsen and Karen Engle (New York, London: Routledge, 1995), 294–313.

17 Nicholas Mirzoeff, *Watching Babylon: The War in Iraq and Global Visual Culture* (New York, London: Routledge, 2005), 119.

18 Michael Ratner and Ellen Ray, *Guantanamo: What the World Should Know* (White River Junction, VT: Chelsea Green Publishing Co., 2004), 57.

19 Ibid., 25.

20 See, for example, David Cole, *Enemy Aliens* (New York, London: The New Press, 2003); Tram Nguyen, *We Are All Suspects Now: Untold Stories from Immigrant Communities after 9/11* (Boston: Beacon Press, 2005); and Susan M. Akram and Kevin Johnson, 'Race, Civil Rights, and Immigration Law after September 11, 2001: The Targeting of Muslims and Arabs,' *NYU Annual Survey of American Law* 58 (2001–3): 295–355.

21 Sharryn Aiken, 'National Security and Canadian Immigration: Deconstructing the Discourse of Trade-Offs,' in *Securing Canada in an Uncertain World: Perspectives, Policies, and Practices*, ed. David DeWitt (Toronto: University of Toronto Press, forthcoming), 13.

22 Interview by author with Janet Dench, Canadian Council for Refugees, Toronto, 20 December 2005.

23 Andrew Brouwer, interview by author, Toronto, 22 December 2005.

24 Janet Dench interview.

25 Mirzoeff, *Watching Babylon*, 121.

26 Ibid., 144.

27 Ibid., 127.
28 Zygmunt Bauman, *Society under Siege* (Cambridge: Polity Press, 2002), 113.
29 Mirzoeff, *Watching Babylon*, 119–21.
30 Nancy Baker, 'National Security versus Civil Liberties,' *Presidential Studies Quarterly* 33, no. 3 (September 2003): 547.
31 Reem Bahdi, 'No Exit: Racial Profiling and Canada's War on Terrorism,' *Osgood Hall Law Journal/Revue d'Osgoode Hall* 41 (2003): 293–317, para. 3. Leti Volpp has shown the same for the American context in 'The Citizen and the Terrorist,' *UCLA L. Review* 49 (2001–2): 1575–1600.
32 Bahdi, 'No Exit,' para. 4.
33 Volpp, 'The Citizen and the Terrorist,' 1578.
34 Badhi ('No Exit') canvases the topography of racial profiling.
35 Legomsky, 'The Ethnic and Religious Profiling of Noncitizens,' 181.
36 Caroline Mallan, 'U.K. Arrests Spur "Profiling" Debate,' *Toronto Star*, 19 August 2006, A2.
37 Sujit Choudrhry, 'Equality in Face of Terror: Ethnic and Racial Profiling and s. 15 of the Charter,' in *The Security of Freedom: Essays on Canada's Anti-Terrorism Bill*, ed. R. Daniels, P. Macklem, and K. Roach (Toronto: University of Toronto Press, 2001), 378.
38 Volpp, 'The Citizen and the Terrorist,' 1576.
39 Edward Said, *Culture and Imperialism* (New York: Alfred A. Knopf, 1993), 295.
40 Karim Karim, *Islamic Peril: Media and Global Violence* (Montreal: Institute of Policy Alternatives, 2003).
41 Zuhair Kashmeri, *The Gulf Within. Canadians, Arabs, Racism and the Gulf War* (Toronto: J. Lorimer, 1991).
42 A review of this scholarship can be found in Gil Gott, 'The Devil We Know: Racial Subordination and National Security Law,' *Villanova Law Review* 50, no. 4 (2005): 1073–1134. See also Susan M. Akram and Kevin R. Johnson, 'Race, Civil Rights and Immigration Law after September 11, 2001: The Targetting of Arabs and Muslims,' *NYU Annual Survey of American Law* (2001–3): 295–355.
43 Gott, 'The Devil We Know,' 1109.
44 Bahdi, 'No Exit,' para. 4 and note 11.
45 Bulent Diken and Carsten Bagge Lausten, *The Culture of Exception: Sociology Facing the Camp* (London, New York: Routledge, 2005), 50
46 Irene M. Silverblatt, *Modern Inquisitions: Bern and the Colonial Origins of the Civilized World* (Durham: Duke University Press, 2005), 5.
47 Ibid., 7.

48 Ibid., 18.
49 Ibid., 37.
50 Ibid., 25.
51 Since there is secret evidence in the interests of national security, the detainee and his counsel are entitled to a summary of evidence approved by the designated judge.
52 Federal Court Hearing Division, 'Statement Summarizing the Information Pursuant to Paragraph 40.1(4)(b) of the Immigration Act' (18 October 2001), 2, note 5.
53 Ibid., 3.
54 Leti Volpp, 'Impossible Subjects: Illegal Aliens and Alien Citizens,' *Michigan Law Review* 103, no. 106 (May 2005): 1591.
55 Federal Court Hearing Division, 'Statement,' 7.
56 Ibid., 9.
57 Carmela Murdocca, 'Foreign Bodies: Race, Canadian Nationalism and the Trope of Disease,' MA thesis, OISE/University of Toronto, 2002, 20. Murdocca relies on Sander Gilman in order to highlight the ways in which representations and metaphors of disease have long been a feature of nationalist discourse.
58 Ibid., 21.
59 Karen Engle, 'Constructing Good Aliens and Good Citizens: Legitimizing the War on Terror(ism),' *University of Colorado Law Review* 75, no. 1 (Winter 2004): 80.
60 Federal Court Hearing Division, 'Statement,' 17.
61 Sherene H. Razack, '"Simple Logic": The Identity Documents Rule and the Fantasy of a Nation Besieged and Betrayed,' *Journal of Law and Social Policy* 15 (2000): 183–211.
62 *Almrei v. Canada (Minister of Citizenship and Immigration)*, [2005] F.C.J. 1994. *Applicant's Application Record*, vol. 3, at 706.
63 Ibid., 717.
64 Ibid., 727–8.
65 Ibid., 736.
66 Ibid., 743.
67 *Almrei v. Canada (Minister of Citizenship and Immigration)*, [2004] F.C.J. 509 at 103.
68 *Almrei v. Canada (Minister of Citizenship and Immigration)*, [2005] F.C.J. 1994.
69 Ibid., 32.
70 Ibid., 35.
71 Ibid., 43.

72 Ibid., 44.
73 Ibid., 45.
74 Ibid., 49.
75 Ibid., 50.
76 Ibid., 100–1.
77 Ibid., 103.
78 Ibid., 106.
79 Ibid., 108.
80 Ibid., 109.
81 Ibid., 116.
82 Ibid., 128.
83 *Almrei v. Canada (Minister of Citizenship and Immigration)*, [2005] F.C.J. 1994, 133.
84 Ibid., 265.
85 Ibid., 268.
86 Ibid., 343.
87 Ibid., 370.
88 Ibid., 376.
89 Ibid., 380.
90 Ibid., 396.
91 Ibid., 398.
92 Ibid., 414.
93 Ibid., 416.
94 Amit S. Rai, 'Of Monsters: Biopower, Terrorism and Excess in Genealogies of Monstrosity,' *Cultural Studies* 18, no. 4 (July 2004): 545–50.
95 Ibid., 550.
96 Stewart Bell, *The Martyr's Oath: The Apprenticeship of a Home Grown Terrorist* (Mississauga: John Wiley and Sons, 2005).
97 See Mackenzie Institute, http://www.mackenzieinstitute.com.
98 François Debrix, 'Tabloid Realism and the Revival of American Security Culture,' in *11 September and Its Aftermath: The Geopolitics of Terror*, ed. Stanley D. Bruun (London, Portland, OR: Frank Cass, 2004), 152.
99 Ibid., 161.
100 Mosse, *Toward the Final Solution*, xi.
101 Debrix, 'Tabloid Realism, 158.
102 Mahmood Mamdani, *Good Muslim, Bad Muslim: America, The Cold War, and the Roots of Terror* (New York: Doubleday, 2004), 22.
103 Faisal Kutty, lawyer, interview by author, Toronto, 17 January 2006.
104 Mamdani, *Good Muslim, Bad Muslim*, 19.
105 Ileana M. Porras, 'On Terrorism: Reflections on Violence and the

Outlaw,' in *After Identity: A Reader on Law and Culture*, ed. Dan
Danielsen and Karen Engle (New York, London: Routledge, 1995), 302.
106 Engle, 'Constructing Good Aliens,' 91.
107 Rai, 'Of Monsters,' 558.
108 *Harkat (Re)*, [2005] F.C.J. 481; Harkat v. Canada (Minister of Citizenship
and Immigration, [2005] F.C.J. 2149; *Harkat (Re)* (F.C.), [2005] 2 F.C.R.
416, [2004] F.C.J. 2101; *Harkat (Re)*, [2004] F.C.J. 2101; *Harkat (Re)* (C.F.),
[2005] 2 R.C.F. 416, [2004] A.C.F. 2101; *Harkat (Re)*, [2005] F.C.J. 1467;
Harkat v. Canada (Minister of Citizenship and Immigration), [2004] F.C.J.
1104.
109 *Harkat (Re)*, [2005] F.C.J. 481 at 105.
110 *Harkat v. Canada (Minister of Citizenship and Immigration)*, [2005] F.C.J.
2149 at 105.
111 *Harkat (Re)*, [2005] F.C.J. 481 at 49.
112 *Harkat v. Canada (Minister of Citizenship and Immigration)*, [2005] F.C.J.
2149 at 48.
113 Ibid., 49.
114 *Harkat (Re)*, [2005] F.C.J. 481 at 49.
115 *Harkat v. Canada (Minister of Citizenship and Immigration)*, [2005] F.C.J.
2149 at 47.
116 Ibid., 52.
117 Ibid., 51.
118 *Harkat (Re)*, [2005] F.C.J. 481 at 49; *Harkat v. Canada (Minister of Citizenship and Immigration)*, [2005] F.C.J. 2149 at 50, 52, 54.
119 *Harkat (Re)*, [2005] F.C.J. 481 at 114.
120 Ibid., 109.
121 Ibid., 49.
122 Ibid., 49.
123 *Harkat v. Canada (Minister of Citizenship and Immigration*, [2005] F.C.J.
2149 at 56, 57.
124 *Canada (Minister of Citizenship and Immigration) v. Mahjoub* (T.D.), [2001]
F.C.J. 1483 at 69.
125 *Canada (Minister of Citizenship and Immigration) v. Mahjoub* (T.D.), [2001]
F.C.J. 1483.
126 *Mahjoub v. Canada (Minister of Citizenship and Immigration)*, [2005] F.C.J.
173, transcript at 2573.
127 Ibid.
128 *Mahjoub v. Canada (Minister of Citizenship and Immigration)*, [2005] F.C.J.
173, ranscript at 2552.
129 *Jaballah (Re)* (F.C.A.), [2005] 1 F.C.R. 560, transcript at 144.

130   Ibid., 165.
131   Ibid., 186
132   Ibid., 268.
133   Ibid., 286.
134   *Jaballah (Re)*, [2001] F.C.J. 1748.
135   *Jaballah (Re)* (T.D.), [2003] 4 F.C. 345.
136   *Charkaoui (Re)* (F.C.), [2004] 1 F.C.R. 528 at 531.
137   Ibid., 530.
138   Ibid., 531.
139   *Charkaoui (Re)*, [2004] F.C.J. 1236.
140   Ibid., 21.
141   *Charkaoui (Re)*, [2005] F.C.J. 269 at para. 62.
142   Ibid., 19.
143   Diken and Lausten, *Culture of Exception*, 80.
144   Ibid.
145   Yegenoglu, *Colonial Fantasies*, 3.

Chapter 2 If It Wasn't for the Sex and the Photos

1   Andrea Dworkin. 'Pornography Happens to Women,' in *Life and Death* (New York: The Free Press, 1997), 132.
2   Sherene Razack, *Dark Threats and White Knights: The Somalia Affair, Peacekeeping and the New Imperialism* (Toronto: University of Toronto Press, 2004).
3   See Judith Butler, *Precarious Life: The Powers of Mourning and Violence* (London, New York: Verso, 2004); Gregory Hooks and Clayton Mosher, 'Outrages against Personal Dignity: Rationalizing Abuse and Torture in the War on Terror,' *Social Forces* 83, no. 4 (June 2005): 1627–46; Michelle Brown, 'Setting the Conditions for Abu Ghraib: The Prison Nation Abroad,' *American Quarterly* 57, no. 3 (September 2005): 973–97.
4   Amy Kaplan, 'Violent Belongings and the Question of Empire Today: Presidential Address to the American Studies Association, October 17, 2003,' *American Quarterly* 56, no. 1 (March 2004): 14; cited in Brown, 'Setting the Conditions', 974–5.
5   Avery F. Gordon, 'Abu Ghraib: Imprisonment and the War on Terror,' *Race & Class* 48, no. 1 (2006): 43.
6   Hannah Arendt, *On the Origins of Totalitarianism* (New York: Harcourt, Brace, Jovanovich, 1973), 452.
7   Ibid., 454.
8   Gordon, 'Abu Ghraib,' 52.

9 Jacobo Timerman, *Prisoner without a Name, Cell without a Number* (New York: Vintage Books, 1982), 96.
10 For a discussion of interlocking oppression in comparison to intersectionality see Sherene Razack, *Looking White People in the Eye: Gender, Race, and Culture in Courtrooms and Classrooms* (Toronto: University of Toronto Press, 1998), 11–12.
11 Jasbir K. Paur, 'Abu Ghraib: Arguing against Exceptionalism,' *Feminist Studies* 30, no. 2 (Summer 2004): 522–34.
12 Revathi Krishnaswamy, *Effeminism: The Economy of Colonial Desire* (Ann Arbor: University of Michigan Press, 1998), 3.
13 Robert Fisk, *The Great War for Civilization: The Conquest of the Middle East* (London: HarperCollins, 2005).
14 Henry A. Giroux, 'What Might Education Mean after Abu Ghraib? Revisiting Adorno's Politics of Education,' *Comparative Studies of South Asia, Africa and the Middle East* 24, no. 1 (2004): 5–24.
15 Ibid., 11–12.
16 Ibid., 17.
17 Ibid., 20.
18 Craig Whitney, 'Introduction,' in *The Abu Ghraib Investigations*, ed. Steven Strasser (New York: Public Affairs, 2005), vi.
19 *The Fay Inquiry*, cited ibid., xv.
20 Whitney, 'Introduction,' ibid., x.
21 Ibid., xiv.
22 See Samuel P. Huntington, *The Clash of Civilizations and the Remaking of World Order* (New York: Touchstone Press, 1997).
23 John Gray, 'Power and Vainglory,' in *Abu Ghraib: The Politics of Torture*, ed. Gray et al. (Berkeley: North Atlantic Books, 2004), 50.
24 Mark Danner, 'The Logic of Torture,' ibid., 31.
25 Ibid., 32.
26. Brooke Warner, 'Abu Ghraib and a New Generation of Soldiers,' ibid., 77.
27 Gray, 'Power and Vainglory.'
28 Seymour Hersh, *Chain of Command: The Road from 9/11 to Abu Ghraib* (New York: HarperCollins, 2004), 24.
29 Ibid., 46.
30 *Final Report of the Independent Panel to Review Department of Defense Operations*. Chairman Hon. James R. Schlesinger (August 2004). http://www.defenselink.mil/news/Aug2004/d20040824finalreport.pdf.
31 On the television program *The Big Picture*, Karpinski said that the pictures were intended for use in future interrogations. CBC television, 13 September 2006.

32 Danner, 'The Logic of Torture,' 33.

33 David Olive, 'Why Record Evil? Abuse Photos Hard to Explain,' *Toronto Star*, 22 May 2004, A1.

34 Susan Willis, 'Quien es mas macho? The Abu Ghraib Photos,' presentation at the Toronto Women's Bookstore, 18 January 2005.

35 Shawn Michelle Smith, *American Archives* (Princeton: Princeton University Press, 1999), 4.

36 Ibid.

37 Omer Bartov, *Germany's War and the Holocaust: Disputed Histories* (Ithaca, London: Cornell University Press, 2003), xi.

38 Proof of complicity is disturbing and when it was found that a few of the photos in the exhibit had been mistakenly labelled, and were in fact crimes of the Soviet secret police, thereby allowing some Germans to claim that the German army had merely striven to protect Germany from the crimes of the Red Army and other Soviet agencies, the opportunity was seized and the exhibit was closed. Although a commission of experts found very few errors, the exhibit, differently organized and titled, was later reopened (Bartov, *Germany's War and the Holocaust*).

39 Norman L. Kleeblatt, 'The Body of Alfred Dreyfus: A Site for France's Displaced Anxieties of Masculinity, Homosexuality and Power,' in *Diaspora and Visual Culture: Representing Africans and Jews*, ed. Nicholas Mirzoeff (London, New York: Routledge, 2000), 76–132.

40 James Allen et al., *Without Sanctuary: Lynching Photographs in America* (Santa Fe, NM: Twin Palms Publishers, 2000).

41 Smith, *American Archives*, 50.

42 Andrew Austin, 'Review Essay. Explanation and Responsibility: Agency and Motive in Lynching and Genocide,' *Journal of Black Studies* 34, no. 5 (May 2004): 719–33.

43 Ibid., 726.

44 Ibid., 727–8.

45 Laura Wexler, 'A Sorry History,' *The Washington Post*, 19 June 2005, B1, http://washingtonpost.com/wp-dyn/content/article/2005/06/18/AR2005061800075_p.

46 Trudier Harris, *Exorcising Blackness: Historical and Literary Lynching and Burning Rituals* (Bloomington: Indiana University Press, 1984), xi.

47 Ibid.

48 Ibid., 14.

49 Ibid., 23.

50 Ibid.

51 Robyn Weigman, *American Anatomies: Theorizing Race and Gender* (Durham, London: Duke University Press, 1995).

52 Gwen Bergner, *Taboo Subjects: Race, Sex, and Psychoanalysis* (Minneapolis: University of Minnesota Press, 2005). Heidi J. Nast, 'Mapping the 'Unconscious': Racism and the Oedipal Family,' *Annals of the Association of American Geographers* 90, no. 2 (2000): 215–55.

53 Lisa Cardyn, 'Sexualized Racism/Gendered Violence: Outraging the Body Politic in the Reconstruction South,' *Michigan Law Review* 100, no. 4 (February 2002): 675.

54 James Baldwin, 'Going to Meet the Man,' in *Going to Meet the Man (Stories)* (New York: The Dial Press, 1965), 227–49.

55 Ibid., 239.

56 Ibid., 235–6.

57 Ibid., 230.

58 Ibid., 249. I replace the letters of the word 'nigger' used by Baldwin in an attempt to reduce the violence and lessen the harm of the word.

59 Robert Young, *Colonial Desire: Hybridity in Theory, Culture and Race* (London, New York: Routledge, 1995), 149.

60 Ibid., 90.

61 Ibid., 5.

62 Gilles Deleuze and Felix Guattari, *Anti-Oedipus: Capitalism and Schizophrenia*, vol. 1 (1972), trans. R. Hurley, M. Seem and H. Lane (New York: Viking, 1977), 33. Cited in Young, *Colonial Desire*, 169.

63 Young, *Colonial Desire*, 171.

64 Ibid., 170.

65 Ibid., 181.

66 Dworkin, 'Pornography Happens to Women,' 130.

67 Ibid., 130–1.

68 Ibid., 132.

69 Cited in Young, *Colonial Desire*,180.

70 Claude Mackay, 'The Lynching' as cited in Harris, *Exorcising Blackness*, 75.

71 William Pinar, '"I Am a Man": The Queer Politics of Race,' *Cultural Studies Critical Methodologies* 3, no. 3 (2003): 271.

72 Ibid., 281.

73 Frantz Fanon, cited ibid., 276.

74 Pinar, '"I Am a Man,"' 274.

75 Harris, *Exoricising Blackness*, 20.

76 Dworkin, 'Pornography Happens to Women,' 158.

77 Pinar, '"I Am a Man,"' 278.

78 Barbara Ehrenreich, 'Feminism's Assumptions Upended,' in *Abu Ghraib*, ed. John Gray et al., 67.

79 Ibid.

80 Zillah Eisenstein. 'Sexual Humiliation, Gender Confusion and the Horrors at Abu Ghraib,' *Znet*, 22 June 2004, http://www.zmag.org/content/showarticle.cfm?SectionID=12&ItemID=5751.

81 Mary Louise Fellows and Sherene H. Razack, 'The Race to Innocence: Confronting Hierarchical Relations Among Women,' *The Journal of Gender, Race and Justice* 1, no. 2 (Spring 1998): 335–52.

82 As Radhika Mohanram asks for the Algerian colonial context: 'Did French women in Algeria come into being only within the context of race and not within gender?' Mohanram answers this question affirmatively, recalling Fanon's description of a French woman's excitement over the capture and anticipated castration of five members of the Algerian National Liberation Front. Radhika Mohanram, *Black Body: Women, Colonialism, and Space* (Minneapolis: University of Minnesota Press, 1999), 71.

83 Razack, '"Outwhiting the White Guys?"' in *Dark Threats and White Knights*.

84 Willis, 'Quien es mas macho? The Abu Ghraib Photos.'

85 Available at http://en.wikipedia.org/wiki/Lynndie_England (accessed June 2005).

86 Yegenoglu, *Colonial Fantasies*, 11.

87 Michael Taussig, 'Culture of Terror – Space of Death: Roger Casement's Putumayo Report and the Explanation of Torture,' in *Violence in War and Peace. An Anthology*, ed. Nancy Scheper-Hughes and Philippe Bourgeois (Malden, MA: Blackwell Publishers, 2004), 40.

88 Ibid., 40.

89 Ibid., 41.

90 Jacobo Timerman, *Prisoner without a Name*.

91 Ibid., 51.

92 Charles Graner, as quoted in Michael A. Fuoco, 'Witnesses Describe Abu Ghraib Abuse: Defense Plays Down Pyramid of Prisoners as Something Cheerleaders across America Do,' *Pittsburgh Post-Gazette*, 11 January 2005.

93 Baldwin, 'Going to Meet the Man,' 236.

Chapter 3 Modern Women as Imperialists

1 George L. Mosse, *Toward the Final Solution: A History of European Racism* (Madison: University of Wisconsin Press, 1978, 1985), xxvii.

2 Meyda Yegenoglu, *Colonial Fantasies: Towards a Feminist Reading of Orientalism* (Cambridge: Cambridge University Press, 1998), 111.
3 Rosemary M. George, 'Homes in the Empire, Empire in the Home,' *Cultural Critique* 26 (1993–4): 97.
4 In addition to Fallaci (2002), Chesler (2003), and Manji (2003) (see n. 13 below) there were A. Dershowitz, *The Case for Israel* (Hoboken, NJ: John Wiley and Sons, 2003), A. Foxman, *Never Again? The Threat of the New Anti-Semitism* (San Francisco: Harper, 2003), P. Iganski and B. Kosmin, *A New Anti-Semitism? Debating Judeophobia in 21st Century Britain* (London: Institute for Jewish Policy Research, 2003).
5 Edward Said, *The Question of Palestine* (New York: Vintage Books, 1992), 25.
6 Étienne Balibar, *We, the People of Europe?* (Princeton: Princeton University Press, 2004), 129.
7 Achille Mbembe, 'Necropolitics,' *Public Culture* 15, no. 1 (2003): 14. Italics in original.
8 Ibid., 40.
9 Ibid., 30.
10 Balibar, *We, the People of Europe?* 34.
11 Yegenoglu, *Colonial Fantasies*, 105.
12 Anonymous email from isalit@rogers.com, personal communication, 11 August 2002.
13 Orianna Fallaci, *The Rage and the Pride* (New York: Rizzoli International Publications Inc., 2002); Phyllis Chesler, *The New Anti-Semitism and What We Must Do about It* (New York: Jossey-Bass, 2003), Irshad Manji, *The Trouble with Islam: A Wake-up Call for Honesty and Change* (Toronto: Random House, 2003).
14 Barbara Walker, 'The Canary Is Choking,' *The Social Contract* (Fall 2002), http://www.thesocialcontract.com/pdf/thirteen-one/xiii-1-60.pdf (accessed 15 November 2003).
15 Samuel P. Huntington, *The Clash of Civilizations and the Remaking of World Order.* (New York: Touchstone Press, 1997).
16 Ibid., 210.
17 Ibid., 264.
18 Edward Said, 'The Clash of Ignorance,' *Media Monitors Network,*11 October 2001, at http://www.mediamonitors.net/edward40.html (accessed 13 August 2003).
19 Huntington, *Clash of Civilizations*, 318.
20 R. Inglehart and P. Norris, 'The True Clash of Civilizations,' *Foreign Policy*, March/April 2003: 67–74.

21 R. Inglehart and P. Norris, *Rising Tide: Gender Equality and Cultural Change around the World* (Cambridge: Cambridge University Press, 2003), 154.

22 Ibid., 158.

23 J. Didion, 'Mr. Bush and the Divine.' *New York Review of Books* 17 (6 November 2003): 81–6.

24 Fallaci, *The Rage and the Pride*, 83.

25 Ibid., 84.

26 Ibid., 36.

27 Oriana Fallaci, 'Anti-Semitism Today,' *Panorama Magazine*, 12 April 2002, http://www.tpi.umn.edu/shifman/fallaci.pdf (accessed 1 May 2007).

28 Rana Kabbani, 'Bible of the Muslim Haters,' *The Guardian*, 11 June 2002. http://www.guardian.co.uk/farright/story/0,11981,731126,00.html (3 April 2004). I do not consider here the reception to Fallaci's work in Italy, although the over 700,000 copies sold in the first two weeks indicate the popular support for her views.

29 See http://www.collapsingworld.org/cw_Gat-Rutter.html.

30 G. Gurely 'The Rage of Oriana Fallaci,' *The New York Observer*, 11 June 2003, http://www.observer.com/pagesstory.asp?ID=6869 (accessed 1 March 2004).

31 R. Dreher, 'Oriana's Screed: Review of *The Rage and the Pride*,' *National Review Online*, 8 October 2002, http://www.nationalreview.com/dreher/dreher101002.asp (accessed 1 March 2004).

32 Ibid.

33 G. Jonas, 'Fallaci Is a Little Heavy on the Rage,' *National Post*, 7 November 2002, A22.

34 Charles Taylor, 'Oriana Fallaci Declares War on Radical Islam,' *Salon.com*, 16 November 2002, http://archive.salon.com/books/feature/2002/11/16fallaci/index_np.html (accessed 14 April 2004).

35 Ibid.

36 See 'Mission Statement' on the Campus Watch website. See also Daniel Pipes, *Militant Islam Reaches America* (New York: W.W. Norton, 2003).

37 See 'Peace Pipes,' *Wall Street Journal*, August 19, 2003.

38 D. Pipes and L. Hedegaard, 'Something Rotten in Denmark?' *New York Post*, 27 August 2002, http://www.danielpipes.org/article/450 (accessed 15 November 2003).

39 Walker, 'The Canary Is Choking.'

40 For a discussion of the Muslim man as rapist of white women in Australia, see Binoy Kampmark, 'Islam, Women and Australia's Discourse of Terror,' *Hecate* 29, no. 1 (2003).

41 Kevin Michael Grace, 'A Multiculturalist Speaks,' *Canadian Heritage*

Alliance Magazine, http://www.canadianheritagealliance.com/channels/articles/grace/speaks.html (accessed 15 November 2003).

42 Chesler, *The New Anti-Semitism*, 1.

43 K.J. Lopez, 'Liberal and Pro-Israel: An Interview with Phyllis Chesler,' *National Review Online*, 25 November 2003, http://www.nationalreview.com/interrogatory/chesler200311250905.asp (accessed 1 March 2004)

44 Chesler, *The New Anti-Semitism*, 77.

45 Ibid., 11.

46 Ibid., 9.

47 Ibid., 71.

48 Lopez, 'Liberal and Pro-Israel,' 2003

49 Chesler, *The New Anti-Semitism*, 11.

50 P. Chesler and D.M. Hughes, 'Feminism in the 21st Century,' *Washington Post* 22 February 2002, B7. For thoughtful critiques on the 'new anti-Semitism,' see B. Klug, 'The Myth of the New Anti-Semitism,' *The Nation*, 15 January 2004. Responding to the point frequently made by Chesler and others that all Jews become conflated with Israel in the minds of those who perpetrate attacks on Jews in France, Klug notes that Israel does see itself as the Jewish collective and not as a state that happens to be Jewish, a view that is shared by Jews outside of Israel. As Klug concludes: 'Not that this justifies, not for one moment, a single incident where Jews are attacked for being Jewish; such attacks are repugnant. But it does provide a context within which to make sense of them without seeing a global "war against the Jews" as Chesler claims.'

51 Chesler and Hughes, 'Feminism in the 21st Century.'

52 C. Kaplan, 'Getting to Know You: Travel, Gender and the Politics of Representation in *Anna and the King of Siam* and *The King and I*,' in *Late Imperial Culture*, ed. R. de la Campa, E.A. Kaplan, and M. Sprinkler (London: Verso Press, 1995), 33–52. M. Yegenoglu, *Colonial Fantasies*, 1998.

53 Manji, *The Trouble with Islam*, 11.

54 Ibid., 12.

55 Ibid., 31.

56 Ibid., 47.

57 Ibid., 48.

58 Ibid., 90.

59 Ibid., 106.

60 Ibid., 123.

61 Ibid., 173.

62 J. Reed, 'Extreme Makeover,' *Vogue Magazine*, November 2003, 465–72.

63 Andrew Sullivan, 'Decent Exposure,' *New York Times*, 25 January 2004, http://www.muslim-refusenik.com/news/nytimes-04-01-25pt1.html (accessed 14 April 2004).

64 Reed, 'Extreme Makeover.'

65 P. Donnelly, 'Muslim Writer Challenges Her Faith,' *The Gazette*, 2 October 2003, http://www.muslim-refusenik.com/news/mtlgazette-oct02 -03.html (accessed 14 April 2004).

66 Daniel Pipes, '(Moderate) Voices of Islam,' *New York Post*, 23 September 2003, http://www.danielpipes.org/article/1255 (accessed 1 March 2004).

67 M. Posner, 'Rousing Islam,' *Globe and Mail*, 16 September 2003, http://www.muslim-refusenik.com/news/globe-sept16-03.html (accessed 14 April 2004).

68 J. Remsen, 'Stirring up Fellow Muslims,' *Philadelphia Inquirer*, 11 January 2004, http://www/philly.com/mld/inquirer/living/religion/7679655 .htm?lc (accessed 14 April 2004).

69 M. Kalman, 'A Muslim Calling for Reform – and She's a Lesbian,' *San Francisco Chronicle*, 19 January 2004 http://www.muslim-refusenik.com/ news/sfchronicle20040119.html (accessed 14 April 2004).

70 *O Magazine*, May 2004.

71 Andrew Sullivan, 'Decent Exposure,' *New York Times*, 25 January 2004, http://www.muslim-refusenik.com/news/nytimes-04-01-25pt1.html (accessed 14 April 2004).

72 J. Podur, 'A Multifaceted Fraud [review of *The Trouble with Islam*],' *Znet*, 5 December 2003, http://www.zmag.org/content/showarticle.cfm ?Item ID=4624 (accessed 14 April 2004).

73 Wahhabism is an ultra-orthodox eighth-century strain of Islam that has recently gained considerable prominence. Bin Ladin subscribes to Wah-habism. See T. Ali, *The Clash of Fundamentalisms: Crusades, Jihads, and Modernity* (London: Verso, 2002).

74 Yegenoglu, *Colonial Fantasies* 135.

75 Ibid., 144.

76 K. Pollitt, 'Introduction', *Nothing Sacred: Women Respond to Religious Fundamentalism and Terror*, ed. B. Reed (New York: Thunder's Mouth Press/Nation Books, 2002), ix

77 C. Beckett and M. Macy, 'Race, Gender and Sexuality: The Oppression of Multiculturalism,' *Women's Studies International Forum* 24, nos. 3/4 (May–August 2001): 311.

78 L. Abu-Lughod, 'Saving Muslim Women or Standing with Them? On Images, Ethics and War in Our Times,' *Insaniyaat* 1, no. 1 (Spring 2003)

http://www.aucegypt.edu/academic/insanyat/Issue %20I/I-article.htm (accessed 15 November 2003).

79 Ibid.

Chapter 4 Racism in the Name of Feminism

1 I use the term culturalization and the adjective culturalist to describe an exclusive focus on culture, understood as frozen in time and separate from systems of domination. For an exploration of culturalization of violence in the law see Sherene Razack, *Looking White People in the Eye: Gender, Race, and Culture in Courtrooms and Classrooms* (Toronto: University of Toronto Press, 1998).

2 Étienne Balibar, *We, the People of Europe?'* (Princeton: Princeton University Press, 2004), 123.

3 Meyda Yegenoglu, *Colonial Fantasies: Towards a Feminist Reading of Orientalism* (Cambridge: Cambridge University Press, 1998), 112.

4 H. Drachmann, 'Haarder Hyldet af Norske Feminister.' *Politikken*, 21 November 2003; http://www.polikem.dk/VisArtikel.iasp?Page ID= 295643 (accessed 14 April 2004).

5 A.Q. Raja, 'Exploiting the Media – Creating Further Infringement,' trans. Ulla Johanson, *VG Nett* (2004), http://www.v.g.no/pub/vgart.hbs?artid= 217461 (accessed 12 April 2004); K. Zaman, 'Kadra, Nadia and Synab Accuse Their Norwegian Helpers: Break with Their Allies,' trans. U. Johanson, *VG Nett* (2004), http://www.vg.no/pub/vgart.hbs?artid=216868 (accessed 12 April 2004).

6 Council of Europe, Parliamentary Assembly, 'Forced Marriages and Child Marriages,' Doc. 9966, 13 October 2003.

7 Hege Storhaug and Human Rights Service, *Human Visas: A Report from the Front Lines of Europe's Integration Crisis*, trans. Bruce Bawer (Norway: KOLOFON AS, 2003); http://www.kolofon.com (accessed 30 January 2004).

8 Unni Wikan, *Generous Betrayal: Politics of Culture in the New Europe.* (Chicago, London: University of Chicago Press, 2002).

9 Storhaug, *Human Visas*, 7.

10 Ibid., 10.

11 Ibid., 27.

12 Ibid., 28–9.

13 Ibid., 62–3.

14 Ibid., 88.

15 Ibid., 98.

16 Ibid., 101.

17 Ibid., 112, 134.

18 Ibid., 172.

19 Ibid., 122.

20 Ibid., 133.

21 Ibid., 160.

22 Ibid., 136–7.

23 Ibid., 180.

24 Ibid., 197.

25 Ibid., 149.

26 'SEIF – SelvhjElp for Innvandrere og Flyktninger,' trans. Ulla Johanson, http://www.seif.no/tvangsekteskap/kriseguide, 15 November 2003.

27 Edward Said, *Culture and Imperialism* (New York: Alfred A. Knopf, 1993), 37–8.

28 Ibid., 295. Said makes this remark in reference to the logic underpinning the Gulf War, a logic of murderous, uncivilized Arabs.

29 George Mosse, *Toward the Final Solution* (Madison: University of Wisconsin Press, 1985), 115.

30 Daniel Jonah Goldhagen, *Hitler's Willing Executioners: Ordinary Germans and the Holocaust* (New York: Alfred A. Knopf, 1996), 49–79.

31 See Claudia Koonz, *The Nazi Conscience* (London: The Belknap Press of Harvard University Press, 2003).

32 Bertel Harder, quoted in Per Egil Hegge, 'When Danes Are Refused Entry to Their Home Country,' trans. U. Johanson, *Aftenposten*, 18 July 2003.

33 Wikan, *Generous Betrayal*.

34 Ibid., 7.

35 Ibid., 27.

36 Ibid., 24.

37 Ibid., 140.

38 Ibid.

39 Ibid., 147.

40 Donald Martin Carter, 'Navigating Citizenship, Review of *Generous Betrayal* by Unni Wikan,' *Anthropological Quarterly* 75, no. 2 (Spring 2002): 410–11.

41 Sherene Razack, 'From the 'Clean Snows of Petawawa': The Violence of Canadian Peacekeepers in Somalia,' *Cultural Anthropology* 15, no. 1 (2000): 127–63.

42 Elisabeth Eide, '"Down There" and "Up Here": "Europe's Others" in Norwegian Feature Stories.' PhD dissertation, 7 November 2002, Institutt for Medier og Kommunikasjon (Ref. no. 73336: Oslo, Norway), 135.

43 Ibid.

44 Marianne Gullestad, 'Invisible Fences: Nationalism, Egalitarianism and Immigration,' 12 October 2000, http://cas.uchicago.edu/workshops/antheur/Gullestad.pdf (accessed 15 November 2003).
45 Ibid., 24.
46 Ibid., 30.
47 Thomas Hylland Eriksen, 'Norway a Multiethnic Country,' http://odin.dep.no/odin/engelsk/norway/social/032091-990909/index-dok000-b-n-a.html (accessed 15 November 2003).
48 Sherene Razack, '"Simple Logic": The Identity Documents Rule and the Fantasy of a Nation Besieged and Betrayed,' *Journal of Law and Social Policy* 15 (2000): 183–211.
49 Saskia Sassen, *Globalization and Its Discontents* (New York: New Press, 1998), xxx.
50 Ibid.
51 Ibid., xxxvi.
52 Wikan, *Generous Betrayal*, 119.
53 Eriksen, 'Norway a Multiethnic Country.'
54 David Theo Goldberg, *The Racial State* (Cambridge, Mass., and Oxford: Blackwell, 2002), 50–1.
55 Razack, '"Simple Logic" and Sherene Razack, 'Making Canada White: Law and the Policing of Bodies of Colour in the 1990s,' *Canadian Journal of Law and Society* 14, no. 1 (Spring 1999): 159–84.
56 Razack, *Looking White People in the Eye*.
57 See Jane Freedman, 'L'Affaire des foulards: Problems of Defining a Feminist Antiracist Strategy in French Schools,' in *Feminism and Anti-Racism: International Struggles for Justice* ed. France Winddance Twine and Kathleen M. Blee (New York: New York University Press, 2001), 295–312.
58 See Bronwyn Winter, 'Women, the Law, and Cultural Relativism in France: The Case of Excision,' *Signs: Journal of Women in Culture and Society* 19, no. 4 (1994): 939–74.
59 A. Suh, 'London Conference Tackles Sensitive Issue of Forced Marriages.' *VOA News*, 2003, at http://www.voanews.com/article.cfm?object ID=7FOCDDIF-C915-44B8-9CCD17F4E9483C5C# (accessed 12 April 2004).
60 Ministry of Industry, Employment and Communications, Stockholm, Sweden, 'Memorandum,' 1 July 2002. See also Mikael Kurkiala, 'Interpreting Honour Killings,' *Anthropology Today* 19, no. 1 (February 2003): 6–7.
61 'Forced Weddings: Difficult Culture Clash,' *Norway Now*, 20 October 1999, http://odin.dep.no/ud/engelsk/publ/periodika.032005-992400/index-dok000-b-n-a.html (accessed 15 November 2003).

62 Salil Tripathi, 'Nuptial Nightmares in London,' *Tehelka* (New Delhi), September 2000, http://www.saliltripathi.com/articles/Sept2000Tehelka.html (accessed 15 November 2003).

63 Abdullahi An Na'im, 'Forced Marriage,' 2000, http://www.soas.ac.uk/honourcrimes/ForcedMarriage.htm (accessed 30 January 2004).

64 Communication en Conseil des Ministres de Nicole Ameline, Ministre déléguée à la parité et à l'égalité professionnelle, 21 January 2003, http://www.lemonde.fr (accessed 31 January 2004).

65 An Na'im, 'Forced Marriage.'

66 Committee on Equal Opportunities for Women and Men, 'Crimes of Honour,' presented to the Council of Europe, Parliamentary Assembly, Rapporteur Mrs Cryer, United Kingdom, SOC 4 June 2002, http://www.soas.ac.uk/honourcrimes/Mat_COEreport_june02.pdf (accessed 15 November 2003).

67 Ibid., para. 3.

68 Ibid., para. 6.

69 Ibid., para. 7.

70 Ibid., para., 39.

71 Ibid., para. 45.

72 Danish immigration minister Bertel Haarder, quoted in A. Osborn, 'Copenhagen Set to Introduce Toughest Immigration Laws,' *DAWN*, 30 June 2002, http://www.dawn.com/2002/06/30/int8.htm (accessed 15 November 2003).

73 In August 2003 the Danish government released a revised plan to combat the practice of forced marriage. The 'Action Plan for 2003–2005 on Forced, Quasi-Forced and Arranged Marriages,' further articulates that a 'multi-faceted initiative' is required to stop such 'cultural and ethnic practices' that includes facilitating dialogue between youths and parents, counselling, intensified efforts by local authorities to criminalize 'unlawful coercion,' clubs for girls, residential activities and further research. Denmark, 'Action Plan for 2003–2005 on Forced, Quasi-Forced and Arranged Marriages,' 15 August 2003.

74 Denmark, Ministry of Refugee, Immigration and Integration Affairs, *Aliens (Consolidation) Act no. 608, 17 July 2002*, s. 9(1). For new and old rules for family reunification see http://www.udlst.dk/english/Family+Reunification/Default.htm (accessed 30 January 2003). For a discussion of the Muslim woman's body and forced marriage in the Danish context, see Helle Laila Rytkonen, 'Europe and Its "Almost-European" Other: A Textual Analysis of Legal and Cultural Practices of Othering in Contemporary Europe.' PhD dissertation, Stanford University, 2002.

75 Denmark, Ministry of Integration, *Bill Amending the Aliens Act, the Marriage Act and Other Acts*, s. 9(1)(ii), 28 February 2002, background paper, 'The Family Reunification Field.'

76 Ibid.

77 Miriam Ticktin draws on David Blatt to make this argument, 'Between Justice and Compassion: "Les Sans Papiers" and the Political Economy of Health, Human Right, and Humanitarianism in France.' PhD dissertation, Department of Cultural and Social Anthropology, Stanford University, 2002, 25.

78 Jon Henley, 'MPs Urge French Ban on Religious Symbols,' *The Guardian*, 14 November 2003.

79 Kamal Ahmed, Gaby Hinsliff, and Oliver Morgan, 'Ministers Plan to End Forced Marriages,' *The Observer*, 4 November 2001, http://observer.guardian.co.uk/politics/story/0,6903,587516,00.html (accessed 15 November 2003).

80 On 1 April 2003 the government raised the age at which a spouse can be brought into Britain from 16 to 18. In the Immigration Rules, section 277 now reads: 'Nothing in these Rules shall be construed as permitting a person to be granted entry clearance, leave to enter, leave to remain or variation of leave as a spouse of another if the applicant will be aged under 16 or the sponsor will be aged under 18 on the date of arrival in the United Kingdom or (as the case may be) on the date on which the leave to remain or variation of leave would be granted.' http://www.ind.homeoffice.gov.uk (accessed 8 April 2004).

81 See, for example, Marianne Gullestad, 'Mohammed Atta and I: Identification, Discrimination and the Formation of Sleepers,' *European Journal of Cultural Studies* 6, no. 4 (2003): 529–48.

82 Ministry of Children and Family Affairs, *Action Plan against Forced Marriages*, Spring 1999, 4; http://odin.dep.no/bfd/engelsk/publ/handbooks/004021-120005/index-ind001-b-f-a.html (accessed 15 November 2003).

83 Ibid.

84 Ibid.

85 L.H.M. Ling, 'Hegemonic Liberalism: Martha Nussbaum, Jorg Haider, and the Struggle for Late Modernity,' paper delivered at the International Studies Association 41st annual convention, Los Angeles, 14–18 March 2000, http://www.geocities.co.jp/CollegeLife-Club/5676/Hegemonic-Liberalism.html (accessed 30 January 2004).

86 Ibid.

87 UN Commission on the Status of Women, 'Statement by Laila Davoy, Minister, Norwegian Ministry of Children and Family Affairs,' New York, 4 March 2002.

88 Lise Grette, 'Norway's Choice of Direction in the Work against Forced Marriage,' introduction to workshop, 12 September 2002, Seventh International Metropolis Conference, 'Togetherness in Difference,' Oslo, Norway. Text on file with author.

89 Ministry of Children and Family Affairs, 'Renewed Initiative against Forced Marriage,' Spring 2002, http://odin.dep.no/archive/bfdvedlegg/01/04/Q1037014.pdf (accessed 15 November 2003).

90 Kirsti Ellefsen, 'Danish Conditions in Norway?' trans. U. Johanson, *Aftenposen*, 25 May 2003.

91 Personal communication, Terje Bjoranger, adviser, Norwegian Directorate of Immigration, 17 December 2003.

92 Ibid. See also Jonathan Tisdall, 'Bondevik May Face Papal Rebuke; Can Change Marriage Law,' http://www.aftenposten.no/english/local/article627274.ece (accessed 17 September 2003).

93 Simen Slette Sunde, 'A Stricter Law against Forced Marriages a Concern,' trans. U. Johanson, *Aftenposten*, 21 May 2003.

94 Norway, Ministry of Justice and the Police, 'Norway's Plan of Action for Combating Trafficking in Women and Children 2003–2005,' November 2002, http://odin.dep.no/archive/jdvedlegg/01/01/Traff067.pdf (15 November 2003).

95 See, for example, Kaye Haw, *Educating Muslim Girls: Shifting Discourses* (Buckingham: Open University Press, 1998); M. Eslea and K. Mukhtar, 'Bullying and Racism among Asian Schoolchildren in Britain,' *Educational Research* 42, no. 2 (Summer 2000): 207.

96 Mosse, *Toward the Final Solution*, xxvii.

97 See An Na'im, 'Forced Marriage.'

98 Anja Bredal, 'Arranged Marriages as a Multicultural Battlefield,' paper prepared for the working conference 'Youth in the Plural City: Individualized and Collectivized Identity Projects,' Rome (25–28 May 1999), 11.

99 Ibid., 16.

100 Yunas Samad and John Eade, 'Community Perceptions of Forced Marriage,' Community Liaison Unit, United Kingdom, 2002, http://www.fco.gov.uk/Files/kfile/clureport.pdf (accessed 15 November 2003).

101 Ibid., 15.

102 Ibid., 48.

103 Ibid., vi.

104 Southall Black Sisters, *Forced Marriage: An Abuse of Human Rights One Year After 'A Choice by Right.'* Interim Report, July 2001, 18.
105 Ibid., 11.
106 Ibid., 12.
107 Didier Fassin observes this dynamic in the French health-care service-provision context. See 'Culturalism as Ideology,' in *Cultural Perspectives on Reproductive Health*, ed. Carla Makhlouf Obermeyer (Oxford: Oxford University Press, 2001), 307.
108 Anne McGillivray and Brenda Comaskey, *Black Eyes All of the Time: Intimate Violence, Aboriginal Women, and the Justice System* (Toronto: University of Toronto Press, 1999), 100.
109 Committee on the Elimination of Violence against Women, press release, 21 January 2003, 'Norway Called a "Haven for Gender Equality," as Women's Anti-Discrimination Committee Examines Reports on Compliance with Convention,' http://www.un.org/News/Press/docs/2003/wom1377.doc.htm (accessed 15 November 2003).
110 Status of Women Canada, 'Fact Sheet: Statistics on Violence against Women in Canada,' 6 December 2003, http://www.swc-cfc.gc.ca/dates/dec6/facts_e.html (accessed 30 January 2004).
111 An-Na'im, 'Forced Marriage.'
112 Fassin, 'Culturalism as Ideology,' 313.

Chapter 5 The Muslims Are Coming

1 Talal Asad, *Formations of the Secular* (Stanford: Stanford University Press, 2003), 17.
2 Unni Wikan, 'Honour Killings and the Problem of Justice in Modern-day Europe,' paper presented at the conference 'Social Development, Social Inequalities and Social Justice,' Jean Piaget Society, 4 June 2004, Toronto, Ontario.
3 Sherene H. Razack, 'Imperilled Muslim Women, Dangerous Muslim Men and Civilised Europeans: Legal and Social Responses to Forced Marriages,' *Feminist Legal Studies* 12, no. 2 (2004): 129–74.
4 *Arbitration Act*, S.O. 1991, c. 17.
5 Prithi Yelaja and Robert Benzie, 'McGuinty: No Sharia Law,' *Toronto Star*, 12 September 2005, A1.
6 Sherene H. Razack, *Dark Threats and White Knights: The Somalia Affair, Peacekeeping, and the New Imperialism* (Toronto: University of Toronto Press, 2004); Balakrishnan Rajagopal, *International Law from Below: Development,*

Social Movements and Third World Resistance (Cambridge, New York: Cambridge University Press, 2003); Inderpal Grewal, 'Women's Rights as Human Rights: Feminist Practices, Global Feminism and Human Rights Regimes in Transnationality,' *Citizenship Studies* 3, no. 3 (1999): 337–54.

7 Inderpal Grewal, *Transnational America: Feminisms, Diasporas, Neoliberalisms* (Durham, London: Duke University Press, 2005), 152.

8 Dene Moore, 'Muslims Visit Quebec Town,' *Toronto Star*, 12 February 2007. Also, communication by e-mail from a member of the Muslim women of the Hidaya association who visited Hérouxville (m_hayder@hotmail.com) (12 February 2007).

9 Binoy Kampmark, 'Islam, Women and Australia's Cultural Discourse of Terror,' *Hecate* 29, no. 1 (2003): 86–105.

10 Marion Boyd, 'Dispute Resolution in Family Law: Protecting Choice, Promoting Inclusion,' December 2004. Online: Ministry of Attorney General, http://www.attorneygeneral.jus.gov.on.ca/english/about/pubs/boyd/executivesummary. pdf.

11 David Warren, 'Multiculturalism – from Britannia to Sharia,' *National Post*, 8 December 2003, A14.

12 Ken Elgert, 'Islamic Law a Step toward Legal Apartheid,' *Edmonton Journal*, 4 December 2003, A19.

13 Sara Harkirpal Singh, 'Religious Law Undermines Loyalty to Canada,' *Vancouver Sun*, 10 December 2003, A23.

14 Ghammim Harris, 'Sharia Is Not a Law by Canadian Standards,' *Vancouver Sun*, 15 December 2003, A15.

15 Boyd, 'Dispute Resolution in Family Law,' 5.

16 Canadian Council of Muslim Women, 'An Open Letter to Premier Dalton McGuinty and Attorney General Michael Bryant,' http://www.ccmw.com/MuslimFamilyLaw/Letter%20to%20Ontario%20Premier%20Attorney%20General.htm.>

17 Ibid.

18 Women Living Under Muslim Laws, 'Call for Action: Support Canadian Women's Struggle against Sharia Courts,' 7 April 2005, http://www.wluml.org/english/actionsfulltxt.shtml?cmd[156]=i-156-180177.

19 Ibid.

20 For example, Leti Volpp has responded to Susan Moller Okin's polemical essay in which Okin argues that multiculturalism is bad for women (an argument that relies upon the case example of forced marriages, among other practices). Okin's position reinstals the West as superior in a number of ways, Volpp points out. First, the West is represented as more

advanced and less patriarchal than Muslim societies, and the immigrant/Muslim woman is represented as a victim of her culture and devoid of agency in contrast to her freer Western sister. Second, the free, autonomous Western woman and her oppressed Third World sister who is mired in tradition 'elides the level of violence intrinsic to the United States.' Third World cultures are essentialized and static and feminist liberation means a life somehow lived outside of culture, or at least outside Third World culture. Within such dichotomies, it is difficult to understand the forces that influence cultural practices and identifying practices that would strengthen women's contestations within culture. Leti Volpp, 'Feminism versus Multiculturalism,' *Columbia Law Review* 101 (June 2001): 1181. See also Bonnie Honig '"My Culture Made Me Do It"': Response to Okin,' in *Is Multiculturalism Bad for Women?* ed. J. Cohen, M. Howard, and M.C. Nussbaum (Princeton, NJ: Princeton University Press, 1999), 35-40

21 Floya Anthias, 'Beyond Feminism and Multiculturalism: Locating Difference and the Politics of Location,' *Women's Studies International Forum* 25, no. 3 (2002): 275.

22 Ibid., 285.

23 Uma Narayan, *Dislocating Cultures: Identities, Traditions, and Third World Feminism* (New York: Routledge, 1997), 33.

24 Pascale Fournier for the Canadian Council of Muslim Women, 'The Reception of Muslim Family Law in Western Liberal States,' 3. Online: www.ccmw.com/Position Papers/Pascale paper.doc

25 Women's Legal Education and Actual Fund (LEAF), 'Submission to Marion Boyd in Relation to Her Review of the *Arbitration Act*,' 17 September 2004, http://www.leaf.ca/legal-pdfs/Ontario%20Arbitration %20Act %20-%20Submission%20to%20Ontario%20Government.pdf. LEAF's revised position was contained in a press release and letter to Michael Bryant, the then attorney general. Women's Legal Education and Action Fund, 'Revised Position in Response to Marion Boyd's Report on the Use of the Ontario Arbitration Act for Religious Arbitration of Family Law (June 2005),' on file with author.

26 Public meeting, 'International Campaign Against Sharia Courts in Canada,' held at Oriole Community Centre, 2975 Don Mills Rd., Toronto, 26 June 2004.

27 Boyd, 'Dispute Resolution in Family Law,' 100.

28 Ibid, 89.

29 Rosie Dimanno, 'Sharia Solution a Fair One, and Not Racist,' *Toronto Star*, 16 September 2005, A2.

30 Lynda Hurst, 'Distortions and Red Herrings,' *Toronto Star*, 17 September 2005, A6.
31 Haroon Siddiqui, 'Sharia Is Gone but Fear and Hostility Remain,' *Toronto Star*, 15 September 2005, A25.
32 Sangeeta Ray, 'Against Earnestness: Performing the Political in Feminist Theory,' *Journal of Practical Feminist Philosophy* 3, no. 1 (February 2003): 68–79.
33 Carol Quillen, 'Reply to Rey Chow and Martha Nussbaum,' *Signs* 27, no.1 (Autumn 2001): 138.
34 Grewal, *Transnational America*, 27.
35 Amina Jamal, 'Transnational Feminism as Critical Practice: A Reading of Feminist Discourses in Pakistan,' *Meridians* 5, no. 2 (Spring 2005): 57–82.
36 Ibid., 75–6.
37 Banu Gokariksel and Katharyne Mitchell, 'Veiling, Secularism, and the Neo-liberal Subject: National Narratives and Supranational Desires in Turkey and France,' *Global Networks* 5, no. 2 (2005): 147–65.
38 See Sherene Razack, '"Your Client Has a Profile": Race and Security in Canada,' working paper, Court Challenges Program, May 2006, on which chapter 1 is based.
39 Talal Asad, 'Reflections on Laïcité and the Public Sphere,' keynote address at the Beirut Conference on Public Spheres, 22–24 October 2004, http://www.islamamerica.org/articles.cfm/article_id/94 (accessed 5/26/2006); also reproduced in part as 'Reflections on Laïcité and the Public Sphere,' *Items and Issues* 5, no. 3 (2005), Social Science Research Council. http://www.ssrc.org/publications/items/v5n5/refelctions2.html (accessed 26 May 2006).
40 Asad, Beirut conference presentation.
41 Ibid.
42 Ibid.
43 Asad, *Formations of the Secular*, 13.
44 Ibid., 14.
45 Étienne Balibar, 'Ambiguous Universality,' *Differences: A Journal of Feminist Cultural Studies* 7, no. 1 (Spring 1995): 48–74.
46 I am grateful to Sedef Arat-Koc for reminding me of this point.
47 Gokariksel and Mitchell, 'Veiling, Secularism, and the Neo-liberal Subject,' 149.
48 Lauren Berlant, *The Queen of America Goes to Washington City* (Durham: Duke University Press, 1997), 192.
49 Richard Delgado and Jean Stefancic, 'Cosmopolitan Inside Out: International Norms and the Struggle for Civil Rights and Local Justice,'

Connecticut Law Review 27, no. 3 (Spring, 1996): 773.

50 Judith Ezekiel, 'Magritte Meets Maghreb: This Is Not a Veil,' *Australian Feminist Studies* 20, no. 47 (July 2005): 233.

51 A. Sivanandan, 'Race, Terror and Civil Society,' *Race & Class* 47, no. 3 (2006): 3.

52 Liz Fekete, 'Anti-Muslim Racism and the European Security State,' *Race & Class* 46, no. 1 (2004): 4.

53 Ezekiel, 'Magritte Meets Maghreb,' 231; Ghassan Hage, *White Nation: Fantasies of White Supremacy in a Multicultural Society* (New York, London: Routledge, 2000).

54 Mike De Sousa, 'Keep Islamic Law out of Canada, Quebec Politicians Urge,' *Montreal Gazette*, 11 March 2005, A1.

55 Sally Armstrong, 'Criminal Justice. Commentary,' *Chatelaine* 77, no. 11 (November 2004): 152–7.

56 Ariane Brunet, "Canada: Women Criticize Sharia," *Gazette* Montreal, 15 April 2005, available from Women Living Under Muslim Laws website, http://www.luml.org/english/newsfulltext.shtml?cmd%5B157%5D= x-157-187721.

57 Ingrid Peritz, 'Ebadi Decries Islamic Law for Canada,' *Globe and Mail*, 14 June 2005, A7.

58 Azizah Al-Hibri, 'Is Western Patriarchal Feminism Good for Third World/Minority Women?' in *Is Multiculturalism Bad for Women?* ed. J. Cohen, M. Howard, and M.C. Nussbaum (Princeton: Princeton University Press, 1999), 45.

59 Sivanandan, 'Race, Terror and Civil Society,' 3.

60 Ezekiel, 'Magritte Meets Maghreb,' 233.

Conclusion

1 Sherene Razack, *Looking White People in the Eye: Gender, Race, and Culture in Courtrooms and Classrooms.* Toronto: University of Toronto Press, 1998.

2 Joy Gordon, 'Cool War: Economic Sanctions as a Weapon of Mass Destruction,' *Harper's Magazine*, November 2002 (repr. March 2007), http://www.harpers.org/CoolWar.html?pg=1.

3 Derek Gregory, *The Colonial Present* (Cambridge, MA: Blackwell Publishing, 2004), 248–9.

4 Giorgio Agamben, *Homo Sacer: Sovereign Power and Bare Life*, trans. Daniel Heller-Roazen (Stanford: Stanford University Press, 1998), 174.

5 Olivia Ward, 'Islam, West Clash Not Inevitable: Poll,' *Toronto Star*, 19 February 2007, A10.
6 Sean Gordon, 'Hijab on Agenda for World Soccer Group,' *Toronto Star*, 28 February 2007, http://www.thestar.com/printArticle/186477.
7 Debra Black, 'Hijab Ban in Soccer Is Upheld.' *Toronto Star*, 4 March 2007, A3.
8 Etienne Balibar, *We, the People of Europe? Reflections on Transnational Citizenship*, trans. J. Swenson (Princeton, Oxford: Princeton University Press, 2004), 60.
9 Canadian Press, 'Canadian Boy, Iranian Parents Held in U.S.,' *Toronto Star*, 2 March 2007, http://www.thestar.com/printArticle/187676.
10 Henry Stancu, 'Toronto Welcomes Detainees,' *Toronto Star*, 22 March 2007, A16.
11 Zygmunt Bauman, *Society under Siege* (Cambridge: Polity Press, 2002), 114.
12 George L. Mosse, *Toward the Final Solution* (Madison: University of Wisconsin Press, 1985), xxviii.

Bibliography

Abu-Lughod, L. 'Saving Muslim Women or Standing with Them? On Images, Ethics, and War in Our Times.' *Insaniyaat* 1, no. 1 (Spring 2003). http://www.aucegypt.edu/academic/insanyat/Issue%20I/I-article.htm (accessed 15 November 2003).

Agamben, Giorgio. *Homo Sacer: Sovereign Power and Bare Life*. Trans. Daniel Heller-Roazen. Stanford: Stanford University Press, 1998.

– *State of Exception*. Trans. Kevin Attell. Chicago: University of Chicago Press, 2005.

Ahmad, Muneer I. 'A Rage Shared by Law: Post-September 11 Racial Violence as Crimes of Passion.' *California Law Review* 92, no. 5 (October 2004): 1259–1330.

Ahmed, Kamal, Gaby Hinsliff, and Oliver Morgan. 'Ministers Plan to End Forced Marriages.' *The Observer*, 4 November 2001. http://observer.guardian.co.uk/politics/story/0,6903,587516,00.html (accessed 15 November 2003).

Aiken, Sharryn. 'From Slavery to Expulsion: Racism, Canadian Immigration Law and the Unfulfilled Promise of Modern Constitutionalism.' In *Interrogating Race and Racism*, ed. V. Agnew. Toronto: University of Toronto Press, 2007.

– 'National Security and Canadian Immigration: Deconstructing the Discourse of Trade-Offs.' In *Securing Canada in an Uncertain World: Perspectives, Policies, and Practice*, ed. David DeWitt. Toronto: University of Toronto Press, forthcoming.

– 'Of Gods and Monsters: National Security and Canadian Refugee Policy.' *Revue québécoise de droit international* 14, no. 2 (2003): 1–51.

Akram, Susan M. 'Scheherezade Meets Kafka: Two Dozen Sordid Tales of Ideological Exclusion.' *Georgetown Immigration Law Journal* 14, no. 51 (1999–2000): 51–113.

Akram, Susan M., and Kevin R. Johnson. 'Race, Civil Rights, and Immigration Law after September 11, 2001: The Targeting of Arabs and Muslims.' *NYU Annual Survey of American Law* 58 (2001–3): 295–355.

Al-Hibri, Azizah. 'Is Western Patriarchal Feminism Good for Third World/Minority Women?' In *Is Multiculturalism Bad for Women?* ed. J. Cohen, M. Howard, and M.C. Nussbaum, 41–6. New Jersey: Princeton University Press, 1999.

Ali, T. *The Clash of Fundamentalisms: Crusades, Jihads, and Modernity.* London: Verso, 2002.

Allen, James, et al. *Without Sanctuary: Lynching Photographs in America.* Santa Fe, NM: Twin Palms Publishers, 2000.

Amnesty International. 'Guantanamo: Lives Torn Apart: The Impact of Indefinite Detention on Detainees and Their Families.' 6 February 2006. http://web.amnesty.org/library/print/ ENGAMR510072006 (accessed 18 March 2006).

An-Na'im, Abdullahi. 'Forced Marriage.' 2000. http://www.soas.ac.uk/ honourcrimes/ForcedMarriage.htm (accessed 30 January 2004).

Anthias, Floya. 'Beyond Feminism and Multiculturalism: Locating Difference and the Politics of Location.' *Women's Studies International Forum* 25, no. 3 (2002): 275–86.

Arendt, Hannah. *Eichmann in Jerusalem: A Report on the Banality of Evil.* New York: Viking Press, 1963; Penguin Books, 1994.

– *On the Origins of Totalitarianism.* New York: Harcourt, Brace, Jovanovich Publishers, 1973.

Armstrong, Sally. 'Criminal Justice. Commentary.' *Chatelaine* 77, no. 11 (November 2004): 152–7.

Asad, Talal. *Formations of the Secular: Christianity, Islam, Modernity.* Stanford: Stanford University Press, 2003.

– 'Reflections on Laicité and the Public Sphere.' Keynote address at the Beirut Conference on Public Spheres, 22–24 October 2004. http://www .islamamerica.org/articles.cfm/article_id/94 (accessed 26 May 2006). Also reproduced in part as 'Reflections on Laicité and the Public Sphere,' *Items and Issues* 5 no. 3 (2005). Social Science Research Council, http://www .ssrc.org/publications/items/v5n5/reflections2.html (accessed 26 May 2006).

Austin, Andrew. 'Review Essay. Explanation and Responsibility: Agency and Motive in Lynching and Genocide.' *Journal of Black Studies* 34, no. 5 (May 2004): 719–33.

Bahdi, Reem. 'No Exit: Racial Profiling and Canada's War on Terrorism.' *Osgoode Hall Law Journal/Revue d'Osgoode Hall* 41 (2003): 293–317.

Baker, Nancy. 'National Security versus Civil Liberties.' *Presidential Studies Quarterly* 33, no. 3 (September 2003): 547–67.

Baldwin, James. 'Going to Meet the Man.' In *Going to Meet the Man (Stories)*, 227–49. New York: The Dial Press, 1965.

Balibar, Étienne. 'Ambiguous Universality.' *Differences: A Journal of Feminist Cultural Studies* 7, no. 1 (Spring 1995): 48–74.

– *We, the People of Europe? Reflections on Transnational Citizenship*. Trans. James Swenson. Princeton, NJ: Princeton University Press, 2004.

Bartov, Omer. *Germany's War and the Holocaust: Disputed Histories*. Ithaca, London: Cornell University Press, 2003.

Bauman, Zygmunt. *Life in Fragments: Essays in Postmodern Morality*. Oxford: Blackwell, 1995.

– *Society under Siege*. Cambridge: Polity Press, 2002.

Beckett, C., and M. Macey. 'Race, Gender and Sexuality: The Oppression of Multiculturalism.' *Women's Studies International Forum* 24, nos. 3/4 (May–August 2001): 309–19.

Bell, Stewart. *The Martyr's Oath: The Apprenticeship of a Home Grown Terrorist*. Mississauga: John Wiley and Sons, 2005.

Berlant, Lauren. *The Queen of America Goes to Washington City*. Durham: Duke University Press, 1997.

Black, Debra. 'Hijab Ban in Soccer Is Upheld.' *Toronto Star*, 4 March 2007, A3.

Bogo, Didier. 'Security and Immigration: Towards a Critique of the Governmentality of Unease.' *Alternatives* 27 (special issue 2002): 63–92.

Boyd, Marion. 'Dispute Resolution in Family Law: Protecting Choice, Promoting Inclusion.' December 2004. Ontario: Ministry of Attorney General. http://www.attorneygeneral.jus.gov.on.ca/english/about/pubs/boyd/executivesummary.pdf.

Bredal, Anja. 'Arranged Marriages as a Multicultural Battlefield.' Paper prepared for the working conference 'Youth in the Plural City: Individualized and Collectivized Identity Projects.' Rome, 25–28 May 1999.

Brown, Michelle. 'Setting the Conditions for Abu Ghraib: The Prison Nation Abroad.' *American Quarterly* 57, no. 3 (September 2005): 973–97.

Brunet, Ariane. 'Canada: Montreal Women Criticize Sharia.' *The Gazette* (Montreal), 15 April 2005. Available from the Women Living Under Muslim Laws website, at http://www.wluml.org/english/newsfulltext.shtml?cmd%5B157%5D=x-157-187721.

Butler, Judith. *Precarious Life: The Powers of Mourning and Violence*. London, New York: Verso Press, 2004.

Campus Watch. Mission Statement. http://www.campus-watch.org (accessed 15 November 2003).

Canada. Office of the Auditor General. *Report of the Auditor General of Canada to the House of Commons, Chapter 5: Citizenship and Immigration Canada – Control and Enforcement.* Ottawa: Office of the Auditor General of Canada, April 2003. http://www.oag-bvg.gc.ca/domino/reports.nsf/html/ 03menu_e.html.

Canada Border Services Agency. 'Fact Sheet: Security Certificates.' April 2005. http://www.cbsa-asfc.gc.ca/newsroom/_factsheets/2005/certificat-e.html (accessed 18 March 2006).

Canadian Arab Federation. 'Arabs in Canada: Proudly Canadian and Marginalized: Report on the Findings and Recommendations of the Study "Arab Canadians: Charting the Future."' April 2002. http://caf.ca (accessed 18 March 2006).

Canadian Council of Muslim Women. 'An Open Letter to Premier Dalton McGuinty and Attorney General Michael Bryant.' http://www.ccmw .com/MuslimFamilyLaw/Letter%20to%20Ontario%20Premier %20Attorney%20General.htm.

– 'Muslim Women in Canada Fact Sheet.' http://www.whrnet.org/ fundamentalisms/docs/issue-muslim_women_fs-0503.html (accessed 18 March 2006).

Canadian Council for Refugees. 'Refugees and Security.' March 2001 (updated February 2003). http://www.web.net/~ccr/security.pdf (accessed 18 March 2006).

Canadian Press. 'Canadian Boy, Iranian Parents Held in U.S.' *Toronto Star*, 2 March, 2007. http://www.thestar.com/printArticle/187676.

– 'U.S. Security Rules Force Quebec Plant to Shuffle Staff.' *Toronto Star*, 12 January 2007, A8.

Canadian Security Intelligence Service. 'General Comments on the Report's Findings.' Mr. Suleyman Goven and the Canadian Security Intelligence Service in the matter of a complaint under section 41 of the Canadian Security Intelligence Service Act before the Honourable Robert Keith Rae. Toronto, 3 April 2000. Expurgated version.

Cardyn, Lisa. 'Sexualized Racism / Gendered Violence: Outraging the Body Politic in the Reconstruction South.' *Michigan Law Review* 100, no. 4 (February 2002): 675–867.

Carter, Donald Martin. 'Navigating Citizenship: Review of *Generous Betrayal* by Unni Wikan.' *Anthropological Quarterly* 75, no. 2 (Spring 2002): 410–11.

CBC News. '59% of Quebecers Say They're Racist: Poll.' 15 January 2007. http://www.cbc.ca/Canada/Montreal/story/2007/01/15/mtl -racism.html.

Chesler, P. *The New Anti-Semitism and What We Must Do about It*. New York: Jossey-Bass, 2003.

– *Women & Madness*. New York: Avon, 1972.

Chesler, P., and D.M. Hughes. 'Feminism in the 21st Century.' *Washington Post*, 22 February 2002, B7.

Chomsky, Noam. 'War on Terror.' Amnesty International Lecture. Dublin, Ireland, 18 January 2006.

Choudrhry, Sujit. 'Equality in Face of Terror: Ethnic and Racial Profiling and s. 15 of the Charter.' In *The Security of Freedom: Essays on Canada's Anti-Terrorism Bill*, ed. R. Daniels, P. Macklem, and Kent Roach, 163–178. Toronto: University of Toronto Press, 2001.

Cole, David. *Enemy Aliens: Double Standards and Constitutional Freedoms in the War on Terrorism*. New York, London: The New Press, 2003.

Committee on the Elimination of Violence against Women. 'Norway Called a 'Haven for Gender Equality,' as Women's Anti-Discrimination Committee Examines Reports on Compliance with Convention.' Press release, 21 January 2003. http://www.un.org/News/Press/docs/2003/wom1377.doc.htm (accessed 15 November, 2003).

Committee on Equal Opportunities for Women and Men. 'Crimes of Honour.' Presented to the Council of Europe, Parliamentary Assembly, Rapporteur Mrs Cryer, United Kingdom, SOC 4 June 2002. http://www.soas.ac.uk/honourcrimes/Mat_COEreport_june02.pdf (15 November 2003).

Communication en Conseil des Ministres de Nicole Ameline, Ministre déléguée à la parité et à l'égalité professionnelle, 21 January 2003. http://www.lemonde.fr (accessed 31 January 2004).

Copeland, Paul, legal counsel. 'Abdullah Almalki Chronology.' Summer 1998. http://www.bccla.org/othercontent/almalkichronology.pdf (accessed 18 March 2006).

'Copenhagen Set to Introduce Toughest Immigration Laws.' *DAWN* 30 June 2002. http://www.dawn.com/2002/06/30/int8.htm (accessed 15 November, 2003).

'Council of Europe, Parliamentary Assembly. 'Forced Marriages and Child Marriages.' Doc. 9966, 13 October 2003.

Crittenden, R.N. Review of *The Clash of Civilizations and the Remaking of World Order*. November 2002, revised; September 2001. http://www.hargravpublishing.com/Civilizations.htm (accessed 15 November 2003).

Danner, Mark. 'The Logic of Torture.' In *Abu Ghraib: The Politics of Torture*, ed. John Gray et al., 17–46. Berkeley: North Atlantic Books, 2004.

Da Silva, D. Ferreira. 'Towards a Critique of the Socio-logos of Justice: The

Analytics of Raciality and the Production of Universality.' *Social Identities* 7, no. 3 (2001): 421–54.

Debrix, Francois. 'Tabloid Realism and the Revival of American Security Culture.' In *11 September and Its Aftermath: The Geopolitics of Terror*, ed. Stanley D. Bruun, 151–90. London, Portland, OR: Frank Cass, 2004.

Deleuze, Gilles, and Felix Guattari. *Anti-Oedipus: Capitalism and Schizophrenia*. Vol. 1 (1972), trans. R. Hurley, M. Seem, and H. Lane. New York: Viking, 1977.

Delgado, Richard, and Jean Stefancic. 'Cosmopolitan Inside Out: International Norms and the Struggle for Civil Rights and Local Justice.' *Connecticut Law Review* 27, no. 3 (Spring 1995): 773.

Denmark. Action Plan for 2003–2005 on Forced, Quasi-Forced and Arranged Marriages.' 2003. http://www.nyidanmark.dk/NR/rdonlyres/05ED3816 -8159-4899-9CBB-CDD2D7BF23AE/0/forced_marriages.pdf (accessed 12 April 2004).

– Ministry of Integration. *Bill Amending the Aliens Act, the Marriage Act and Other Acts*, s. 9(1)(ii), 28 February 2002. Background paper, 'The Family Reunification Field.' http://www.flygtning.dk/publikationer/hoering/ unhcr.pdf (accessed 12 April 2004).

– Ministry of Refugee, Immigration and Integration Affairs *Aliens (Consolidation) Act no. 608, 17 July 2002*, s. 9(1). Available at http://www.udlst.dk/ english/Family+Reunification/Default.htm (accessed 30 January 2003).

Derrida, Jacques. *Rogues: Two Essays on Reason*. Trans. Pascale-Anne Brault and Michael Naas. California: Stanford University Press, 2005.

Dershowitz, A. *The Case for Israel*. Hoboken, NJ: John Wiley and Sons, 2003.

De Sousa, Mike. 'Keep Islamic Law Out of Canada, Quebec Politicians Urge.' *Montreal Gazette*, 11 March 2005, A1.

Didion, J. 'Mr. Bush and the Divine.' *New York Review of Books* 17 (6 November 2003): 81–6.

Diken, Bulent, and Carsten Bagge Lausten. *The Culture of Exception: Sociology Facing the Camp*. London, New York: Routledge, 2005.

– 'Zones of Indistinction: Security, Terror, and Bare Life.' *Space & Culture* 5, no. 3 (August 2002): 290–307.

Dimanno, Rosie. 'Sharia Solution a Fair One, and Not Racist.' *Toronto Star*, 16 September 2005, A2.

Donnelly, P. 'Muslim Writer Challenges Her Faith.' *The Gazette*, 2 October 2003. http://www.muslim-refusenik.com/news/mtlgazette-oct02-03.html (accessed 14 April 2004).

Drachmann, H. 'Haarder Hyldet af Norske Feminister.' *Politikken* 2003.

http://www.poliken.dk/VisArtikel.iasp?PageID=295643 (accessed 14 April 2004).

Dreher, R. 'Oriana's Screed: Review of *The Rage and the Pride.' National Review Online* 8 (October 2002). http://www.nationalreview.com/dreher/dreher101002.asp (accessed 1 March 2004).

Dubois, W.E.B. *The Souls of Black Folk* (1903). Repr.. New York: Fawcett Publications, 1962.

Dworkin, Andrea. 'Pornography Happens to Women.' In *Life and Death*, 126–138. New York: The Free Press, 1997.

Ehrenreich, Barbara. 'Feminism's Assumptions Upended.' In *Abu Ghraib: The Politics of Torture*, ed. John Gray et al., 65–70. Berkeley: North Atlantic Books, 2004.

Eide, Elisabeth. '"Down There" and "Up Here": "Europe's Others" in Norwegian Feature Stories.' PhD dissertation, Institutt for Medier og Kommunikasjon (Ref. no. 73336, Oslo, Norway, 2002.

Eisenstein, Zillah. 'Sexual Humiliation, Gender Confusion and the Horrors at Abu Ghraib.' Znet, 22 June 2004. http://www.zmag.org/content/showarticle.cfm?SectionID=12&ItemID=5751.

Elgert, Ken. 'Islamic Law a Step toward Legal Apartheid?' *Edmonton Journal*, 4 December 2003, A19.

Ellefsen, Kirsti. 'Danish Conditions in Norway?' Trans. Ulla Johanson. *Aftenposen* 25 (May 2003).

Engle, Karen. 'Constructing Good Aliens and Good Citizens: Legitimizing the War on Terror(ism).' *University of Colorado Law Review* 75 no. 1 (Winter 2004): 59–114.

Eriksen, Thomas Hylland. 'Norway a Multi-ethnic Country.' News of Norway, issue 1, 2001. http://www.norway.org/News/archive/2000/2000101ethnic.html (accessed 15 November 2003).

Eslea, M., and K. Mukhtar. 'Bullying and Racism among Asian Schoolchildren in Britain.' *Educational Research* 42, no. 2 (July 2000): 207–17.

Ezekiel, Judith. 'Magritte Meets Maghreb: This Is Not a Veil.' *Australian Feminist Studies* 20, no. 47 (July 2005): 231–43.

Fallaci, O. 'Anti-Semitism Today.' *Panorama Magazine*, 12 April 2002. http://www.tpi.umn.edu/shifman/fallaci.pdf (accessed 14 May 2007).

– *The Rage and the Pride*. New York: Rizzoli International Publications Inc., 2002.

Fanon, Frantz. *The Wretched of the Earth*. New York: Grove Press, 1963.

Farley, Anthony Paul. 'The Black Body as Fetish Object.' *Orlando Law Review* 76 (1997): 457–530.

220   Bibliography

Fassin, Didier. 'Culturalism as Ideology.' In *Cultural Perspectives on Reproductive Health*, ed. Carla Makhlouf Obermeyer, 300–18. Oxford: Oxford University Press, 2001.

Fekete, Liz. 'Anti-Muslim Racism and the European Security State.' *Race & Class* 46, no. 1 (2004): 3–29.

Fellows, Mary Louise, and Sherene H. Razack. 'The Race to Innocence: Confronting Hierarchical Relations among Women.' *Journal of Gender, Race and Justice* 1, no. 2 (Spring 1998): 335–52.

Final Report of the Independent Panel to Review Department of Defense Operations. Honorable James R. Schlesinger, Chairman, August 2004. 126 pages. http://www.defenselink.mil/news/Aug2004/d20040824finalreport.pdf.

'Forced Weddings: Difficult Culture Clash.' *Norway Now*, 20 October 1999. http://odin.dep.no/ud/engelsk/publ/periodika.032005-992400/index -dok000-b-n-a.html (accessed 15 November 2003).

Foucault, Michel. 'Society Must Be Defended.' In *Lectures at the College de France 1975–1976*, ed. Mauro Bertani and Alessandro Fontana, trans. David Macey. New York: Picador, 2003.

Fournier, Pascale (for the Canadian Council of Muslim Women). 'The Reception of Muslim Family Law in Western Liberal States.' http://www.ccmw .com/Position%20Papers/Pascale%20paper.doc.

Foxman, A. *Never Again? The Threat of the New Anti-Semitism*. San Francisco: Harper, 2003.

Freedman, Jane. 'L'Affaire des foulards: Problems of Defining a Feminist Antiracist Strategy in French Schools.' In *Feminism and Anti-Racism: International Struggles for Justice*, ed. France Winddance Twine and Kathleen M. Blee, 295–312. New York: New York University Press, 2001.

Fuoco, Michael A. 'Witnesses Describe Abu Ghraib Abuse: Defense Plays Down Pyramid of Prisoners as Something Cheerleaders across America Do.' *Pittsburg Post-Gazette*, 11 January 2005.

George, Rosemary M. 'Homes in the Empire, Empire in the Home.' *Cultural Critique* 26 (Winter 1993–4): 95–129.

Gilroy, Paul. *Between Camps: Race, Identity, and Nationalism*. London: Allen Lane, 2000. (Also known as *Against Race: Imagining Political Culture beyond the Color Line*, Harvard University Press.)

Giroux, Henry A. 'What Might Education Mean after Abu Ghraib? Revisiting Adorno's Politics of Education.' *Comparative Studies of South Asia, Africa and the Middle East* 24, no. 1 (2004): 5–24.

Globe and Mail. Editorial. 'Why Hassan Almrei Still Sits in Detention.' 8 December 2005, A28.

Godoy, Angelina Snodgrass. 'Converging on the Poles: Contemporary Punishment and Democracy in Hemispheric Perspective.' *Law and Social Inquiry* 30 (2005): 515–48.

Gokariksel, Banu, and Katharyne Mitchell. 'Veiling, Secularism, and the Neoliberal Subject: National Narratives and Supranational Desires in Turkey and France.' *Global Networks* 5, no. 2 (2005): 147–65.

Goldberg, David. '"Killing Me Softly": Civility/Race/Violence.' *Review of Education, Pedagogy, and Cultural Studies* 27 (2005): 337–66.

– *The Racial State.* Cambridge, MA: Blackwell, 2002.

– *Racist Culture: Philosophy and the Politics of Meaning.* Cambridge, MA: Blackwell, 1993.

Goldhagen, Daniel Jonah. *Hitler's Willing Executioners: Ordinary Germans and the Holocaust.* New York: Alfred A. Knopf, 1996.

Goldstein, R. 'Letter: Richard Goldstein Replies to Charles Taylor's "Oriana Fallaci Declares War on Radical Islam."' *Salon.com*, 21 November 2002. http://archive.salon.com/books/letters/2002/11/21/goldstein_reply (accessed 14 April 2004).

Gordon, Avery F. 'Abu Ghraib: Imprisonment and the War on Terror.' *Race & Class* 48, no. 1 (2006): 42–59.

Gordon, Joy. 'Cool War: Economic Sanctions as a Weapon of Mass Destruction.' *Harper's Magazine*, November 2002 (repr. March 2007). http://www.harpers.org/CoolWar.html?pg=1.

Gordon, Sean. 'Hijab on Agenda for World Soccer Group.' *Toronto Star*, 28 February 2007. http://www.thestar.com/printArticle/186477.

– 'Quebec Town Spawns Uneasy Debate.' *Toronto Star*, 5 February 2007, A1, A4.

Gott, Gil.'The Devil We Know: Racial Subordination and National Security Law.' *Villanova Law Review* 50, no. 4 (2005): 1073–134.

Grace, K.M. 'A Multiculturalist Speaks.' *Canadian Heritage Alliance Magazine.* http://www.canadianheritagealliance.com/channels/articles/grace/speaks.html (accessed 15 November 2003).

Gray, John. 'Power and Vainglory.' In *Abu Ghraib: The Politics of Torture*, ed. Gray et al., 47–55. Berkeley: North Atlantic Books, 2004.

Gregory, Derek. *The Colonial Present.* Cambridge, MA: Blackwell Publishing, 2004.

Grette, Lise. 'Norway's Choice of Direction in the Work against Forced Marriage.' Introduction to workshop, Seventh International Metropolis Conference, 'Togetherness in Difference,' Oslo, Norway, 12 September 2002.

Grewal, Inderpal. *Transnational America: Feminisms, Diasporas, Neoliberalisms.* Durham, London: Duke University Press, 2005.

– 'Women's Rights as Human Rights: Feminist Practices, Global Feminism and Human Rights Regimes in Transnationality.' *Citizenship Studies* 3, no. 3 (1999): 337–54.

Gullestad, Marianne. 'Invisible Fences: Nationalism, Egalitarianism and Immigration.' Anthropology of Europe Workshop Archives. 12 October 2000. http://cas.uchicago.edu/workshops/antheur/Gullestad.pdf (accessed 15 November 2003).

– 'Mohammed Atta and I: Identification, Discrimination and the Formation of Sleepers.' *European Journal of Cultural Studies* 6, no. 4 (2003): 529–48.

Gurely, G. 'The Rage of Oriana Fallaci.' *New York Observer*, 11 June 2003. http://www.observer.com/pagesstory.asp?ID=6869 (accessed 1 March 2004).

Ghassan,Hage. *White Nation: Fantasies of White Supremacy in a Multicultural Society.* New York, London: Routledge, 2000.

Hamdi, Mohammed, Anu Bose, Nayyar Javed, Jo-Anne Lee, and Lise Martin. 'The Impact of the National Security Agenda on Racialized Women: Bringing US out of the Policy Ghetto and into the Development of National Policy, Strategies and Solutions.' Canadian Research Institute for the Advancement of Women and the National Organization of Immigrant and Visible Minority Women of Canada. Fall 2005.

Hansen, Thomas Blom. 'Sovereigns beyond the State: On Legality and Authority in Urban India.' In *Sovereign Bodies: Citizens, Migrants, and States in the Postcolonial World*, ed. Thomas Hansen and Finn Stepputat, 169–91. Princeton: Princeton University Press, 2005.

Hansen, Thomas Blom, and Finn Stepputat. 'Introduction.' In *Sovereign Bodies: Citizens, Migrants, and States in the Postcolonial World*, ed. Hansen and Stepputat, 1–38. Princeton: Princeton University Press, 2005.

Hardt, Michael, and Antonio Negri, *Empire*. London and Cambridge: Harvard University Press, 2000.

Harris, Ghammim. 'Sharia Is Not a Law by Canadian Standards.' *Vancouver Sun*, 15 December 2003, A15.

Harris, Trudier. *Exorcising Blackness: Historical and Literary Lynching and Burning Rituals*. Bloomington: Indiana University Press, 1984.

Haw, Kaye. *Educating Muslim Girls: Shifting Discourses*. Buckingham: Open University Press, 1998.

Hegge, Per Egil. 'When Danes Are Refused Entry to Their Home Country.' Trans. Ulla Johanson. *Aftenposten*, 18 July 2003.

Helly, Denise. 'Are Muslims Discriminated against in Canada since September 2001?' *Journal of Canadian Ethnic Studies* 36, no. 1 (Fall 2004): 24–47.

Henley, Jon. 'MPs Urge French Ban on Religious Symbols.' *The Guardian*, 14 November 2003.

Hersh, Seymour. *Chain of Command: The Road from 9/11 to Abu Ghraib*. New York: HarperCollins, 2004.

Hindess, Barry. 'Citizenship and Empire.' In *Sovereign Bodies: Citizens, Migrants, and States in the Postcolonial World*, ed. Thomas Blom Hansen and Fian Stepputat, 241–56. Princeton, NJ: Princeton University Press, 2005.

Honig, Bonnie. ' 'My Culture Made Me Do It': Response to Okin.' In *Is Multiculturalism Bad for Women?* Ed. Joshua Cohen, Matthew Howard, and Martha C. Nussbaum, 35–40. Princeton, NJ: Princeton University Press, 1999.

Hooks, Gregory, and Clayton Mosher. 'Outrages against Personal Dignity: Rationalizing Abuse and Torture in the War on Terror.' *Social Forces* 83, no. 4 (June 2005): 1627–46.

Huntington, Samuel P. *The Clash of Civilizations and the Remaking of World Order*. New York: Touchstone Press, 1997.

Hurst, Lynda. 'Distortions and Red Herrings.' *Toronto Star*, 17 September 2005, A6.

Hussain, Nasser. *The Jurisprudence of Emergency: Colonialism and the Rule of Law*. Ann Arbor: University of Michigan Press, 2003.

– 'Towards a Jurisprudence of Emergency: Colonialism and the Rule of Law.' *Law and Critique* 10 (1999): 93–115.

Iganski, P., and B. Kosmin. *A New Anti-Semitism? Debating Judeophobia in 21st Century Britain*. London: Institute for Jewish Policy Research, 2003.

Inglehart, R., and Norris, P. *Rising Tide: Gender Equality and Cultural Change around the World*. Cambridge: Cambridge University Press, 2003.

– 'The True Clash of Civilizations.' *Foreign Policy*, March/April 2003: 67–74.

Inter-American Commission on Human Rights. *Report on the Situation of Human Rights of Asylum Seekers within the Canadian Refugee Determination System*. 28 February 2000. http://www.cidh.org/countryrep/canada 2000en/table-of-contents.htm (accessed 16 March 2006).

'International Campaign Against Sharia Courts in Canada.' Public meeting held at Oriole Community Centre, 2975 Don Mills Rd, Toronto. 26 June 2004.

International Forum on Forced Marriages. Great Britain, 2003. http://www.britain-info.org/culturaldiversity/xq/asp/SarticleType.1/Article_ID.3814/qx/ar (26 July 2003).

Jackman, Barbara, legal counsel. 'Ahmad El Maati Chronology,' April 2001. http://www.bccla.org/othercontent/elmaatichronology.pdf (accessed 18 March 2006).

– 'One Measure of Justice in Canada: Judicial Protection for Non-Citizens.' Paper presented at the Canadian Bar Association annual conference, Banff, Alberta, April 2005.

Jamal, Amina. 'Transnational Feminism as Critical Practice: A Reading of Feminist Discourses in Pakistan.' *Meridians* 5, no. 2 (Spring 2005): 57–82.

Jonas, G. 'Fallaci Is a Little Heavy on the Rage.' *National Post*, 7 November 2002, A22. http://www.nationalpost.com (accessed 1 March 2004).

Kabbani, R. 'Bible of the Muslim Haters.' *The Guardian*, 11 June 2002. http://www.guardian.co.uk/farright/story/0,11981,731126,00.html (accessed 3 April 2004).

Kalman, M. 'A Muslim Calling for Reform – and She's a Lesbian.' *San Francisco Chronicle*, 19 January 2004. http://www.muslim-refusenik.com/news/sfchronicle20040119.html (accessed 14 April 2004).

Kampmark, Binoy. 'Islam, Women and Australia's Cultural Discourse of Terror.' *Hecate* 29, no. 1 (2003): 86–105.

Kaplan, Amy. 'Violent Belongings and the Question of Empire Today – Presidential Address to the American Studies Association, October 17, 2003.' *American Quarterly* 56, no. 1 (March 2004): 1–18.

Kaplan, C. 'Getting to Know You: Travel, Gender and the Politics of Representation in *Anna and the King of Siam* and *The King and I.*' In *Late Imperial Culture*, ed. R. de la Campa, E.A. Kaplan, and M. Sprinkler, 33–52. London: Verso, 1995.

Karim, Karim. *Islamic Peril: Media and Global Violence.* Montreal: Institute of Policy Alternatives, 2003.

Kashmeri, Zuhair. *The Gulf Within: Canadians, Arabs, Racism and the Gulf War.* Toronto: J. Lorimer, 1991.

Kelley, Ninette, and Michael Trebilcock. *The Making of the Mosaic: A History of Canadian Immigration Policy.* Toronto: University of Toronto Press, 2000.

Khalema, Nene Ernest, and Jenny Wannas-Jones. 'Under the Prism of Suspicion: Minority Voices in Post-September 11.' *Journal of Muslim Minority Affairs* 23, no. 1 (April 2003): 25–39.

Kleeblatt, Norman L. 'The Body of Alfred Dreyfus: A Site for France's Displaced Anxieties of Masculinity, Homosexuality and Power.' In *Diaspora and Visual Culture: Representing Africans and Jews*, ed. Nicholas Mirzoeff, 76–132. London, New York: Routledge, 2000.

Klug, B. 'The Myth of the New Anti-Semitism.' *The Nation*, 15 January 2004. http://www.thenation.com/doc.mhtml?i=20040202&s=klug (accessed 1 March 2004)

Koonz, Claudia. *The Nazi Conscience.* London: The Belknap Press of Harvard University Press, 2003.

Krishnaswamy, Revathi. *Effeminism: The Economy of Colonial Desire.* Ann Arbor: University of Michigan Press, 1998.

Kurkiala, Mikael. 'Interpreting Honour Killings.' *Anthropology Today* 19, no. 1 (February 2003): 6–7.

Legomsky, Stephen H. 'The Ethnic and Religious Profiling of Noncitizens: National Security and International Human Rights.' *Boston College Third World Law Journal* 25 (2005): 161–220.

Ling, L.H.M. 'Hegemonic Liberalism: Martha Nussbaum, Jorg Haider, and the Struggle for Late Modernity.' Paper delivered at the International Studies Association 41st annual convention, Los Angeles, 14–18, March 2000. http://www.geocities.co.jp/CollegeLife-Club/5676/Hegemonic -Liberalism.html (accessed 30 January 2004).

Lopez, K.J. 'Liberal and Pro-Israel: An Interview with Phyllis Chesler.' *National Review Online*, 25 November, 2003. http://www.nationalreview .com/interrogatory/chesler200311250905.asp (accessed 1 March 2004).

Mahler, Jonathan. 'The Bush Administration vs. Salim Hamdan.' *New York Times Magazine*, 8 January 2006, 44.

Mallan, Caroline. 'U.K. Arrests Spur "Profiling Debate."' *Toronto Star*, 19 August 2006, A2.

Mamdani, Mahmood. *Good Muslim, Bad Muslim: America, the Cold War, and the Roots of Terror*. New York: Doubleday, 2004.

Manji, I. *The Trouble with Islam: A Wake-up Call for Honesty and Change*. Toronto: Random House, 2003.

Mbembe, Achille. 'Necropolitics.' Trans. Libby Meintjes. *Public Culture* 15, no. 1 (2003): 11–40.

– *On the Postcolony*. Berkeley: University of California Press, 2001.

McGillivray, Anne, and Brenda Comaskey. *Black Eyes All of the Time: Intimate Violence, Aboriginal Women, and the Justice System*. Toronto: University of Toronto Press, 1999.

Mirzoeff, Nicholas. *Watching Babylon: The War in Iraq and Global Visual Culture*. New York, London: Routledge, 2005.

Mohanram, Radhika. *Black Body: Women, Colonialism, and Space*. Minneapolis: University of Minnesota Press, 1999.

Moore, Dene. 'Muslims Visit Quebec Town.' *Toronto Star*, 12 February 2007.

– 'Quebec Town Bans Kirpans, Stoning Women.' *Globe and Mail*, 30 January 2007, A12.

Mosse, George L. *Toward the Final Solution. A History of European Racism*. Madison: University of Wisconsin Press, 1978, 1985.

Murdocca, Carmela. 'Foreign Bodies: Race, Canadian Nationalism and the Trope of Disease.' MA thesis, OISE/University of Toronto, 2002.

Narayan, Uma. *Dislocating Cultures: Identities, Traditions, and Third World Feminism*. New York: Routledge, 1997.

National Post. Editorial. 'Much Ado About Sharia.' 13 December 2003, A25.

Neal, Andrew W. 'Foucault in Guantanamo: Towards an Archaeology of the Exception.' *Security Dialogue* 37, no. 1 (2006): 31–46.

Nguyen, Tram. *We Are All Suspects Now. Untold Stories from Immigrant Communities after 9/11*. Boston: Beacon Press, 2005.

Norway. Ministry of Justice and the Police. 'Norway's Plan of Action for Combating Trafficking in Women and Children 2003–2005.' November 2002. http://odin.dep.no/archive/jdvedlegg/01/01/Traff067.pdf (accessed 15 November 2003).

– Ministry of Children and Family Affairs. 'Action Plan against Forced Marriages.' Spring 1999. http://odin.dep.no/bfd/engelsk/publ/handbooks/004021-120005/index-ind001-b-f-a.html (accessed 15 November 2003).

– 'Renewed Initiative against Forced Marriage 2002.' Spring 2002. http://odin.dep.no/archive/bfdvedlegg/01/04/Q1037014.pdf (accessed 15 November 2003).

Olive, David. 'Why Record Evil? Abuse Photos Hard to Explain.' *Toronto Star*, 22 May 2004, A1.

Ong, Aihwa. *Neoliberalism as Exception: Mutations in Citizenship and Sovereignty*. Durham, London: Duke University Press, 2006.

– 'Splintering Cosmopolitanism: Asian Immigrants and Zones of Autonomy in the American West.' In *Sovereign Bodies: Citizens, Migrants, and States in the Postcolonial World*, ed. Thomas Blom Hansen and Fian Stepputat, 257–75. Princeton, NJ: Princeton University Press, 2005.

O'Neil, Brendan. 'After Guantanamo.' BBC News, 25 January 2005. http://news.bbc.co.uk/1/hi/magazine/4203803.stm (accessed 18 March 2005).

Oprah Magazine. 'The First Annual Chutzpah Awards.' May 2004, 234, 240.

Osborn, A. 'Copenhagen Set to Introduce Toughest Immigration Laws.' DAWN, 2002. http://www.dawn.com/202/06/30int8.htm (accessed 12 April 2004).

Paur, Jasbir K. 'Abu Ghraib: Arguing against Exceptionalism.' *Feminist Studies* 30, no. 2 (Summer 2004): 522–34.

Peritz, Ingrid. 'Ebadi Decries Islamic Law for Canada.' *Globe and Mail*, 14 June 2005, A7.

Perkins, Tara. 'Royal Bank Caught by American Sanctions.' *Toronto Star*, 17 January 2007, F1.

Pinar, William. '"I Am a Man": The Queer Politics of Race.' *Cultural Studies Critical Methodologies* 3, no. 3 (2003): 271–86.

Pipes, D. *Militant Islam Reaches America*. New York: W.W. Norton, 2003.

– '(Moderate) Voices of Islam.' *New York Post*, 23 September 2003.
http://www.danielpipes.org/article/1255 (accessed 1 March 2004).

Pipes, D., and L. Hedegaard. 'Something Rotten in Denmark?' *New York Post*, 27 August 2002. http://www.danielpipes.org/article/450 (accessed 15 November 2003).

Podur, J. '"A Multifaceted Fraud": Reviewing Irshad Manji's *The Trouble With Islam*, parts 1 and 2, *Znet*, 5 December 2003, http://www.zmag.org/content/showarticle.cfm?ItemID=4624 (accessed 14 April 2004).

Pollitt, K. 'Introduction.' In *Nothing Sacred: Women Respond to Religious Fundamentalism and Terror*, ed. B. Reed, ix–xiv. New York: Thunder's Mouth Press / Nation Books, 2002.

Porras, Ileana M. 'On Terrorism: Reflections on Violence and the Outlaw.' In *After Identity: A Reader on Law and Culture*, ed. Dan Danielsen and Karen Engle, 294–313. New York, London: Routledge, 1995.

Posner, M. 'Rousing Islam.' *Globe and Mail*, 16 September 2003. http://www.muslim-refusenik.com/news/globe-sept16-03.html (accessed 14 April 2004).

Pratt, Anna. *Securing Borders: Detention and Deportation in Canada*. Vancouver: UBC Press, 2005.

Quillen, Carol. 'Reply to Rey Chow and Martha Nussbaum.' *Signs* 27, no. 1 (Autumn 2001): 87–124.

Rai, Amit S. 'Of Monsters: Biopower, Terrorism and Excess in Genealogies of Monstrosity.' *Cultural Studies* 18, no. 4 (July 2004): 538–70.

Raja, A.Q. 'Exploiting the media. Creating Further Infringement.' *VG Nett*, 2004. http://www.vg.no/pub/vgart.hbs?artid+217461 (accessed 12 April 2004).

Rajagopal, Balakrishnan. *International Law from Below: Development, Social Movements and Third World Resistance*. Cambridge, New York: Cambridge University Press, 2003.

Rao, Govind. 'Inventing Enemies: Project Thread and Canadian "Security."' *Canadian Dimension* 38, no. 1 (January 2004): 9.

Ratner, Michael, and Ellen Ray. *Guantanamo: What the World Should Know*. White River Junction, VT: Chelsea Green Publishing Co., 2004.

Ray, Sangeeta. 'Against Earnestness: Performing the Political in Feminist Theory.' *Journal of Practical Feminist Philosophy* 3, no.1 (February 2003): 68–79.

Razack, Sherene H. *Dark Threats and White Knights: The Somalia Affair, Peacekeeping, and the New Imperialism*. Toronto: University of Toronto Press, 2004.

– 'From the 'Clean Snows of Petawawa': The Violence of Canadian Peacekeepers in Somalia.' *Cultural Anthropology* 15, no. 1 (2000): 127–63.

– 'Imperilled Muslim Women, Dangerous Muslim Men and Civilised Europeans: Legal and Social Responses to Forced Marriages.' *Feminist Legal Studies* 12, no. 2 (2004): 129–74.

- *Looking White People in the Eye: Gender, Race, and Culture in Courtrooms and Classrooms.* Toronto: University of Toronto Press, 1998.
- 'Making Canada White: Law and the Policing of Bodies of Colour in the 1990s.' *Canadian Journal of Law and Society* 14, no. 1 (Spring 1999): 159–84.
- '"Simple Logic": The Identity Documents Rule and the Fantasy of a Nation Besieged and Betrayed.' *Journal of Law and Social Policy* 15 (2000): 183–211.
- 'A Violent Culture or Culturalized Racism?' *Studies in Practical Philosophy* 3, no. 1 (February 2003): 80–104.
- 'When Place Becomes Race.' In *Race, Space and the Law: Unmapping a White Settler Society*, ed. S. Razack, 1–6. Toronto: Between the Lines, 2002.
- '"Your Client Has a Profile": Race and Security in Canada.' Working paper, Court Challenges Program, May 2006.

Reed, J. 'Extreme Makeover.' *Vogue Magazine*, November 2003, 465–72, 510.

Remsen, J. 'Stirring up Fellow Muslims.' *Philadelphia Inquirer*, 11 January 2004. http://www.philly.com/mld/inquirer/living/religion/7679655.htm?lc (accessed 14 April 2004).

Roy, Oliver. *Globalized Islam: The Search for a New Ummah.* New York: Columbia University Press, 2004.

Rytkonen, Helle Laila. 'Europe and Its "Almost-European" Other: A Textual Analysis of Legal and Cultural Practices of Othering in Contemporary Europe.' PhD dissertation, Stanford University, 2002.

Said, Edward W. 'The Clash of Ignorance.' *Media Monitors Network*, 11 October 2001. http://www.mediamonitors.net/edward40.html (accessed 13 August 2003).

- *Culture and Imperialism.* New York: Alfred A. Knopf, 1993.
- *The Question of Palestine.* New York: Vintage Books, 1979, 1992.

Samad, Yunas, and John Eade. 'Community Perceptions of Forced Marriage.' Community Liaison Unit, United Kingdom, 2002. http://www.fco.gov.uk/Files/kfile/clureport.pdf (accessed 15 November 2003).

Sassen, Saskia. *Globalization and Its Discontents.* New York: New Press, 1998.

Shepherd, Michelle. 'Man held without Charges Granted Bail.' *Toronto Star*, 7 March 2007, A1, A17.

- 'RCMP Clears Itself in "Terror Cell" Sweep: Police Concludes Probe Was Justified.' *Toronto Star*, 6 October 2004, A01.

Shepherd, Michelle, and Peter Edwards. 'Terror Suspects May Be Freed.' *Toronto Star*, 28 August 2003.

Siddiqui, Haroon. 'Sharia Is Gone but Fear and Hostility Remain.' *Toronto Star*, 15 September 2005, A25.

Siddiqui, Tabassum. 'Testimony Begins for 3 in Class Suit against U.S.' *Toronto Star*, 5 April 2006, A4.

Silverblatt, Irene M. *Modern Inquisitions: Peru and the Colonial Origins of the Civilized World*. Durham, NC: Duke University Press, 2005.

Singh, Sara Harkirpal. 'Religious Law Undermines Loyalty to Canada.' *Vancouver Sun*, 10 December 2003, A23.

Sivanandan, A. 'Race, Terror and Civil Society.' *Race & Class* 47, no. 3 (2006): 1–8.

Skukovsky, Paul. 'Terrorism Suspect's Suit Tells of U.S. Abuse: Documents in Guantanamo Case Describe Extreme Isolation.' *Seattle Post Intelligencer Reporter*, 6 August 2004. http://seattlepi.nwsource.com/local/185134 _guantanamo06.html.

Smith, Shawn Michelle. *American Archives*. Princeton: Princeton University Press, 1999.

Southall Black Sisters. *Forced Marriage: An Abuse of Human Rights One Year after 'A Choice by Right.' Interim Report*. July 2001.

Stancu, Henry. 'Toronto Welcomes Detainees.' *Toronto Star*, 22 March 2007, A16.

Status of Women Canada. 'Fact Sheet: Statistics on Violence against Women in Canada December 6, 2003.' http://www.swc-cfc.gc.ca/dates/dec6/facts _e.html (accessed 30 January 2004).

Storhaug, Hege, and Human Rights Service. *Human Visas: A Report from the Front Lines of Europe's Integration Crisis*. Trans Bruce Bawer. Norway: KOLOFON AS, 2003. www.kolofon.com (accessed 30 January 2004).

Strasser, Steven. *The Abu Ghraib Investigations*. New York: Public Affairs, 2005.

Suh, A. 'London Conference Tackles Sensitive Issue of Forced Marriages.' VOA News, 2003. http://www.voanews.com/article.cfm?objectID +7F0CDD1F-C915-44B8-9CCD17F4E9483C5C# (accessed 12 April 2004).

Sullivan, Andrew. 'Decent Exposure.' *New York Times*, 25 January 2004. http://www.muslim-refusenik.com/news/nytimes-04-01-25pt1.html (accessed 14 April 2004).

Sunde, Simen Slette.'A Stricter Law against Forced Marriages a Concern.' Trans. Ulla Johanson. *Aftenposten*, 21 May 2003.

Taussig, Michael. 'Culture of Terror – Space of Death: Roger Casement's Putumayo Report and the Explanation of Torture.' In *Violence in War and Peace: An Anthology*, ed. Nancy Scheper-Hughes and Philippe Bourgeois, 39–53. Malden, MA: Blackwell Publishers, 2004.

Taylor, C. 'Oriana Fallaci Declares War on Radical Islam.' *Salon.com*, 16 November 2002. http://archive.salon.com/books/feature/2002/11/16/ fallaci/index_np.html (accessed 14 April 2004).

Ticktin, Miriam. 'Between Justice and Compassion: "Les Sans Papiers" and the Political Economy of Health, Human Right and Humanitarianism in France.' PhD dissertation, Department of Cultural and Social Anthropology, Stanford University, 2002.

Timerman, Jacobo. *Prisoner without a Name, Cell without a Number.* Trans. Tony Talbot. New York: Alfred A Knopf Inc., 1981; Vintage Books, 1982.

Tisdall, Jonathan. 'Bondevik May Face Papal Rebuke. Can Change Marriage Law.' *Aftenposten*: News from Norway, 17 September 2003, 12:17. http://aftenposten.no/english/local/article627274 (accessed 17 September 2003).

Toronto Police Services. *Overview: 2001 Hate Bias Crime Statistical Report.* Toronto: Toronto Police Services, 2002.

Tripathi, Salil. 'Nuptial Nightmares in London.' *Tehelka* (New Delhi), September 2000. http://www.saliltripathi.com/articles/Sept2000Tehelka.html (accessed 15 November 2003).

United Nations Commission on the Status of Women. 'Statement by Laila Davoy, Minister, Norwegian Ministry of Children and Family Affairs.' New York, 4 March 2002.

Van Munster, Rens. 'The War on Terrorism: When the Exception Becomes the Rule.' *International Journal for the Semiotics of Law* 17 (2004): 141–53.

Voegelin, Eric. 'The Growth of the Race Idea.' *Review of Politics* 1, no. 3 (July 1940): 283–317.

Volpp, Leti. 'The Citizen and the Terrorist.' *UCLA Law Review* 49 (2001–2): 1575–1600.

– 'Feminism versus Multiculturalism.' *Columbia Law Review* 101 (June 2001): 1181–1218.

– 'Impossible Subjects: Illegal Aliens and Alien Citizens.' *Michigan Law Review* 103, no. 106 (May 2005): 1582–1630.

Walker, B. 'The Canary Is Choking.' *The Social Contract*, Fall 2002. http://www.thesocialcontract.com/pdf/thirteen-one/xiii-1-60.pdf (accessed 15 November 2003).

Walkom, Thomas. 'Anti-terror Provisions Could Rise Once More.' *Toronto Star*, 3 March 2007, F3.

Wall, James M. 'No Peace Pipe: The Stated Goal of Bush Appointee Daniel Pipes – an Israeli Victory and a Palestinian Defeat.' *Christian Century*, 20 September 2003.

Ward, Olivia. 'Islam, West Clash Not Inevitable: Poll.' *Toronto Star*, 19 February 2007, A10.

Warner, Brooke. 'Abu Ghraib and a New Generation of Soldiers.' In *Abu Ghraib: The Politics of Torture*, ed. John Gray et al., 71–86. Berkeley: North Atlantic Books, 2004.

Warren, David. 'Multiculturalism – from Britannia to Sharia.' *National Post*, 8 December 2003, A14.

Weigman, Robyn. *American Anatomies: Theorizing Race and Gender.* Durham, NC, and London: Duke University Press, 1995.

Wexler, Laura. 'A Sorry History.' *Washington Post*, 19 June 2005, B1. http://washingtonpost.com/wp-dyn/content/article/2005/06/18/AR2005061800075_p.

Whitney, Craig. 'Introduction.' In *The Abu Ghraib Investigations*, ed. Steven Strasser, vi. New York: Public Affairs, 2005.

Wikan, Unni. *Generous Betrayal: Politics of Culture in the New Europe.* Chicago, London: University of Chicago Press, 2002.

– 'Honour Killings and the Problem of Justice in Modern-day Europe.' Paper presented at the conference 'Social Development, Social Inequalities and Social Justice,' Jean Piaget Society, 4 June 2004, Toronto, Ontario.

Wilhelm, Trevor, and Dalson Chen. 'Hate Crime or Free Speech?' *Windsor Star*, 13 January 2007. http://www.canada.com/windsorstar/news/story.html?id=465428a2-657b-4732-b12f-e07548dda592.

Willis, Susan. 'Quien es mas macho? The Abu Ghraib Photos.' Presentation at the Toronto Women's Bookstore, 18 January 2005.

Winter, Bronwyn. 'Women, the Law, and Cultural Relativism in France: The Case of Excision.' *Signs: Journal of Women in Culture and Society* 19, no. 4 (1994): 939–74.

Women's Legal Education and Action Fund (LEAF). 'Submission to Marion Boyd in Relation to Her Review of the *Arbitration Act*,' 17 September 2004. http://www.leaf.ca/legal-pdfs/Ontario%20Arbitration%20Act%20=%20Submission%20to%20Ontario%20Government.pdf.

Women Living Under Muslim Laws. 'Call for Action: Support Canadian Women's Struggle against Sharia Courts.' 7 April 2005. http://www.wluml.org/english/actionsfulltxt.shtml?cmd[156]=i-156-180177.

Yegenoglu, M. *Colonial Fantasies: Towards a Feminist Reading of Orientalism.* Cambridge: Cambridge University Press, 1998.

Yelaja, Prithi, and Robert Benzie. 'McGuinty: No Sharia Law.' *Toronto Star*, 12 September 2005, A1.

Young, Robert. *Colonial Desire: Hybridity in Theory, Culture and Race.* London, New York: Routledge, 1995.

Zaman, K. 'Kadra, Nadia and Synab Accuse Their Norwegian helpers: Break with Their Allies.' *VG Nett*, 2004. http://www.wgno.pub.vgart.hbs?artid=216868 (accessed 12 April 2004).

Legal References

Almrei v. Canada (Attorney General), [2003] O.J. 5198.
Almrei v. Canada (Minister of Citizenship and Immigration), [2004] F.C.J. 509.
Almrei v. Canada (Minister of Citizenship and Immigration) (F.C.), [2004] 4 F.C.R. 327.
Almrei v. Canada (Minister of Citizenship and Immigration) [2005] F.C.J. 213.
Almrei v. Canada (Minister of Citizenship and Immigration) [2005] F.C.J. 437.
Almrei v. Canada (Minister of Citizenship and Immigration) [2005] F.C.J. 1994.
Almrei v. Canada (Minister of Citizenship and Immigration) (F.C.A.), [2005] 3 F.C.R. 142.
Almrei (Re) [2001] A.C.F. no 1772.
Almrei v. Canada (Minister of Citizenship and Immigration and the Solicitor General of Canada). FCA. *Applicant's Application Record*, vol. 3, 479–784.
Almrei Detention Conditions Affidavit, 10 November 2002.
Arbitration Act, S.O. 1991, c. 17.
Bill C-86, *Immigration Act*. (passed June 1992).
Canada (Minister of Citizenship and Immigration) v. Jaballah, [1999] F.C.J. 1681.
Canada (Minister of Citizenship and Immigration) v. Jaballah, [2003] F.C.J. 1274.
Canada (Minister of Citizenship and Immigration) v. Mahjoub, [2001] F.C.J. 79.
Canada (Minister of Citizenship and Immigration) v. Mahjoub, [2001] F.C.J. 1483.
Canada (Minister of Citizenship and Immigration) v. Mahjoub, [2001] S.C.C.A. 151.
Canada (Minister of Citizenship and Immigration) v. Mahjoub (T.D.), [2001] 4 F.C. 644.
Canada (Minister of Citizenship and Immigration) v. Mahjoub, [2003] F.C.J. No. 1183.
Canada (Minister of Citizenship and Immigration) v. Mahjoub, [2004] F.C.J. 448.
Canada (Minister of Citizenship and Immigration) v. Mahjoub (F.C.), [2004] 1 F.C.R. 493.
Charkaoui v. Canada (Minister of Citizenship and Immigration), [2004] F.C.J. 1571.
Charkaoui v. Canada (Minister of Citizenship and Immigration), [2004] 1 F.C.R. 451.
Charkaoui (Re), [2003] F.C.J. 1815.
Charkaoui (Re), [2003] F.C.J. 2060.
Charkaoui (Re), [2004] F.C.J. 78.
Charkaoui (Re), [2004] F.C.J. 338.
Charkaoui (Re), [2004] F.C.J. 405.
Charkaoui (Re), [2004] F.C.J. 757.
Charkaoui (Re), [2004] F.C.J. 1090.

Charkaoui (Re), [2004] F.C.J. 1236.

Charkaoui (Re), [2004] F.C.J. 1549.

Charkaoui (Re), [2004] F.C.J. 1548.

Charkaoui (Re), [2004] F.C.J. 1686.

Charkaoui (Re), [2004] F.C.J. 1922.

Charkaoui (Re) (F.C.), [2004] 3 F.C.R. 32.

Charkaoui (Re) (F.C.), [2004] 1 F.C.R. 528.

Charkaoui (Re), [2005] F.C.J. 139.

Charkaoui (Re), [2005] F.C.J. 269.

Charkaoui (Re) (F.C.A.), [2005] 2 F.C.R. 299.

Federal Court Hearing Division. 'Statement Summarizing the Information Pursuant to Paragraph 40.1(4)(b) of the Immigration Act.' 18 October 2001.

Harkat v. Canada (Minister of Citizenship and Immigration), [2004] F.C.J. 1104.

Harkat v. Canada (Minister of Citizenship and Immigration), [2005] F.C.J. 2149.

Harkat (Re), [2004] F.C.J. 2101.

Harkat (Re), [2005] F.C.J. 481.

Harkat (Re), [2005] F.C.J. 1467.

Harkat (Re) (F.C.), [2005] 2 F.C.R. 416.

Harkat (Re) (F.C.), [2005] 2 R.C.F. 416, [2004] A.C.F. 2101.

Immigration and Refugee Protection Act, S.C. 2001, c. 27. http://www.laws .justice.gc.ca/en/1-2.5/index.html.

Jaballah v. Canada (Attorney General), [2005] O.J. 3681.

Jaballah v. Canada (Minister of Citizenship and Immigration), [2000] F.C.J. 1577.

Jaballah v. Canada (Minister of Citizenship and Immigration), [2003] F.C.J. 420.

Jaballah v. Canada (Minister of Citizenship and Immigration), [2003] F.C.J. 1495.

Jaballah (Re), [2001] F.C.J. No. 1748.

Jaballah (Re) (T.D.), [2003] 4 F.C. 345.

Jaballah (Re) (T.D.), [2004] F.C.J. 1199.

Jaballah (Re), [2005] F.C.J. 500.

Jaballah (Re) (F.C.A.), [2005] 1 F.C.R. 560.

Mahmoud Jaballah v. Attorney General of Ontario, Application for Release, 7 September 2005.

Mahjoub v. Canada (Minister of Citizenship and Immigration), [2004] F.C.J. 1335.

Mahjoub v. Canada (Minister of Citizenship and Immigration), [2005] F.C.J. 173.

Proceedings of the Special Senate Committee on the Anti-terrorism Act, Issue no. 3. Ottawa, 7 March 2005.

– Issue no. 13. Ottawa, 13 June 2005..

Regaldo-Brito v. Minister of Employment and Immigration, [1987] 1 F.C. 80 (C.A.).

Suresh v. Canada (Minister of Citizenship and Immigration), [2002] 1 S.C.R. 3.

Index

Eichmann, Adolf, 9
Eisenstein, Zillah, 76–7
empire: as gendered, 17–18; ideas
    harnessed to project of, 177; im-
    portance of culture clash in, 89;
    no one stands outside of, 21; role
    of feminists in, 86, 148; the term,
    12–13; white women's role in,
    76–7, 83. *See also* colonialism
enemy combatants, 29
England, Lyndie, 59, 67, 77
Engle, Karen, 38, 49–50
Enron, 101
Europe: and the civilized European,
    5; as culturally superior, 93–5;
    European racism as system of
    thought, 10–11. *See also* individual
    countries
European Apartheid, 109
extraordinary rendition, 29
Ezekiel, Judith, 166–7, 170

Fallaci, Orianna, 101–2, 104; *The
    Rage and the Pride*, 87–8, 91–3, 95,
    98
family (heterosexual), 47
family reunification, 20, 110–16, 120,
    123, 126, 129–30, 134–6, 203n74
Fanon, Frantz, 75, 79, 195n82
Farley, Anthony, 150
'fascist poetics,' 79
Fassin, Didier, 144
Fay Inquiry, 65
female genital mutilation, 88, 99,
    104, 108, 126, 144
feminists: explaining Abu Ghraib,
    76–8; on forced marriage, 120,
    141–4; as liberal internationalists,
    157; narrative of pre-modernity to
    modernity, 102–6; opposition to

faith-based arbitration, 21; racism
    and Western, 87; relying on
    culture-clash logic, 103–6; role in
    empire building, 86, 148–9, 177;
    saving Muslim women, 17–18;
    shared terrain with far right, 107;
    in support of Israel, 97–101;
    writing about violent Muslim
    men, 83–5. *See also* Sharia law in
    Canadian context
Fisk, Robert, 63
forced marriage. *See under* marriage
Foucault, Michel, 10–11, 15, 21
Fournier, Pascale, 154
France, 108, 127, 144, 152, 170. *See
    also* Dreyfus; hijab / wearing of
    the veil
freedom: of Western women com-
    pared to Muslim women, 116; as
    the West's distinctive attribute, 49
French Muslim Council, 170

gender: in confinement of Muslims,
    16; double standard for minority
    groups, 169; in empire building,
    83, 104–5; and European superi-
    ority, 89–91; as fatal flaw in
    Muslim world, 90; hegemonic
    masculinity, 64; as an issue in
    Norway, 119–20; masculinity in
    sexualized racial violence, 70–5;
    in process of colonization, 63; in
    project of empire, 17–18, 177; as
    technology of war on terror, 20;
    white women in sexualized vio-
    lence, 19, 65–7, 75–8; women
    entering privileged space, 86;
    women's rights in Islam, 98–103.
    See also Sharia law in Canadian
    context